Dipping into the Wells

The story of the two Chiltern villages
of Stoke Row and Highmoor
seen through the memories of their inhabitants

Angela Spencer-Harper

With Best Wishes from Angela

Robert Boyd
PUBLICATIONS

Published by
Robert Boyd Publications
260 Colwell Drive
Witney
Oxfordshire OX28 5LW

First published September 1999
Reprinted with amendments, September 2000
Second reprint, September 2004

ISBN 1 899536 35 3

Printed and bound at the Alden Press, Oxford

Dipping into the Wells

An illustrated story of the two Chiltern villages

of Stoke Row and Highmoor

seen through the memories of their inhabitants

Contents

To the late Bill George of Stoke Row and Ada Britnell of Highmoor,

two people typical of the many that I have interviewed,

some of whom have now gone on to 'higher service' .

All of them have availed me of the richness of their experiences.

Without their help, this volume would never have been written.

The picture on the front cover is taken from an engraving, published in the *Berks and Oxon Advertiser* on 1 March 1872, along with a report of the celebrations in Stoke Row, following the recovery of HRH Prince of Wales from typhoid fever.

The Maharajah of Benares sent £200 to fund this event and requested that 27 February 1872 be set aside as a public holiday. The drawing was done before the gold elephant was added to the well machinery.

This newspaper cutting is now in the Centre for Oxfordshire Studies at the Westgate Library, Oxford and reproduced with permission.

Dipping into the Wells

Acknowledgements are due:

To all the many people whose names appear in this book and my late friend, the Henley photographer and teacher, Tony Smith. Since Tony's death, David Beasley has not only carefully reproduced almost all the 1300 photographs in my collection; he and his wife, Ann, have become our firm friends. His patience and help in preparing all the photographs for this book are very much appreciated.

I owe a great debt of gratitude to Dr Malcolm Graham, Head of the Centre for Oxfordshire Studies, not only for writing the Foreword, but for all his help over many years. I would like also to mention Nuala la Vertue of the Oxfordshire Photographic Archive for all her assistance – we've had many a laugh together. Dr Liz Finn and all the staff of the Oxfordshire Archives have been very patient with my endless enquiries and I especially thank Liz for her review on the back cover.

The staff of the Bodleian Library and many other museums and libraries have also been very helpful. These include Henley Library, Beaulieu Motor Museum, the Imperial War Museum and the Victoria and Albert Museum. John Rhodes was kind enough to allow me to use illustrations from *Oxfordshire Brickmakers* and I thank him for those. I am also grateful to Geoff Boyson, for his historical notes and to Francis Sheppard for information taken from his book *Brakspear's Brewery 1779 - 1979*, as well as to Michael Parsons, former Managing Director, and Tony Verey, Estates Manager, of Brakspear's Brewery, Henley, for their assistance.

Many thanks to David Spencer, Lecturer in Geography at Reading University, Rev Brian Weaver, Vicar of Highmoor Church, and to Noel Baker, for his permission to use extracts from the books written by his father, Mr John H Baker. Also to Avril Bryant for her several sketches, to Gundrada Sheridan for drawing the maps and to Laureen Williamson for permission to quote from her writings. I am grateful too to John Whitehead and Paul Lacey for information on and photographs of buses, as well as to Ken Poyton for the use of his photograph of the Maharajah's Well.

I owe a huge debt to Tony Hall for reading through this book and making many constructive suggestions and to Dr Jim McWhirter for reading the chapter on Health.

Bob Boyd, who arranged the printing and publishing of this book, has been very generous with his time and valuable advice, born of his long experience in this field. Having never previously published a book myself, and certainly never gone through the process of making one 'camera-ready', I have been most grateful to him for his invaluable support through the latter stages of this project.

All this work on the computer would not have been possible without the programming help given to me by our eldest son, Philip – thanks a million, Prof!

And certainly my heartfelt thanks go to my dear husband, Bob, without whose unfailing patience and painstaking proof-reading of this book, many more ambiguities would have appeared. His constant support is, as always, appreciated with love.

Foreword

The product of 15 years' research, Angela Spencer-Harper's book is a very welcome study of two Chiltern villages that have remained off the beaten track for most historians. The Victoria History of the County of Oxford has still to cover the parishes in the Binfield and Langtree Hundreds and most of the published literature about Stoke Row concentrates on the wonderfully exotic Maharajah's Well, erected at the expense of the Maharajah of Benares in 1863-64. Hardly anything has been published about Highmoor, a chapelry of Bix and Rotherfield Greys until 1860.

The absence of published work might suggest that these villages simply have no history but Angela has triumphantly proved otherwise. Her volume makes fascinating use of interviews with more than 60 local people and includes over 350 photographs from the large collection that she has assembled over the years. It is predominantly a people's history recalling a more neighbourly and picturesque past but a decidedly less comfortable one with long working hours and the daily drudgery of fetching water from a well.

Local memories bring the history of both villages to life and they range across many topics including schools, churches and chapel, work and play and experiences of wartime. They recall vibrant communities with characters like James Cox, the elder at Stoke Row Chapel, who would always halt the Sunday sermon at noon by announcing the last hymn; even a horse with a taste for beer is remembered as a regular visitor to the Crooked Billet.

Such recollections may sometimes be fallible but the importance of this book is that it documents so much that could never be gleaned from other sources. We need many more Angelas delving as sympathetically into the histories of their villages before the process of 'gentrification' changes them beyond recall and the passage of time leaves us with only fragmentary records of what went before.

Malcolm Graham
Head of Oxfordshire Studies
Oxfordshire County Council
April 1999

Introduction

On picking up this book, some people will ask themselves, "Why the story of *two* villages?" The answer lies in the fact that our house, 'The Old Place', lies on the boundary between Stoke Row and Highmoor and so we have always felt we owe allegiance to both. We moved here early in 1979 and soon afterwards I was introduced to Miss Dolly Franklin, who had lived here as a child from 1908 to 1930. I brought her to our house and tape recorded her memories of life here. Later I transcribed them on to paper, and when the *Stoke Row News* was appealing for contributions, with Dolly's permission, I published her recollections in several instalments. The result was that other people suggested more likely subjects for interviewing in both Stoke Row and Highmoor and so I have been able to write, and publish in the *Stoke Row News*, the memoirs of over sixty local residents.

In the early days I was often shown photographs of families, friends, schools, churches, buildings and so on. Then I met Tony Smith of Henley who had taught at Gillott's School and who helped me by copying these photographs until his untimely death in February 1993, which was a terrible blow to us all. A few months afterwards, however, David Beasley, himself having built up a vast acquisition of photographs and information and published books about Wallingford, came to my rescue and helped me continue my labour of love by reproducing more borrowed photographs. I now have a collection of over 1300, together with more than 500 colour ones that I have taken myself, of buildings in the two villages and the subjects of the memoirs.

As a result of several newspaper articles and photographic exhibitions, I have been encouraged to write this book and hope that it will appeal to readers much further afield than just these two Oxfordshire villages. It does not purport to be a scholastic history. As a relative newcomer, the most I have done is to use the memories of the people who have lived here for many years and in some cases, several generations, to tell the story of their own villages.

I have also done much research at Oxford, although documentary evidence is slight for the most part. The main exception to this has been the many papers relating to the Maharajah's Well, three log books for Stoke Row School and one for Highmoor School. For this reason the chapter on the schools is quite long and detailed, because these books are so revealing. Although, perhaps for want of a better word, I often refer to this as my 'work', it has been and still is, a source of great joy and interest to me. Sometimes it becomes almost like a jigsaw puzzle, for which I am constantly finding new pieces and yet some still remain infuriatingly missing!

I have met many people, at all levels and from all walks of life during my researches, enjoyed many a cup of coffee, or tea and had many a laugh! Also I have been able to do it all at my leisure – after a lifetime of working in an office, it is wonderful to have such a flexible and pleasant pastime!

Angela Spencer-Harper.

1. Local Maps

This book is the story of two small villages, once thought of as being 'hidden' high up in the Chiltern Hills. They lie deep in the beech woods of South Oxfordshire, roughly in the centre of a square made by the towns of Henley-on-Thames to the east, Wallingford to the west, Reading to the south and Watlington to the north. Each of the first three towns is on the Thames, which sweeps in a curve around the south of this area. Having said that, many of the old villagers, especially the women, rarely saw the river and knew little of the towns and country beyond their own boundaries.

I have read many local history books – always buying one for what ever part of the country I happen to be staying in. Most of them are very good, many better than this one, but some of their authors, knowing their own home ground well and believing that the people who will buy and read the book will only be locals and know the area as well as they, fail to supply even a simple hand-drawn map.

Therefore I am extremely grateful to Michael Reade for permission to use these maps, which are taken from the Reade manuscripts, and show the ancient parish boundaries. Also to Gundrada Sheridan for drawing the other two, of Stoke Row and Highmoor. I hope they will all enable the reader to relate to the book, especially if he or she lives outside the immediate locality.

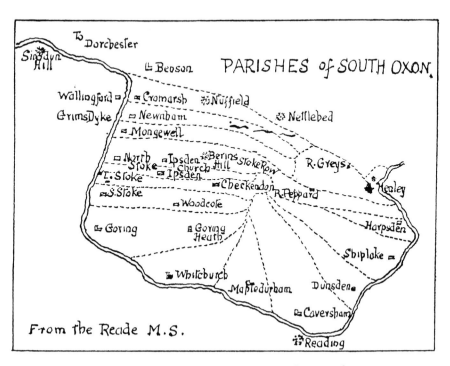

The Parishes of South Oxfordshire, from the Reade manuscript.
By kind permission of Mr Michael Reade of Ipsden.

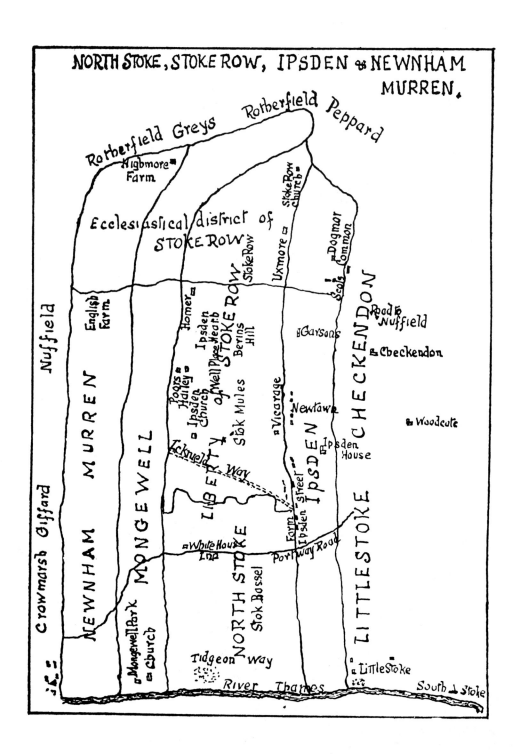

The Ancient Parishes of North Stoke, South Stoke, Ipsden and Newnham Murren from the Reade manuscript. By kind permission of Mr Michael Reade of Ipsden.

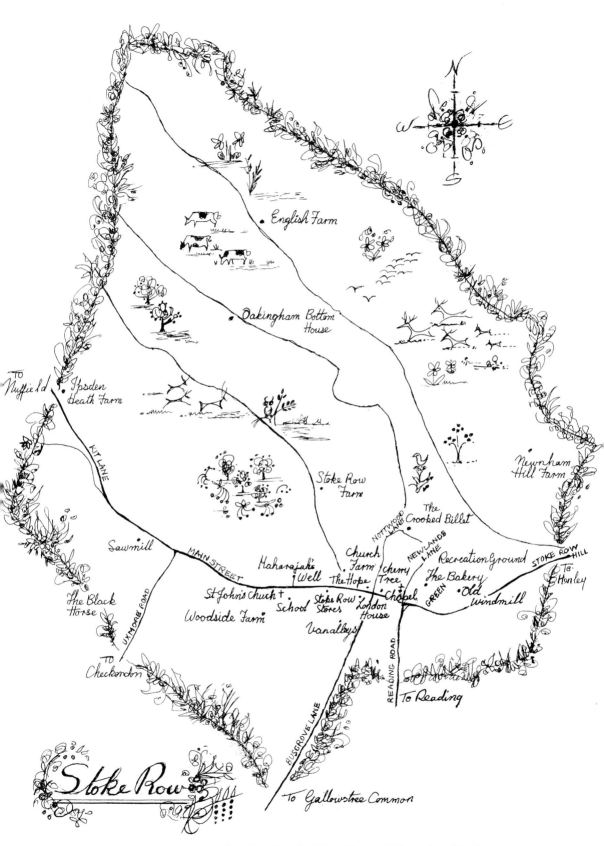

Stoke Row. Drawn by Gundrada Sheridan of Sheridan Designs.

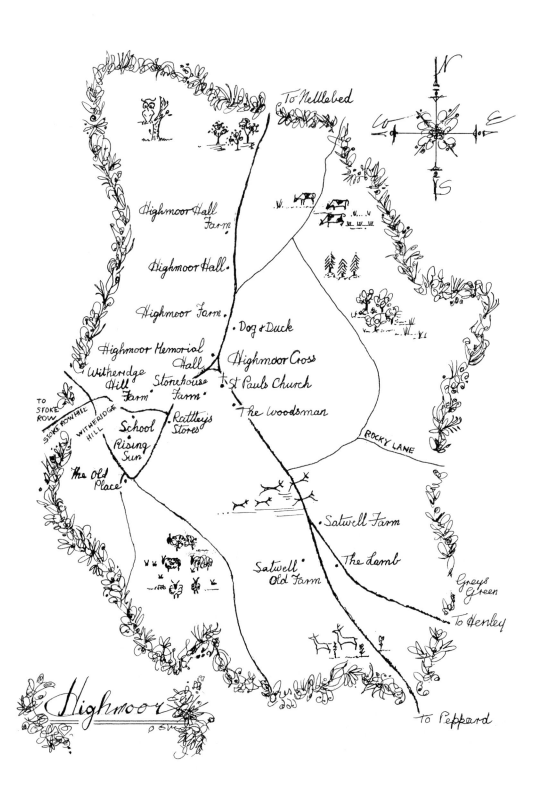

Highmoor. Drawn by Gundrada Sheridan of Sheridan Designs.

4

2.   A Brief Background History of the Area

The adjacent villages of Stoke Row and Highmoor are situated on the south western edge of the Chiltern Hills. The soil is mainly clay, chalk, some sand and flint. An earthquake was recorded in the Chilterns in December 1250 caused by a huge subsidence of clay into an enormous cavity in the chalk.

Quite a few *puddingstones* are to be found in this locality. These conglomerates are in fact a residue from the Ice Age. There is a very large one on the right hand side of the hill as you go from the bottom of Witheridge Hill up to Stoke Row. Bill George told me that in the early days of this century several local men tried to put chains around this rock in order to pull it out, using the power of a steam engine, "but it wouldn't budge an inch – I reckon it goes down very deep, like an iceberg." There is another in Greyhone Wood, just below Beech Hollow and yet another en route to Bromsden Farm in Lower Highmoor Woods near the old chalk pit.

In her section of the 1995 *Stoke Row Village Appraisal*, entitled 'The History of Our Village', Laureen Williamson who has done quite a lot of research into the history of Stoke Row, explains how the name came into being: "The first known reference to a place called Stoke Row is in 1435 in connection with a land transaction when Row is spelled 'Rewe'... The earliest known boundary divisions, which are believed to date to Saxon times, ie before 1066, had the territory of Stoke Row (and Ipsden) encompassed within the Parish of North Stoke which at that time was known simply as 'Stoches' or 'Stoke', meaning 'a place' or 'a farm'. The 'Row' part of Stoke Row is either from the Saxon 'Ruh', meaning outback, or from the Norman French 'Rue' meaning a street, road or row."

Several flint tools have been found in the area but one in particular from the New Stone Age period, was found near Church Farm, Cox's Lane, Stoke Row in 1949 by a Mr Fairey who was digging a hole for a fence post. It is now in the Reading Museum. Mr Leslie Cram, one of the archaeologists there, pointed out to me how it had been flaked to make the shape, was chipped to create an edge and then ground on a sarsen or any rough stone to make it smooth. (There are sarsen stones in the grounds of Uxmore House which were probably found locally).

After that the tool had been chipped again along the edge to sharpen it and to make it fit snugly into the shaft of a wooden stick handle, which would have given it more leverage. With this tool the New Stone Age man would have made other tools from wood such as bows, arrows, ploughs, (perhaps tipped with flint heads) and maybe some of the first tent pegs!

A New Stone Age Axe, of the type found at Stoke Row

Geoff Boyson spent a considerable amount of time in the Oxfordshire Archives studying the history of this area when he was Editor of the *Stoke Row News*. His notes about the region, albeit unreferenced, were spiced with his own special brand of humour and published in our village magazine under the following headings:

The Bronze Age (1500 – 350 BC)

The Bronze Age craftsmen were skilled in the working of bronze tools and equipment and also of gold brooches, pins and earrings. They used a two-ox plough and cast bronze to make socketed axes (one was found at North Stoke in 1886) as well as beaten bronze shields and pots. They wove cloth, probably from nettle fibre (grown at Nettlebed?) and later from wool. Bronze Age folk almost certainly used the Icknield Way and the Ridgeway as trade routes to other parts of the country. They cremated their dead. A bronze urn was found at North Stoke under a round barrow, a few also occur in the Bix/Stonor area.

The Iron Age (550 – 75 BC)

Was it one of Old King Cole's retinue who lost the golden torque found in 1960 at Moulsford? This is a large horseshoe shaped ornament made about 1200 BC from four twisted bars of gold/silver natural alloy, probably from Ireland.

About seven centuries later, people of similar Celtic stock began to settle in Britain. They were primarily farmers, but they introduced the working of a comparatively abundant ore – iron, most of which was probably extracted from the Forest of Dean.

Their carpenters' and blacksmiths' tools and techniques were remarkably similar to those used by hand craftsmen today and examples of their work, ie chariot wheels, weapons and decorative ironware, show a high degree of skill and artistry.

The farm was the centre of family life and aerial photographs have revealed the pattern of their fields at North and South Stoke and all along the Berkshire Downs and Chiltern Hills. In this area many new hilltop forts were built and older ones reconstructed. Bozedown Camp and Blewburton Hill are examples, whilst the Uffington Camp on Whitehorse Hill is the best known. They stretch at intervals from Marlow to Avebury. Tribal warfare may have been rife, one indication being that iron sword blanks were standard 'currency'. Cast bronze coins were used at a later stage.

The Belgae (75 BC)

Up to this time immigrants came as settlers, more or less content to share the land with the natives, but now came the warlike tribes of mixed Celtic/Teuton stock, who were conquerors. At first came the Catuvellauni who controlled territory from East Anglia to the Thames. Their king was Cassivellaunus, probably the first individual Briton to have his name in historical records.

A chieftain called Tasciovanus built an important town near St Albans, whilst Goring, Henley, Wallingford and Dorchester were also tribal centres established perhaps by Cunobelin.

Later other tribes came up from the south to found the kingdom of Atrebates with their headquarters at Calleva (Silchester).

The Romano-British

A coin of Pupienus (238 AD) was found in digging the enclosure of the Maharajah's Well at Stoke Row, and large quantities of Roman pot sherds were found near this village, so possibly this may have been a habitation site. Not all Britons were antagonistic to the invading Romans. Some tribes may have become mercenaries, for in an account by Dion Cassius of the Battle of Wallingford in 43 AD the Roman, Aulus Plautius, commanded his 'Celti' to swim the river, fully armed, at night, to slaughter Caractacus's chariot horses and the Catavellauni were defeated.

A small British settlement probably existed at Stoke Row, called Dagmer (the place of the diggers), the principal occupation being the extraction of clay for plain domestic pottery. Early historians found large quantities of broken pottery in Stoke Row of the Romano-British type and more was found in Swan Wood, Highmoor, which is thought to be the site of a Romano-British farmstead. For many centuries Stoke Row potters were still producing ware significantly Roman in style.

The art of budding cherries also came from the Romans. Pliny, in his book of Natural History, wrote: 'The Cerasus (cherry) was taken to Rome from Pontus in Asia about 73 BC and was transplanted into Britain about 120 years later in AD 47.'

A small military outpost was set up by the Romans at Berin's Hill, where coins and pottery have been found near a Roman style well. More recently, a tiled floor was discovered by two keen amateur archaeologists, Lady Lowe and Mrs Kennington. The river names Thames and Thame in the Chiltern hills derive from the Celtic language. Wallingford was the town of the 'Wealh', a name describing Britons who were under the influence of the Romans.

The Dark Ages

The local Belgae seem to have survived to some extent the conquest of the Romans, the Saxons and the Danes. They were allowed to remain in the 'Uplands', which were known as the Celta Coombe or Ciltria Solna by the Saxons and the Celt Terrae by the Normans.

The 'Prettanni' were described as 'tall, blue-eyed, with fair or reddish hair' by the Roman historian Appian, who did not consider the occupation a very good bargain: 'even a hundred years after the conquest, they are costing us more than we gain.'

CHERRY TREES
HIGHMORE

Cherry Trees at Highmoor. This photograph was taken for a postcard in the 1930s. It shows the road (now the B481) looking from Highmoor Hall down to the Dog and Duck public house, and illustrates the extent to which the verges were kept cropped by animals owned by local folk. Goats, donkeys and even the odd cow were tethered to one spot at a time but were moved at intervals throughout the day. Thanks to the Romans, the cherry trees provided a livelihood for the women of the villages, who picked them and sold them in Reading and Henley. The trees are still pretty today. By kind permission of Hilary Fisher.

In 496, King Arthur, who commanded a well-equipped army of cavalry, repelled the Saxons at the battle of Badon, probably near Marlborough, but in 571 the Saxon Ceawlin, prince of the Gewissae, ousted the Britons from their stronghold at Bensitune (Benson).

The Benedictine monk Berinus came to the notice of the Saxon Prince Cynegesil and was invited to found an Abbey at Dorchester about 631. He also built a number of wooden churches, all of which were probably later burnt down by the Danes. (Wallingford and Dunsden churches were destroyed in 1006). Berinus baptised Cynegesil's sons – Cwicholm in 636 and Cuthrod in 639. Berin's Hill, which runs from Stoke Row to Ipsden, was probably named after this saint.

The Princess Frideswide (680–735) became the first Abbess of a monastery at Oxford, from which she is supposed to have fled to a swineherd's holding at Binsey to escape an unwelcome Royal marriage. In 779, Offa, King of the Mercians, captured the royal estate of Bensington (Benson) from Cynewulf, King of Wessex.

Later the Danes captured Reading and stationed an army there. Skirmett and Fingest are Danish for 'the meeting place on the hill' – the name Witheridge is also thought to be Scandinavian. It means 'Willow Ridge' and it is interesting to note that a local plantswoman told me recently she had found eight types of willow growing in gardens on Witheridge Hill.

The Saxon king, Ethelred II, having failed to appease the local Danes with 'Danegeld', massacred many of them in St Frideswide's church at Oxford, where they were seeking sanctuary. Edward the Confessor, who was Oxfordshire born, ordered a register of the parishes in South Oxon. It was made use of by the Saxon clerks who compiled the local Doomsday survey for the Normans."

These interesting notes by Geoff Boyson give us a brief background against which the villages are set. Life seemed to have gone on very quietly up here in the Chiltern hills and most of the succeeding years can only be interpreted through the following few references found in the Oxfordshire Archives during my researches.

Law and Order in Stoke Row

For the most part this area was only sparsely settled. Most folk were hardworking woodmen or potters but some were engaged in less honest activities. A Florentine traveller, Brunetto Latino, writing of his journey from London to Oxford in the 13th century, stated:

"Our journey was with some difficulty and danger, made in two days, for the roads are bad and we had to climb hills of hazardous ascent and which to descend are doubly perilous. We passed through woods which are dangerous places as they are infested with robbers."

Nevertheless, some semblance of order seems to have existed by 1683, when "James Goswell, Tithingman of Stoke Row, was ordered by Matthew Allnutt, Constable, to whip Joseph Robson, as a rough and vagabond and escort him from the Parish."

At the Oxford Quarter Sessions in 1688, "Clement Cox, constable of Stoke Row, was presented by the Chief Constable. Thomas Leaver, did not present his returns."

Another reference, also found in the Oxfordshire Archives states: "Thomas Frewin died in 1771. He had been Parish Clerk for 48 years and a Parish Constable." Quite a remarkable length of service to a community by the standards of the time – even today, when people live longer, few can say they have given that amount of time to their parish.

But at the Quarter Sessions in the same year, "John Baker, Tithingman and William Barker, labourer, allowed to escape from their custody a one James Frewin, who had been arrested when caught stealing sacks of beans and given into their charge by James Smith." One wonders if James Frewin was a less law abiding relative of Thomas above!

Stoke Row Common (now more usually called the Village Green) in about 1900.
By kind permission of Avril Bryant.

In 1806 the Constable was Moses Allnutt, the Tithingman James Whittick and the Hayward John Whittick. Although the meanings of the names Constable and Tithingman are fairly obvious, the 'Hayward' had nothing to do with hay but was custodian of the village properties. The word comes from the Anglo-Saxon 'haeg' meaning enclosure and gives us the modern word 'hedge'.

According to the *Oxford Chronicle* of 22 March 1862, a one Richard Green appeared "Before the Borough Bench; before E Reynolds, Esq, Mayor of Wallingford, R Payne, Esq and J Hilliard Esq. Richard Green of Stoke Row was summonsed by Inspector Johnson for leaving his horse and cart in the streets of Wallingford longer than was necessary. Fined 5s and 12.6d costs."

At a Meeting of the Vestry of Ipsden Church on Easter Monday 10 April 1871, "the following resolution relating to the fixing of the pounds in the Upland and Lowland and the appointment of the Hayward, was agreed by the Overseer, Churchwardens and others of the Parish present this day assembled:

1st: the site of the Upland Pound on the public ground above and close to the public pond opposite the *farm now occupied by John Simmons should be chosen and John Wilson of Stoke Row, road man, should be appointed Hayward.

10

2nd: that, provisionally, the site at the south corner of **the Sawpit ground, by the side of Ipsden Street, be chosen and Mr William Batten be appointed Hayward." (*Church Farm, Cox's Lane, Stoke Row. **Site not known, but may have been in Kit Lane, Stoke Row).

This was signed by Mr E A Reade, Chairman, and the signatures below were: Samuel B Pickett, William Batten, George Hope, James Cox and Thomas Painter.

Clothing the Poor of Stoke Row

Today, when clothes are thrown away as soon as they are out of fashion, it is hard to realise that in Victorian times some of the villagers often had barely enough garments to keep them warm. In 1876 a 'Blanket Charity' was founded by Mr Dodd of Hailey who bequeathed the sum of £400, the interest from which was to provide blankets, half for the poor of Ipsden and half for those of Stoke Row.

From the Minutes of the Vestry Meeting, Ipsden Church on 29 March, 1876: "Mr Philip Charles Dodd communicated to the meeting that his father Mr William John Dodd late of Hailey, in the Parish of Ipsden, bequeathed of his last will a legacy of £400, free of legacy duty, to the poor of Ipsden and Stoke Row, the proceeds of which, invested in Government Securities, to be distributed usually at Christmas in the form of Blankets and Flannel Stuff to the poor of Ipsden and Stoke Row without distinction of creed, the Vicar and Church Wardens of Ipsden to be ex-officio Trustees."

The Vicar and Churchwardens received a cheque for the amount and gave a formal receipt. This was signed "G Stanwell, Vicar" and also bore the signatures of "E A Reade, Samuel B Pickett, Geo Hope, James Cox, Richard Parsons and William Batten." Records still exist for a Clothing Club which was run at Stoke Row between the years 1852 and 1876.

The Stoke Row Windmill

Some mention should be made of the Stoke Row Windmill. It is believed to have been in use until 1840 and was a brick-built domed affair that stood beside Windmill Cottage, in the far corner of the Village Green. James Blackall and Samuel Whittick were both mentioned as 'Millers of Stoke Row' in the Chapel Conveyance of 1815. An underground passage is reputed to have linked the mill to Windmill Cottage and Miss Cicely Turner remembered "there was always a diagonal path across the Common. The last miller's name was Miller Munday."

Jacob Bauer recalled playing in the old building when he was a child but the mill eventually fell into disrepair and was probably dismantled and 'Millstone Cottages' were built on the site. The doorsteps of these semi-detached houses are made from the millstones from the mill. (See chapter on Bodging and Other Trades).

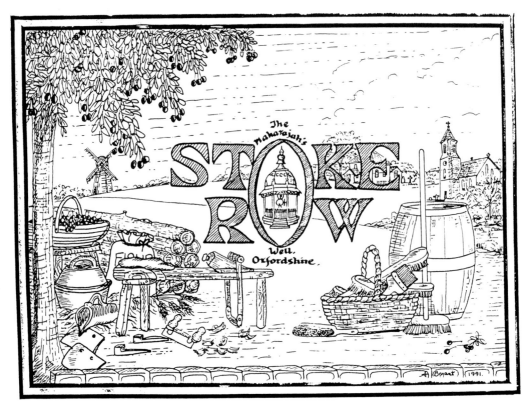

'Traditional Crafts of Stoke Row'. Drawn by Avril Bryant.

Highmoor

"Originally all the land at Highmoor like that of Nettlebed was owned by the Stonor Estate. (In Norman times the Stonors and their relatives held land going from Stonor House down to Caversham, an area of about 5 miles wide by 15 miles long)." (*Victoria County History* Vol II pp 43–44). Alas, as Lord Camoys explained to me in a letter: "The Stonor papers have not yet been catalogued and so we cannot allow anybody to see them."

The Grim's Ditch which was probably created by Iron Age settlers as a defensive earthworks and boundary, runs from Mongewell all the way to Henley. Traces of it can be found in many places including Nuffield and Highmoor, "though the Highmoor end is of an entirely different character from the west end of the ditch, so may not be part of the whole." (VCH II (1907) 'Grim's Ditch 'B', p 339). It is listed in the Sites and Monuments Record at Oxford and forms the boundary that separates Highmoor from Nettlebed.

The name of Highmoor is perhaps not as it seems, a high moorland, because it has always been heathland or beechwoods, but a 'high mere' (pronounced 'merrie' in Anglo-Saxon) or high pond. In the 1661 deeds of Highmoor Hall it is named as Hymer House and in 1855 as Hymor Hall.

12

The Victoria County History has not yet been completed for this part of Oxfordshire, indeed it has hardly been started, but some references to Highmoor were found by Professor W O Hassell of the Bodleian Library and entered in his notes at the VCH office in 1969: "Highmoor comes under Rotherfield Peppard, which itself comes within the Diocese of Lincoln." However, other references state that, administratively, Highmoor was in the Parish of Rotherfield Greys in the Binfield Hundred.

In 1894 Thomas Stonor of Stonor House sold large portions of land in Highmoor and in 1906, soon after Robert Fleming, the banker, came to Nettlebed he bought 'Joyce Grove' and all the farmland, woodland and cottages of Nettlebed and Highmoor. One elderly local person remembered that some of the owners of the cottages sold them for "a handful of gold coins." In 1940 Major Philip Fleming, grandson of Robert Fleming, sold 'Joyce Grove' and the family moved to 'Merrimoles', just inside the Highmoor boundary. Sometime after the war the Fleming Estate Yard was moved there too.

There were, in fact, several large ponds at Highmoor, though they are now largely dry and overgrown. The one by the Dog and Duck was recently cleared, cleaned and reinstated by the Chiltern Society Conservation Volunteers, making an attractive feature at this point on the Highmoor to Nettlebed road.

Witheridge Hill, as seen from Colemore Lane, which runs from the foot of Witheridge Hill to the Unicorn public house at Peppard. This picture comes from a catalogue published by Simmons and Sons in 1913, long before 'Beech Hollow' was built. There were few trees, the gorse was carefully burned off each year and animals were allowed to graze all over the hill.

13

Much of Highmoor was common land and on this pigs, goats, donkeys, cattle and the occasional horse were grazed, thus keeping down the young trees. With the coming of the Second World War this type of husbandry has died out and trees have soon sprung up each side of the Highmoor to Nettlebed Road and on Witheridge Hill. Thanks to the activities of the Conservators, the Nettlebed and District Commons (Preservation) Act 1906 has largely been adhered to and the Friends of the Nettlebed and District Commons are very keen to ensure that this land is carefully managed, so that all may enjoy it.

The Demography of Stoke Row

Until 1952 Stoke Row was in the Parish of Ipsden which itself was a part of the Langtree Hundred. The first population figures available are for Ipsden as a whole and this was 3442 acres and so it would be very difficult to gauge the exact population of Stoke Row. These figures, extracted each decade from Post Office Directories, are for Ipsden, which appears to have been far less populated than the adjoining parish of Rotherfield Greys:

1801: 476.   1811: 481.   1821: 583.   1831: 582.   1841: 610.

However, by 1841 the Census gave a much clearer picture and the figures from 1851 were given for the village of Stoke Row itself:

1851: 437.   1861: 386.   1871: 482.   1881: 520.   1891: 577.
1901: 512.   1911: 522.   1921: (with Ipsden) 708.   1931: 620.
1941: No census (WW2).   1951: 710 (with Ipsden).   1961: 580.
1971: 655.   1981: 654.   1991: 600.

The Demography of Highmoor

Until 1952 Highmoor was part of the Parish of Rotherfield Greys which came under the Binfield Hundred. This area was 2927 acres. Again therefore it is very hard to estimate the population of Highmoor itself. These are the figures for Rotherfield Greys:

1801: 677.   1811: 668.   1821: 717.   1831: 1145.   1841: 1535.
1851: 1518.   1861: 1629.

After this date Highmoor was assessed on its own, with the exception of 1881, when for some unknown reason it was again included with Rotherfield Greys. This is a pity, because it is the missing link between the relatively high figure of 341 in 1871 and the sharp drop to 270 in 1891, possibly due to hardship on the land.

Thereafter the population appears to have been more or less stable, with perhaps only the gentle rise expected of an age when families were large.

1871: 341.   1881: 1909 (inc R Greys).   1891: 270.   1901: 275.   1911: 289.
1921: 291.   1931: 273.   1941: No census (WW2).
1951: 346 (inc R Greys).   1961: 349.   1971: 364.   1981: 346.
1991: 307.

David Spencer, Lecturer in Geography at the University of Reading, who kindly supplied me with the post Second World War figures, points out: "between 1961 and 1991 the number of private households in Highmoor rose by 15 at a time when the population itself was declining. The number of dwellings had increased by 28, these including conversions of barns and other farm buildings. Houses themselves tend to be enlarged but households are smaller, due to single parent families and elderly widows and widowers living on longer on their own. This tendency can be seen throughout South Oxfordshire."

Changes in Village Life

Up until the early part of the 20th century, the church records show that the majority of the villagers married boys and girls from their own or nearby villages. A few exceptions were for example where a girl had been brought from further away by train to work in 'the big house'.

It is easy for us to forget that it was the advent of the bicycle which brought new-found freedom to the average villager – probably only equated with the coming of cheap cars after the Second World War. If a man had a bicycle it meant he could cycle to work, certainly further than he could walk and where he could perhaps earn more money. It not only enabled him to travel more quickly and further but also to travel with greater ease which was a boon to men who worked manually all day, often for long hours. They had carbide lamps to light their way in the dark and these always had to be kept clean. In terms of village life, the 'bike' was almost a revolution.

We come more up to date by quoting from the memories of Rev Cyril Isherwood, Vicar of Stoke Row Church, writing in the *Stoke Row News* in 1980 and thinking back to when he first came here:

"In those days many would have their doors open all day and we were always welcome. I remember so clearly one old woman who was a cripple and lived in one of the houses in Ishree Terrace. She always had a teapot on the stove at her side all day and from time to time would add more water – I am not sure about tea – so that by the end of the day the tea must not only have been brewed but stewed!

Now in 1980, I look around and see Stoke Row completely changed from the way that I knew it during the years 1891 to 1900. Where we had a potato field and a scrub field, all down the west side of School Lane from the churchyard to Woodside cottages,

15

there is now a bungalow and a row of houses. Where the school children's playground was, opposite the school, is now a row of Council bungalows. Where there was a field with cherry trees is now a garage, shop and houses. Where there was once a small farmstead is now a terrace.

The orchard at the side of 'The Cherry Tree' has lost some of its fine old cherry trees and has been built on with a row of houses. The old forge which was at the corner of Newlands Lane is now a private house and other new houses have been built nearby. In Nottwood Lane where there were once one or two old houses there are also a number of new houses.

The once quiet village street has become a highway with a constant flow of traffic day and night including some of the heaviest and longest of vehicles, so that we have to watch very carefully before we can cross. No more are there oil lamps and candles but electricity – for cooking, heating and washing. A majority of the houses are on the telephone. In all this and more, Stoke Row has completely changed its character. The wonderful Well remains a monument to past benefactors and the church ever carries on the Christian faith and sacraments.

In all that I have written I have tried to give some idea of what was once a small hamlet but is now a populous dormitory suburb."

And what of the future?

I suppose if the inhabitants of Stoke Row and Highmoor several generations back were to return to these villages they probably would recognise them, although they would be astonished and terrified at the sight of motor-cars being driven at 50 mph and more, especially on the B481 through Highmoor, a road along which they once bowled their hoops and spun their tops.

'Onward to the 21st Century'. Drawn by Avril Bryant for the 1995 Stoke Row Appraisal.

16

I believe another thing which would surprise them would be the number of trees that have grown up in recent years. A picture drawn in about 1865 shows that there was a clear view from behind the Maharajah's Well past Stoke Row farm almost to the horizon. As we have seen from the photograph on a previous page there were hardly any trees on Witheridge Hill before the Second World War, just gorse which was burned off regularly in controlled fires. A few cows or donkeys grazed both the Commons and the verges, keeping them neatly shorn.

There is no doubt that physically, times were very hard for the occupants of the old cottages, certainly going back to before the First World War, but they did all have one great compensation, that of neighbourliness especially during periods of hardship. The companionship created by larger families and the fact that people had to work together as a team in many different situations, compensated for much that was otherwise grim. Most of the several hundred people that I have interviewed remember the discomforts but, above all, they think back to an age when neighbours had time for a kindly word and children were free to roam anywhere in complete safety.

I expect former villagers would be perplexed too by the high walls that have recently begun to appear especially at Highmoor, around what are now very large dwellings but were formerly just little cottages with a low hedge in front. These walls are usually accompanied by solid or wrought iron gates with security entry systems. Whereas in the old days village folk could see and give a cheery wave to one another from a distance, say from the houses at Lower Highmoor to the Dog and Duck, many people now live in what they feel to be secure homes, entering and leaving by car but never seeing their neighbours.

Let us fervently hope that the future of our villages does not lie in the growing American practice of having notices at the entrance to their estates, roads and houses bearing the chilling words '**Armed Response**'.

3. Interesting Inhabitants

When people think of villages, they usually think of a village green, thatched cottages, a church and maybe a manor house, but the most important part of a village is its inhabitants. Of all the chapters in this book, choosing the photographs for this one was the most difficult, for I have so many pictures of local folk, rich and poor, at work and at leisure.

Some of them are real characters into whose faces hardship had chiselled deep lines and hollow cheeks. People were, and had to be, tough in those times when creature comforts were few, except for the well-to-do.

Maud and Mabel Page in about 1900. Mabel went to live with her grandparents, Mr and Mrs George Page of Stonehouse, Highmoor, when her mother died. Mabel will be celebrating her 105th birthday in June 1999. Kindly lent by Mrs Kathleen Dyer (nee Howells).

Edith, Lily, Ellen and William Green in about 1915. They lived at 'Brickbats' (now 'Clare Cottage') on Stoke Row Hill, but this photograph was probably taken at Highmoor School. Kindly lent by Mrs Kathleen Kucor (nee Brakspear).

Miss Winifred Cox, daughter of James Cox, the Stoke Row builder and joiner. This delightful photograph was taken about 1911. Reproduced by kind permission of Miss Winifred Cox.

Eric Gillett, aged about three. This little boy was son of the Post-mistress and owner of The London House Stores, Stoke Row. Kindly lent by Mrs Tayler (nee Johnson).

These two photographs are in sharp contrast. Above is a simple country wedding, of Mrs May Wells (who was widowed young) to Jim Green. The lady and gentleman on either side of the bride and groom are Mr and Mrs Plumridge, mother and father of the bride. Mrs Plumridge is holding baby Rosemary Wells; the other ladies are unknown. By kind permission of Rosemary Jadkawska (nee Wells).

Quite different, though not far removed in time, was the wedding of Harry Cox, of the well-to-do family of builders who lived at 'The Rest' (later known as 'Bodgers' and now 'Virginia Cottage') to Miss Louisa Winship. By kind permission of Miss Winifred Cox.

Another wedding group – this was a bit later, in April 1925. The coachman is unknown, but next to him is young Jack Brakspear. Standing: Jim Green and unknown bridesmaid, the groom William Brakspear and his bride Edith (nee Green), Helen ('Nell') Brakspear and Francis Earle. Taken outside 'Brickbats' (now 'Clare Cottage'), Stoke Row Hill. Kindly lent by Mrs Kathleen Kucor (nee Brakspear).

This idyllic photograph of a country family was taken as they sat on the Grim's Ditch at Highmoor in about 1910. Left to right: Louisa, Ada and Annie Wells, Mrs Susan Wells (nee Saunders), Rosie Cox (daughter of 'Dablo' Cox). Beside them is Sidney Saunders and Ed'ard Wells, with the family donkey. By kind permission of Mrs Louisa Stevens (nee Wells).

21

Family life featured strongly in both villages. Here is the Lester family, outside their home, 'Laurel Cottage' on Stoke Row Hill in about 1890. At that time this was just half of the present house. The men are: Joe Lester and Tom Wheatley. Ladies: Mrs Emily Carter, Mrs Ada Lester and the children are Ada Carter, Harriet Lester and Albert Carter. By kind permission of John Holroyd.

Almost their next door neighbours, at 'Brickbats' (now 'Clare Cottage') further down the hill, were the Green family. Mr and Mrs Jonas Green and their ten children. The baby on Mrs Green's lap is Edith Green.   Kindly lent by Mrs Kathleen Kucor.

Two Stoke Row families. This is the George family. Ruby and Bill George and their daughter Gillian. Next to her is Bill's sister, Winnie and Gillian's husband, Jim Gavin. The children are: Mark and Debbie (twins), Stewart (at the back) and Malcolm and Debbie (twins). With the children is 'Grandma', Mrs Adeline Blanch George (nee Walters). By kind permission of Bill George, to whom this book is also dedicated.

This is a beautifully posed photograph, probably taken in about 1890 by the stile which was then at the end of School Lane, Stoke Row. It depicts Mr and Mrs Tucker and their four children and two friends. The young lad is George Tucker and the older is Bert Beasley (or Fred Brooker?) The girls are Elizabeth Main (who later married George Gibbons), Polly, Lucy and Elizabeth Tucker. By kind permission of Mrs Elsie Wickham.

23

Work played the most important part in village life, at least, for most people. This photograph is of Rose Green, probably carrying water from the well into her home, which is today called 'Snowdrop Cottage', on Witheridge Hill. The date is unknown. Photograph kindly lent by Mr Fred Allum.

Another very hardworking soul was Mrs Jemima ('Granny') Webb, who lived in one of the original 'Greenman Cottages' which used to stand at right angles to the B 481, opposite The Dog and Duck at Highmoor. They have since been rebuilt and now face the road. She is seen here carrying a bundle of firewood, known as a 'faggot' or 'burden'. When splitting wood she could often be heard to say: "I 'ates them aak'ard bits!" This lovely photograph was taken by Mr A Pilati, who was the butler at Highmoor Park. He entitled the picture 'Fagotting Granny'. Kindly lent by Mrs Ada Britnell (nee Wells).

The old folk were full of sayings. Percy Stallwood, a member of possibly the oldest family in Stoke Row, was born in about 1900. His great-grandfather was a forester and was known as a 'long-headed man' (a clever man).

Josh Main, who was born at 'Clayhill' on Stoke Row Hill told me: "A man I knew couldn't cook shaving water!" and that the traditional greeting in Stoke Row and Highmoor, until quite recently, was: "'Ow be an?"

However, it was from Mrs Ada Britnell that I learned most of the local proverbs, such as: "You've got to have eyes in the backs of your elbows when you've got young children about" and "It's the back end of summer now" (autumn).

Arthur ('Art') Britnell used to say, when someone asked after his well-being: "Bad a-bed and wuss up!" Ted Evans told me that the outside toilet was usually called the 'Dunaken'. Could this have been from the Scottish phrase 'Do ne ken' ('Do not know') – perhaps an answer given to children when they asked where another person had gone to? Other local phrases for the lavatory included 'Sitting on the Throne' and the 'Houses of Parliament!'

Noel Baker told me that when his mother used to light the stove at Highmoor School, she often had difficulty in getting the fire going. Tom Allum would then say to her, comfortingly: "She'll go, Missus, when she gets a holt!" Another popular saying on a winter's day was: "It's a coat colder today!" Our first milkman, on seeing a car go by at great speed, used to shake his head sorrowfully, saying: "'E ough'er 'ave been there afore 'e started!"

Mrs Margaret Allum (nee Busby), c 1920. In 1911, when her husband John Allum was 36 years old, he had an accident on a bicycle and died of his injuries. His widow was left with three children. She died in 1948. Photograph kindly lent by Mrs Sally Crocker (nee Allum).

'Brusher' Slade of Highmoor

One Highmoor personality, 'Brusher' Slade, lived with his old mother *'Granny Slade' in one of the two cottages which now form one, called Cherry Tree Cottage on Witheridge Hill. (*Not to be confused with 'Granny Slade' of Stoke Row). He was often to be found at The Woodman and we get an interesting account of him from John H Baker in his book *A School on the Ground Floor*:

"The custom of some inns in those days often fluctuated according to the favours of a few popular characters whom the other customers found entertaining. One particular favourite was a very hearty beer drinker nicknamed 'Brusher'. He pretended to talk in a half-witted way, making ludicrous remarks about anything or anybody, which invariably caused hilarious laughter among the company. 'Brusher' was a natural buffoon. He had a curious vein of humour. His appearance and gestures contributed to the general effect of his talk, as he sat slouched on the settle, his short clay pipe stuck in the corner of his mouth, his worn cap pushed back on his head, and his face masked with grimaces.

His simpleton pose concealed a very astute and cunning wit. Although a stout handyman labourer, with considerable muscular strength, he never worked for a regular employer, but always took emergency jobs of some urgency which offered higher than ordinary wages. He threw his weight where it brought the best rewards. He valued his freedom more than anything else and had no fancy for a life of restraint and regimentation.

He succeeded in completely fooling the medical officers when called up for service in 1914. He put up such a performance that he was classed as mentally deficient, so idiotic were his answers and general behaviour. A soldier's life was not for 'Brusher'. His labour proved a useful asset during the war years of man shortage on the farms and in the woods. No doubt his intractable character, even at his best, would have made him a misfit in the army. His two brothers, men of a more simple and straightforward nature, passed the medical test and served throughout the war. 'Brusher' was no ordinary fool, he was a fool in jest.

'Brusher' was not always faithful to The Woodman, though it was his second home and favourite pub. His way of employment made him a rover, and he sometimes felt the urge to roam for his beer and company to other pubs in the neighbourhood. It was a quiet night in The Woodman when he had one of his roaming fits. Custom, that is, customers, went where 'Brusher' went. The company followed him as crows follow the plough." 'Brusher' lived at what is today known as 'Cherry Tree Cottage' on Witheridge Hill.

Another well-known character in Highmoor was Edward James Francis Wells, always known as 'Ed'ard'. He was a tent-peg maker and had lived a very hard life, working out in the woods in all weathers. In later life he turned and sold rolling pins.

As Ed'ard grew older, he became unsteady on his 'bike', so he bought himself a tricycle. These photographs were taken by Mr A Pilati.

Later on, the Vicar gave Ed'ard a pram to transport his wood around the village. He died at the grand age of 95 in 1968. Both these photographs were kindly lent by Mrs Louie Stevens (nee Wells).

Despite, or perhaps because of, much hardship, marriages lasted a long time in 'the old days'. One couple who celebrated their Golden Wedding, and there have been quite a few, were Richard and Annie Slade. As can be seen from these two pictures,

they matured into a comfortable and happy way of life, even though they had to work very hard. In his book *The Ipsden Country*, Mr J H Baker described the Slades under the thinly disguised name of Sladen. "Mrs Sladen was a typical motherly housewife, a good and friendly neighbour. It was second nature to her to lend a hand to anyone who needed help. If it brought small monetary rewards from those who could afford to pay, well and good, but she never asked for payment for her services. Her husband, some ten years older than herself, was a real rustic character and had a countryman's philosophy."

These two photographs show Richard and Annie Slade in their early days and on the day of their Golden Wedding. They lived in both Highmoor and Stoke Row. The top photograph was kindly lent by Mrs Beryl Grismanauskas (nee Slade) and the lower one by Mrs Nellie Elliott (nee Edwards).

Another couple who celebrated 50 years of marriage, some years ago though, were Edward ('Ed'ard) Wells and his wife Susan (nee Saunders). Here they are seen in their youth...

...and on the day of their Golden Wedding. Both photographs by kind permission of Mrs Louisa Stevens (nee Wells).

This is Mrs Susan Wells (nee Saunders) in middle life. This picture was taken by Mr Pilati, the butler at Highmoor Park, when Mrs Wells was working at the Dog and Duck, Highmoor. By kind permission of Mrs Ada Britnell (nee Wells).

The strong resemblance between mother and daughter can be seen quite clearly here. This is Susan Wells' daughter, Mrs Ada Britnell of Highmoor, who is one of the two people to whom this book is dedicated, being typical of the many people who helped me with this work. Kindly lent by Louisa Stevens (nee Wells).

Two Highmoor sisters in about 1930. This professional Art Deco portrait is of fashionably dressed Edith Treadwell...

...and this is her equally pretty sister, Mercy Treadwell. Both photographs by kind permission of Mrs Lily Bishop (nee Treadwell).

Quite a few couples in Stoke Row and Highmoor have celebrated their Golden and even Diamond Weddings. This is Ted and Beattie Evans (nee Rogers) when they were courting in 1930. Ted grew up in Stoke Row and Beattie nearby at Kingwood Common.

This is Ted and Beattie celebrating their 65th Wedding Anniversary in October 1996. Both photographs kindly lent by Ted and Beattie Evans.

George and Mavis Stevens feature several times in this book, especially in the chapter on Wars, as George was a PoW in Germany throughout most of the Second World War and Mavis served in the Land Army. Here they are in their garden, after the war...

... and on the day of their Golden Wedding in June 1996.
By kind permission of the Henley Standard.

This charming picture is of 'Granny and Grandad' Wells feeding their cat. It was taken at Tudor Cottage. Lower Highmoor in about 1880. It is believed that they were the parents of 'Ed'ard' Wells. By kind permission of Mrs Rosemary Jadkawska (nee Wells).

Another lovely picture – this is one of my favourites. It shows 'Grandad' Wise and 'Little Cousin George' enjoying 'beaver' (elevenses) together at Highmoor, c 1930. Grandad Wise was born in 1855. By kind permission of Mrs Suzanne Cordery.

Many Stoke Rovians and Highmoorians have lived to a great age, including a number of men who have been well over 90 when they died. Les Powell told me it was said of Stoke Rovians many years ago: "If you didn't live until you were 80, you weren't trying!"

However, the prize must go to Mrs Mabel Cox, who will be celebrating her 105th birthday on 8 June 1999. A picture of Mabel as a young girl appears on the first page of this chapter. She was brought up by her grandparents at Stonehouse Farm, Highmoor. At the age of 21 she married Frederick Cox and they had three children, Mabel has outlived two of them. During the Second World War, she cooked meals for workers in a factory hidden in the local woodlands and delivered milk in an Austin Seven. Many evenings she played the piano with a local dance band called the Swing Sextet. Mabel played the organ at Stoke Row Chapel from the age of 14, retiring officially at the age of 86 – a span of 72 years. She still played occasionally at the age of 97! When Frederick returned to Stoke Row after the war, they moved into 'Victoria Cottage' on the Village Green and she has lived there ever since.

According to a report in the Henley Standard, she attributes her long life to "good plain food." (She also receives a great deal of care from her son, Alan!)

Mabel Cox is seen her on her 100th birthday, holding up her telegram from the Queen on 8 June 1994. This lady also received a cable from President Clinton. By kind permission of the Henley Standard.

4.   Dipping into the Wells

The Maharajah's Well

It all began in Benares (now Varanasi) in Northern India in about 1850, when Edward Anderdon Reade, fifth son of the Squire of Ipsden, (of which Stoke Row was then a part) who was at that time Lieutenant-Governor of the North Western Provinces, was chatting to the Maharajah of Benares about water shortage problems.

According to Mr Reade's version of the story in the *Oxford Times* of 1872: "The scenery (in part of Benares) is not unlike that of the Chiltern Hills; the inconveniences, owing to deficiency of water supply were the same. The measures the Maharajah was adopting for the relief of his people were the subject of much of our conversation, in the course of which it would seem I must have mentioned the results of boyish knowledge in the upland of my own district, such as the people being dependent for water retained in dirty ponds and deserted clay-pits. In dry seasons the water used in cooking in one cottage was passed on to do the like office in others, urchins being cruelly thumped for furtive quenchings of thirst and washing days being indefinitely postponed."

About ten years after the above conversation had taken place, the Maharajah offered to set up a charity to help the people of England. He felt a high regard for this country, partly because he had been educated here, and for the folk of Stoke Row in particular, probably because of his friendship with Mr Reade. Thus it came about that a noble gentleman in India became benefactor to a small Chiltern village. Although the resultant Well proved to be a great boon to the villagers one can only muse on the astonishment that the superstructure must have caused in a part of England that probably knew very little about India at all, except that it was part of the British Empire, coloured pink on the schoolroom map!

The Maharajah of Benares, circa 1865. The original of this photograph was kindly donated to the author by Miss Catherine Hope.

In 1979, Rev Cyril Isherwood, Vicar of Stoke Row 1941-80, who grew up in the village, wrote in the *Stoke Row News*:

"I do not think any of us can realise how difficult life must have been in the little hamlet of Stoke Row during the long hot dry summers of the last century, before the Well was sunk. The only means of water were small tanks in peoples' gardens, which caught the water from the roofs of their houses, or the ponds around the village. But as all these depended on rain, they would soon begin to dry up. So there were days when people would have to go out with yokes on their shoulders and a bucket on each side and literally search for water which could be used for washing or cooking but not for drinking. But as the summer went on this would become a difficult problem to solve. There was, and still is, a pond called the Tea Pond, which seems to have been the most reliable for tea drinkers.

Mr Edward Anderdon Reade of Ipsden. Original also kindly donated by Miss Hope.

When the Vicarage was built, a deep tank was dug in the backyard to hold the water which fell from the roof of the Vicarage and a pump put over the sink in the scullery for drawing up the water. But, as with all other wells, this too depended on the rainfall. The men of the village would be able to get their ale at one of the pubs, the women and children would no doubt drink some home-made ale, as the children were not allowed to drink the water and were severely punished if they did.

And so it came to pass that the Maharajah, wishing to give a substantial charity to England, decided to give a Well where he understood that it was so badly needed. Accordingly, on 10 March 1863 a beginning was made on the digging by John Wilder Ltd of Wallingford. No doubt the work was helped by some Stoke Row men, but I can only vouch for 'Grandpa' Grace and Jimmy Wells. Chalk was reached after digging through 25ft of clay and gravel subsoil and persisted to 300 ft, except for layers of sand at 128 ft and 228 ft, each about 8ft deep, but finally, below 300 ft, a mixture of chalk and shells was found, through which the spring water flowed in.

There was usually 15 to 25 ft of water and it was considered that a daily yield of 600 to 700 gallons of water was to be had. The system of having two buckets, one going up and the other going down, was designed by Mr Reade and Mr Richard Wilder. Also it was Mr Reade who designed the superstructure, which is unique and like no other in England, and of which Stoke Row is justly proud."

Only someone who has lived through a severe drought or who has spent time in a very hot and dry country can imagine what it must have been like in Stoke Row in the last century, when winters were extremely cold, with great falls of snow, and summers were long, hot, dry and dusty.

Rev Isherwood again: "How wonderful it must have been when, at last, the people could come and draw the beautiful, clear spring water. It was quite an event when a father or mother came with a yoke over their shoulders and a bucket on each side to wind the handles for about 10 minutes to bring up one bucket whilst the other went down and the children would look forward to coming to see it done. I can remember so well, on a beautiful summer evening, having a drink of the lovely, clear water which, in summer, was ice cold, but in winter would often be slightly steaming!"

The Maharajah's Well, c 1865. The man standing by it is thought to be a Mr Gill, who went down the well to inspect it when it was finished. Photograph by Henry Jenkins of Wallingford. Kindly loaned by Mrs Joan Watkins (nee Powell).

Rev Isherwood recalled: "when we came to Stoke Row in 1891 the Well had been in use for some years, but there was still the problem of rinsing water for washing, so when our well began to run dry someone would have to go with their yoke and buckets to find a pond, where there was water suitable for washing purposes. During one of those very hot summers, when there were seven weeks of perfect weather, some extra water was brought up from Goring in a tub-shaped conveyance on wheels, but we were only allowed one or two buckets for which, if I remember rightly, we were charged 2d a bucket and, as we had a horse, they did not go far.

As there was no bathroom in the Vicarage, we had our bath either in our bedroom or in the nursery, or even before the kitchen fire in winter. The water had to be heated, either by the kitchen range or else on a 'Beatrice' paraffin heater. But, as the water from the Well could only be used for drinking or cooking, we had to rely on water from our own tank, collected from rain off the roof of our house, or else water from some pond.

In those hot dry summers, at the end of the last century, the ponds began to dry up, so that I can remember having a bath with water of a distinctly clay colour with some stewed tadpoles! Well, it was wet and warm and we just had to accept it as such."

The Well Warden's Cottage

When the Well was sunk, a small single-storey house, with an octagonal roof, was built for the Keeper of the Key of the Well. Between 1864 and 1878 there were two Wardens, a Mrs Whittick, followed by Mr and Mrs William East. Then, in 1878, Mr and Mrs Robert Hewitt came. They remained custodians of the Well until they passed away and their place was taken by their niece, Miss Cecily Turner, who continued to live with them in the cottage and care for the well until her death in 1972.

In adult life, Miss Turner became a teacher at the village school and the task of caring for the Well probably became less onerous as the years went by. By this time most people knew how to use the Well and were familiar with the rules which were posted up near to it.

These included a list of ten instructions for raising the water and ended:

7. Children of tender age are best kept outside the well buildings and on no account let dogs enter it.

8. When strangers come inside to see the water drawn, caution them to keep clear of the handles of the draw wheel on both sides.

9. On leaving the well lock the gate.

10. Thank God for His gift of pure water; and remember that the giver of this well asks nothing more of you than to observe these proper precautions.

W A Reade, Trustee
1st June 1866

Mrs Doris Long (nee Barefoot) of Hayling Island, told me that, in the 1920s, she used to go from her home in Reading to stay with Miss Turner, who was her aunt. It was her job to "whiten the ledge around the base of the Well with 'step whitener'."

In 1964 Heather Townsend, then 11 years old, and a member of the family who voluntarily cared for the Well grounds for many years, lived opposite the Well and was very friendly with Miss Turner.

In an essay she reminisced on happy times spent with this lady in the little octagonal cottage, and wrote: "While talking to Miss Turner I found out that the well was originally to have been built nearer to the road, but the sides fell in, so they built it where it stands today. Several ancient coins were found during the digging, though nobody knows what happened to them.

As a small child, I can recall Miss Turner telling me that one day a man came to draw water from the Well. Unfortunately, he was wearing a hat which, when he leaned over, fell into the Well. He told Miss Turner of this and when, several weeks later, someone else was drawing water and the hat came up in the bucket, she was able to put their minds at rest that nobody had fallen into the Well.

During a water shortage, water from the Well was allowed to the villagers only. The ration was two buckets full per person; some people came collect theirs in carts."

Bringing water home from the Well: William Wixen, senior, William Wixen, junior and young Arthur Wixen, c 1928. By kind permission of Arthur Wixen.

The Well Orchard

In India the custom was to provide an orchard, so that the Well keeper could make a livelihood from the sale of the fruit and the Well could be maintained. Rev Isherwood tells us that the same was done here: "£200 was spent in buying the Cherry Orchard, next to the Well to help bring funds for the upkeep and maintenance of it. Women would go up the high ladders and pick the cherries for 3/6d a day, and the cherries were sold for 2.1/2d per pound. Later men were paid to do this work, and the profits from the sale of the cherries went to the maintenance of the Well. For many years this orchard was a very pretty sight. People would come out from Reading in charabancs, both in the spring to see the cherry blossom and again in the summer to buy the fruit."

From Heather Townsend's essay again, "Miss Turner told me that in the Well ground the fish-shaped pond, surrounded by railings, used to contain several golden carp. (The Maharajah's crest is two golden carp and the moon). Unfortunately, one winter the frost and ice killed them.

There was also a large round mound, which was used as a bandstand. In the cherry season someone would be up at dawn and with either with a pop-gun or a rattle they frightened the starlings which would come in flocks if not scared away. That was called 'bird starving'."

I also found out, looking around at the many documents hanging on the walls of Miss Turner's cottage, that there were regulations for the Well, one of which was that only cows were to graze in the Well Orchard because they are sacred in India.

Miss Turner said that, during Queen Victoria's reign, the Viceroy of India, Lord Hobhouse, came to see the Well. When he returned to India he put an article into an Indian magazine about the Well, her aunt and the garden from which he took away some herbs."

Mrs Long also recalled that the Well Orchard had a set number of cherry trees in it and if one was lost it had to be replaced, "so as to keep the number up".

Further Celebrations

The Maharajah continued to be generous to the village. In 1872, when the Prince of Wales had survived typhoid fever, the Indian potentate sent the enormous sum of £200 for public celebrations of the fact.

The Berks and Oxon Advertiser of 1 March 1872 reported "The proceedings commenced at 10 o'clock, at which hour a special service was celebrated in the pretty little church... At the conclusion of the service, the Maharajah's dole, consisting of half a pound of tea, one pound of sugar, two loaves of bread, two pounds of bacon and a good pair of blankets, marked 'Ishree' (the first name of the Maharajah), was proceeded with, and this handsome gift was made to every cottage in the parish, to the number of 149.

At one o'clock luncheon was served in the club room at the Cherry Tree Inn, to the gentry and yeomanry of the neighbourhood, to which 34 guests sat down... Once they had eaten, the gentry repaired to Mr Godwin's, on whose premises a long covered shed had been fitted up, in which the labourers of the district, to the number of about 150, sat down to a capital lunch. After this the children indulged in various sports and prizes were awarded to the victors in different games...

Then, after an interval, followed the illuminations, which had been entrusted to Messrs C T Brock and Co, the well known pyrotechnists of the Crystal Palace. It is due to them and their assistants that we may sum up the whole matter in one word – perfection. ...All combined to make a happy day for Stoke Row. The weather was fine, the night was still, the wind just right to keep the smoke from the spectators..."

In 1882 Queen Victoria was the victim of an attempt on her life. Again, the Maharajah's generosity provided a splendid celebration, this time for the school-children and their mothers. How sad it was that after that date, probably following the death of the Maharajah, nothing more was heard from Benares for over 60 years. Then contact was made again almost by chance and resulted in the visit of the Duke of Edinburgh to the village, of which more anon.

In 1882 the Maharajah provided the Stoke Row school children with a tea-party and gifts, to celebrate Queen Victoria's survival of an attempt on her life. This picture is rather dark, but it is still possible to see the enormous variety of clothing and especially hats, worn by the children, who are obviously in their Sunday best. Kindly lent by Laureen Williamson.

The Value of Water

In 1906 mains water was brought to parts of Stoke Row from Woodcote, but to the Vicar and his family "it was not like the beautiful spring water of the Well."

Mrs Joan Watkins (nee Powell), who lived at Southview, in School Lane, recalled how valuable water was in the long hot summers of her childhood. One such summer was 1921 by which time she would have been four years old.

Although water from the Maharajah's Well was available in the middle of the village, it was a long way to walk with two buckets on a yoke. "However", she told me, "my mother had a brother, Will, who, with his wife Dolly, lived in Reading and they had a motorbike with a sidecar. In this, every night during all the summers of the 1920s, they used to bring up two water-carrying cans, specially made for this job, each about 15" long x 4" wide x 2'6" high, with taps at the bottom and a box of a dozen quart beer bottles, all filled with water from the taps at Reading." Joan remembered her mother saying one night when she came home from school, "You can have boiled potatoes or a cup of tea, I've only got enough water for one or the other."

During the winter snows, the children were encouraged to make huge snowballs which were left in the middle of the garden. From these their father would chip off snow, in order to plant out his spring seedlings. There was, of course, no water closet indoors at Southview, just a 'privy' or 'up the garden', which her father emptied once a year "late in the evening when the moon was bright!"

In 1927 another pipeline was laid from Nettlebed and, as more and more houses were connected to the piped supply, so the Well became less used. On 18th February 1939 *The London Evening Standard* printed a photograph of (another) Mrs Powell, who lived at No. 1 Wellside Villas. This lady sadly admitted that she had given up using the Well because she "found the labour-saving appeal of the tap too strong!"

She explained: "The water is wonderfully pure, but it is not worth the trouble involved. It takes nearly a quarter of an hour to draw a bucketful because of the great distance to the bottom. The windlass is so hard to turn that I need two people to help me." In the early part of the Second World War it was discovered that the cable which drew the buckets up had rusted and so it was then removed.

The Centenary Celebrations

When the Queen visited Varanasi in 1961, the Maharajah mentioned that the centenary year of his great-grandfather's benefaction was only a few years away. He asked H R H Prince Philip, Duke of Edinburgh if he would be kind enough to visit the little Chiltern village when the time came. The Duke readily agreed and the Maharajah presented her Majesty with an ivory model of the Well, which the Duke brought with him when he came on Wednesday, 8 April, 1964.

For the village it was probably the biggest highlight in its life since the opening of the Well one hundred years before. The Duke arrived on the Village Green in a red helicopter which he piloted himself from Windsor. Fortunately the weather was beautiful for the occasion. *The Reading and Berkshire Chronicle* reported it thus "Captured, single-handed, one village – by the Duke of Edinburgh. This is what happened to Stoke Row, the little Oxfordshire village which opened its heart to welcome the Duke when he attended the Maharajah's Well centenary celebration." Ever since that day, the *Stoke Row News* has commemorated the event by having a helicopter coloured red in the top left hand corner of its cover.

The 3rd USAAF Headquarters Band provided music for much of the day. At the Well the Duke met the Maharajah's envoy, Mr B Sahi, his wife and their 14 year old son. Mr Sahi then presented the Duke with a sealed urn of water from the Ganges and other gifts. A cable of good wishes from the Maharajah was then read out loud. One of the hosts for the day was Michael Reade, great-grandson of the original co-founder of the project. The Duke then drew a bucket of water from the Well under the supervision of Mr J H Wilder, the great-nephew of Richard Wilder whose Wallingford firm had installed the mechanism some 100 years previously.

Miss Turner, teacher at Stoke Row School and Well Warden, seen here outside the little Well Warden's cottage, c 1938.

The Duke leaving the little Well Warden's Cottage. Mrs Sahi was waiting for him outside. By kind permission of Edwin Stallwood.

The Duke and Miss Turner, the Well Keeper, leave her cottage together, to take part in the procession. By kind permission of Edwin Stallwood.

This water was mixed with the Ganges water and a bottle of it still stands in the Cherry Tree public house, where the Duke partook of refreshment later in the day.

A commemorative service was conducted by Revd Cyril Isherwood, who had been Vicar of Stoke Row for as long as anyone could remember. After a few words by the Bishop of Dorchester, the Duke planted a cherry tree in the Well Orchard.

Later, he went to the Village Hall, where he met about 70 of the older residents, many of whom were able to tell him of the days when they drew water from the Well and were glad of it.

The Duke of Edinburgh's helicopter awaits his departure from the Village Green.
By kind permission of Edwin Stallwood.

After the Duke departed, Stoke Row continued its celebrations with children's games and tea. A film about Varanasi (Benares) was then shown in the Village Hall. The day was rounded off with a dance and barbecue. Percy and Ivy Collis were awarded First Prize for the best decorated house in the village. "We were very proud of that!" Mrs Collis told me.

Heather Townsend's essay concluded: "Lastly, I asked Miss Turner of her recollections of the Centenary Celebrations. She told me that several glass jars of Purple Heart cherries from the Well Orchard were sent to Buckingham Palace and the name of Purple Hearts caused the Duke much amusement. Also she said they decorated her cottage, but although it was nice when it was finished, it was rather a nuisance at the time. She said that it was a great honour to meet the Duke and the Indian guests, one of whom was cousin to the present Maharajah, who was unable to come. In the cottage, there are many documents. One is from the Maharajah confirming that Miss Turner's uncle was Well Warden. There are also many pictures, one of which was signed by the Duke during the Centenary Celebrations."

The Restoration of the Well

Although the Well was "tidied up for the occasion", there was little doubt by the mid-1970s that it was beginning to deteriorate. Miss Turner, the last Well Warden, had died in 1972, and no-one in this age of home comforts fancied living in the tiny cottage which was damp and without modern facilities.

In May 1979 an Appeal was launched for £20,000 to restore the Well structure and to make substantial improvements to the cottage. A number of people took out covenants. All sorts of fund-raising events were held, one of which was an *Old Tyme Music Hall*, starring actor George Cole, a village resident, and comedian Roy Hudd, who was then living in nearby Nettlebed. The most significant money-spinners, however, were a series of Steam Engine Rallies, organised by the great steam enthusiast family, the Greenaways, and their innumerable friends. These Rallies have continued each year since and are now a regular part of summer life in the village.

About two years later almost all the money had been found and work began on the restoration of the superstructure. Local builder Maurice Robins and his staff sealed a 'time capsule' in a cavity in the new well surround. This contained items which, it was hoped, would preserve a taste of national and local life of the time.

The *Henley Standard*, on 24 July 1981 reported: "...the canopy, its supports, the iron superstructure and the elephant which surmounts the well cover have been dismantled. Their restoration is being organised by blacksmith John Hill at Broadplatt, who is doing some of the work himself and sending some out to specialists.

The columns are being shot-blasted and hot-dip galvanised; the original golf-leaf finish of the elephant has been found to be too damaged to salvage, so it is being cleaned and will be re-gilded..."

When the whole edifice was finally reassembled in March 1982 the villagers flocked to see the dome being lifted into place.

The Well dome being lowered into place, March 1982. Kindly lent by Gerald O'Leary.

About the same time an extension, with bedroom and bathroom was put on to the rear of the tiny octagonal cottage. Later, a permanent Well Warden was found.

Restoration work on the Well Warden's cottage. The extension provided a much-needed bedroom and bathroom. By kind permission of Gerald O'Leary.

The Maharajah's Well Today

The Well, which is still in the care of its Trustees, has since been repainted and regilded. The whole property is tended by the present Well Warden, Joan Bint, who keeps the gardens looking neat.

A little book, lovingly written by Laureen Williamson, who also wrote a larger version as part of the fund-raising project, is available for visitors who come in large numbers in the summer. They marvel at this wonderful oriental edifice and the pretty little cottage which stands beside it, looking for all the world like a brick-built inspiration for one of Coalport's miniature china pastille burners!

The Maharajah's Well, under snow.
Photograph kindly lent by Ken Poyton

The Highmoor Village Well

In comparison to the Maharajah's Well, Highmoor Well is unpretentious. Nevertheless, it is one of the few local wells to have its own proper well house.

It is said that it, too, caved in as it was being dug, though it is not known whether any men died during the work. Rev H G Munro, Rector of Rotherfield Peppard, appears to have paid for the sinking of the well. It is said that if a piece of rope, the same length as the depth of the well, were laid from the Well House towards the Memorial Hall, it would extend to the middle of the Village Green.

Murray's Handbook for Travellers, Oxford, 1894, states: "Highmoor: A well was sunk in 1865 by the Rev H G Munro, 284 ft in depth, covered by a small hexagonal brick well-house.

Miss Elwes of Highmoor Hall paid for the erection of the Highmoor Well House, a neat brick structure of octagonal shape, surmounted by a weather vane. On one side is a drinking fountain, supplied by a cistern from within, and on the other a wall letter box has been placed for the convenience of parishioners. Inside a bronze tablet reads:

"To the glory of God and to the honour of His holy apostle Paul
this Well was dedicated for the use of this Parish
A D MDCCCLXV"

*Local artist Avril Bryant imagined this scene taking place
when the Highmoor Well was opened in 1865.*

49

The well was operated by a double-handed wheel, with steps on either side, probably made by Wilders of Wallingford. It needed two people to operate it, one standing at each side.

In the chapter on Transport there is a photograph taken in about 1920 which shows the original wellhouse, with its attractive 'lantern'. Mr and Mrs Russell of Stonehouse Cottages, were the last people to care for the well. According to Mrs Ada Britnell, "Their daughter, Mabel, was the last person to draw water from the well, because as she did so, in 1953, the rope broke and it was never replaced."

Thereafter the well fell into disrepair. In 1973 the roof was repaired at a cost of £130. This was paid for by the Parish Council, but the local rates could only afford roofing felt and the beauty of the original tiled roof, with its lantern, was lost. To prevent vandalism, the little windows were cemented in and glazing bars painted on.

In 1991 the then owners of 'Well Cottage' had a new wing added to their house and had a new garage built. This echoes, in an octagonal manner, the design of the well house, which unfortunately they were not able to restore.

In 1996 it was discovered that the Well had been registered by a previous owner as being within the curtilege of 'Well Cottage' and it was immediately decided that a fund should be started with the aim of restoring the Well and returning it to the village. A number of fund-raising events took place over the following three years.

Today the plan to restore the Highmoor Well, complete with its winding gear, is already under way and it is hoped that before very long this pretty little well house will be returned to its former glory and once again become the pride of Highmoor.

Left: the rear of the Highmoor Well house, taken in about 1950 by Mr McLeod from his garden at Well Cottage where he and his wife lived.
Right: This photograph was taken by the author in 1984. It shows the recently felted roof without its attractive 'lantern' top, the concreted windows and little drinking cup recess.

5. The Villages at Prayer

The Church of St John the Evangelist, at Stoke Row is a Listed Building, Grade II and was built in 1846. The exterior is built of stone and flint and is somewhat austere, but the interior is very attractive and in the east, behind the altar, there is a beautiful stained glass window.

Notes made by Professor W O Hassell of the Bodleian Library, and entered in his file when he was obviously hoping to start on the South-east Oxfordshire section of the Victoria County History, point out: "When England was divided into parishes in the 7th century, Newnham Murren and Mongewell were among these, with their riparian (riverside) lengths being presumably set by those of the old Saxon estates. The upper parts of Newnham Murren and Mongewell were incorporated into the ecclesiastical parish of St John the Evangelist, Stoke Row in 1849."

In a letter to me, Dr Malcolm G A Vale, Fellow and Tutor in History and Keeper of the Archives, at St John's College, Oxford, explained: "St John's College, Oxford acquired the land on which the Church and Vicarage are built, as well as the Glebe land at the side, as part of its holdings in Stoke Row and Ipsden in March 1580 when the land was bought from Sir John Arundell, Knight, of Lanherne, Cornwall. The relevant deeds are in the Muniments Room at St John's Oxford."

There is a notice inside the church, let into the wall by the door, which reads:

Stoke Row Parish or Consolidated Chapelry
was formed in the upper part of
Ipsden, Newnham Murren and Mongewell
for all ecclesiastical purposes.

This church of St John the Evangelist
was built in 1846 and
consecrated by Bishop Wilberforce
on St Frideswide's Day 19th October 1848.

The Living is in the patronage of St John's College, Cambridge.

The Oxford Chronicle reported on 30th June 1846: "On Thursday last, the 27th inst, the ceremony of laying the foundation stone of the new church at Stoke-row, in the parish of Ipsden, Oxon, was performed by Miss Reade of Ipsden House. A very large company attended and the address to the congregation, by the Rev Hopkins of Nuffield, was highly impressive, and made its way with great force to the understanding of every class of his hearers. A cold lunch was afterwards provided by John Reade, Esq and wines, etc. by Mr Meyers of the Lamb Inn, Wallingford, in a tent erected by Mr Clarke, the builder, where a large party enjoyed themselves and expressed their satisfaction at the various arrangements."

The Church of St John, the Evangelist, Stoke Row. This photograph was taken from the bedroom of a house opposite, in about 1930. It shows the Schoolmaster's house on the left, and the Council houses in School Lane, which were built in 1920. By kind permission of Mrs Kathleen Dyer (nee Howells).

Rev Cyril Isherwood, Vicar from 1941 until his death in 1980, wrote a short history of the church in the *Stoke Row News* of 1979 - 80: "Until 1844, there was no Church (or School) in Stoke Row. The Mother Church was at St Mary, the Virgin, Ipsden, then called Yppesdene, four miles away. Then it was that the Vicar, Rev Richard Twopenny, felt that it was time the little hamlet of Stoke Row should have its own church, but was faced with the difficulty of raising sufficient funds for the building and also fixing the boundary of the parish. In this important work he was helped by Bishop Wilberforce of Oxford and Mr John Reade, of Ipsden House, and his family who helped most generously.

A number of friends who were interested also gave help and without their support it would not have been possible to commence building. The land for the Vicarage, Church and School was given by St John the Baptist College, Oxford. The cost of building the church was estimated at £2,500. The building was commenced on 27 June 1844, but the church was not consecrated until St Frideswide's Day, 19 October 1848 and was dedicated to St John the Evangelist.

As 'the gift' of Ipsden Parish was acquired by St John's College, Cambridge, by patent of Henry VIII, through the influence of Bishop Fisher of Rochester, in October 1522, so that of Stoke Row automatically came under that College.

From 1846 to 1850 the Sacraments were administered by Rev Isaac Cole. There is no record as to when the Vicarage was built, but I believe it was not inhabited until 1850, when the Rev James Arrowsmith became Vicar, and remained so until 1891.

The first baptism was on 20 November 1846 of Ann Bond; the first wedding was on 1 December 1849 of William Heynard and Emmeline Stallwood, and the first burial was 6 November 1846 of William Berry, aged 82.

The beautiful hanging crucifix, the work of the people of Oberammergau, (now in the Vestry) was presented to the Church by the Vicar of Reading in 1952.

The clock in the tower was a gift of the Rev H H Appleford, who followed my father as Vicar in 1901. It was made by Mr T Hartley in his workshop, a converted stable near Shillingford. Every part (except the foundry work) was made by hand. It was assembled in the tower in 1925 and still, night and day, gives to all around the times of the hour."

The interior of St John's Church – this photograph was probably taken about the time of the First World War and shows many interesting features, most of which are not there today. The Union flag, of course, the oil lamps, the frieze around the walls at shoulder height, the small pipe organ, the medallions on the wall behind the altar and the paintings of the saints, which were later replaced by excerpts from the scriptures. The rose window, which appears to have been attractive even then, was redesigned in 1954. Kindly lent by the Rural History Centre.

53

The Tenor Bell

At the Vestry Meeting on 23 March 1858 at Ipsden: "It was proposed by Mr W B Reade and seconded by Mr Pickett that the Tenor Bell of Ipsden be exchanged for the bell now in use at the District Church of Stoke Row; and that the last-named bell, with the cracked Ipsden bell, be recast and fixed in Ipsden Church; the expence (sic) paid out of the Church Rate." The Parochial Church Council at that time consisted of Rev R Twopenny, who was Chairman, W B Reade, Samuel B Pickett, Philip J Dodd, John Wilder and G Hope."

The attractive Rose Window, designed and made by Barbara Batt in 1954. It depicts the Star, local flora, holly and bluebells.

The Rose Window

In his article, Rev Isherwood did not mention the colourful Rose Window. However, I quote from the church guide: "This window, above the altar, was the work of Barbara Batt who not only designed it but also cut out all the 1226 pieces of glass that form the window.

One of the problems in forming the design was to incorporate two natural forms, bluebells and holly – natives of Stoke Row – into a geometric form Rose Window. This was done by making a border of bluebells and intersecting holly in the background, so that they looked correct from whatever angle they were viewed. The window was dedicated in 1954."

Vicars of St John the Evangelist

One of the panels just inside the church door names the Bishops of Oxford and the Vicars of Stoke Row, but only up to 1941. Les Powell pointed out: "many of the Vicars of Stoke Row Church had names with three syllables in them!" I have added to the following list the names of the Bishops and Vicars who have come since then.

Bishops of Oxford	Vicars of Stoke Row
1846 Samuel Wilberforce	1846 John Cole
1870 John F Mackarkness	1850 James Arrowsmith
1888 William Stubbs	1891 Richard Isherwood
1901 Francis Paget	1901 Herbert H Appleford
1911 Charles Gore	1911 Thomas W Hutchinson
1919 Herbert Burge	1931 Reginald SCH Woods
1925 Thomas Strong	1941 Cyril Isherwood
1937 Kenneth E Kirk	1980 David Salt
1955 Harry J Carpenter	1984 Donald Shepherd
1971 Kenneth J Woolcombe	1995 David R Osborn
1978 Patrick C Rodger	1998 J Alan Johnson
1987 Richard D Harries	

Mrs Doris Long (nee Barefoot) lived in Reading when she was a little girl and used to come and stay with her aunt, Miss Cecily Turner, in the school holidays. She remembered that she used to play billiards with the son of Rev Thomas Hutchinson (1911-31) in the Vicarage during the 1920s. This boy was rather backward and shy, but very musical – he used to play the organ. He didn't mix much with people but he once told my aunt that he 'looked forward to my visits', which I felt was rather an honour!"

She also recollected a less-than-reverent occasion during one of her sojourns in Stoke Row, probably about 1925, when Rev Hutchinson's son was playing the organ and her aunt Cecily was singing in the Choir. Doris and her friend Winnie Powell (who lived in Wellside Villas) sat in the front pew. "It was very cold in there and my feet were freezing, so I took off my fur-backed gloves and my shoes. I put the gloves over my toes, which I then wiggled, after giving Win a nudge, and she burst out laughing! Oh dear, you should have seen the looks on the faces turned towards us and didn't we get told off afterwards!"

Rev Reginald S C H Woods (1931 - 41) was a very kind person who paid a great deal of attention to small details which gave happiness to many people. For instance, to each couple that he married he gave a postcard with the details of their wedding day upon it. One of these was lent to me by Mrs Ruby Brown, now of Wroxham, Norfolk. He also did this for wedding anniversaries, baptisms and other special occasions. Fred Powell recalled a Sunday School outing on a river steamer from Reading to Goring during the time of Rev S C H Woods. Mrs Mary Foreman, Headmistress of Stoke Row School 1939 - 44, remembered that when she first came here at the outbreak of war "One of the first people to welcome me to the School was the Rev Woods." She described him as "a lovely man, a real Christian, always ready to help anyone. He would rather have had holes in the soles of his shoes than see anyone remain worse off than himself.

Although he was a bachelor he had a room at the Vicarage where he had a lot of toys for children, a full set of soldiers, sailors and all sorts of other toys which entranced youngsters when they went to visit him." She and many other people were very sad when in 1941 Rev Woods married a widow and moved away.

Rev Cyril Isherwood followed Rev Woods and was almost a legend by the time we moved here. Sadly, he died soon afterwards, on 12 April 1980. He was certainly a very remarkable man. Born in 1886, he was still the practising Vicar of Stoke Row at the age of 94 and was renowned for cycling around the village. He was 66 years a priest and on high days and holidays he wore a tail coat and top hat. He was a bachelor who got up at 6.20 am most days and took a service in the church each weekday morning and four services on a Sunday. He gave talks to the pupils of Stoke Row School twice a week and visited anyone who he heard was ill. He was able to walk miles, even at 90 years of age. He was thought at that time to be one of the oldest priests in England and lived to exactly the same age as his father who had also been Vicar of Stoke Row (1891 - 1901) and was active in the ministry right up until his death. They are both buried in the churchyard at Meppershall, Bedfordshire, with others of their family.

Cyril Isherwood lived with his sister, Miss Kitty Isherwood, in the old Vicarage until she died at the age of 92 in 1972. 'Miss Kitty', as she was always respectfully known, taught Sunday School and was affectionately remembered for the way in which she helped many local people when they were going through difficult times. When she was much younger she had been a supporter of the Suffragette movement.

A Victorian country parson and his family. The Isherwoods at home in Meppershall, Beds. c 1895. The young boy later became Rev Cyril Isherwood, Vicar of Stoke Row.

In the vestry of St John's, there are photographs of some of the previous Vicars. Most of them look quite formidable and all of them were graduates of St John's College, Cambridge as 'the gift' (right to appoint the Vicar) came under this college.

Rev Richard Isherwood, Vicar of Stoke Row, 1890 - 1900, and his son, Cyril, who grew up in Stoke Row and returned to become Vicar, 1941 - 80. Kindly lent by Rev Donald Shepherd.

Rev Herbert Harben Appleford
Vicar of Stoke Row 1901 - 1911

Rev Thomas William Hutchinson
Vicar of Stoke Row 1911 - 1931

The Bishop of Dorchester visited St John's Church, Stoke Row in about 1935. With him are the Vicar, Rev S C H Woods, and Mr George Arthur Lambourne, who was Church Warden for 45 years. By kind permission of Cecil Lambourne.

Rose Stallwood (later Mrs Rose Textor) and Eileen Saunders (later Mrs Eileen Harris), being confirmed at St John's, Stoke Row in 1937. By kind permission of Rose Textor.

The only double wedding to take place at Stoke Row, on 24 September, 1938. The bride and groom on the left were Rose Carter and Reg Fulbrook and the couple on the right were Lily Carter and John Hayward. By kind permission of Mrs Lily Tayler. (nee Johnson).

An unusual baptism, conducted by Rev Cyril Isherwood on 2 September 1956. It was that of Bolajoko Adegombo Olujinka Laeinde. His parents came from Lagos and his father was training in administration with the Reading Corporation. He later returned to become Chief Executive of Lagos and later went into the church. By kind permission of Mr L J Burling.

Rev David Salt was the Rector of SS Peter and Paul at Checkendon and Vicar of St John's from 1980 to 1984. He came here from missionary work in the South Pacific and left to go to Hungerford. He was very highly thought of there for the way in which he responded to the dreadful 'Hungerford Massacre'. He and his wife later returned to Harpsden, Henley and retired in 1994.

Rev Donald Shepherd came to Stoke Row in 1984 and stayed until 1995, when he retired, with his wife, to the Cotswolds. In the eleven years that he was both Rector of Checkendon and Vicar of Stoke Row, he had been instrumental in the formation of the Langtree Team of Churches. When they retired in June 1995, he and his wife were presented with, among other gifts, a water-colour of a bluebell wood and other scenes around Checkendon, painted by local artist Robert Lobley.

The computer-literate Rev Alan Johnson, who had been with Toc H, came in mid-1998. He brought with him several popular initiatives and is already proving himself to be a caring man, who has become interested and involved in the parish.

Rev Donald Shepherd and his wife, Sylvia, receive their retirement gift from senior congregation member Philip Brownrigg. By kind permission of the Henley Standard.

St Paul's Church, Highmoor

The Post Office Directory of 1864 describes this little church very succinctly, when it states: "The church of St Paul is in the Early English style, consisting of nave and chancel: it was erected, together with the parsonage house, solely at the expense of Rev Joseph Smith BD, the previous Rector of this parish, and was opened for divine service in 1859; Mr Joseph Morris of Reading was the architect and Mr Robert Owthwaite of Henley-on-Thames, the builder."

Richard Slade, senior, remembered: "The first Vicar was a Rev Munro. It is believed that he was previously a Curate at Rotherfield Greys."

In 1877 *Harrods Royal County Directory* listed Rev John M Collard as Vicar and noted that "the living has an annual value of £80, plus the parsonage." A year later, Rev Thomas Henry Lee-Warner became the Vicar of Highmoor and stayed here for 12 years, until his death aged 63, on 11 March 1890, His wife, Henrietta Jane Lee-Warner, died on 22 August 1897, aged 60. They are both buried at Highmoor.

Highmoor Church in 1865, soon after it was built. The Vicarage, nowadays almost entirely hidden by trees, stands starkly to the rear. This photograph was taken from a photocopy which was made from a glass plate negative. Kindly lent by Mrs Monger.

The Post Office Directory of 1887 gave a very full description of this little church:
"Highmoor is an ecclesiastical parish, formed 3 August 1860, out of the civil parishes of Rotherfield Greys and Bix; it is two miles north-west from Greys Church and four and a half miles north-west from Henley-on-Thames, in the Southern division of the county; Henley petty sessional division, Henley county court district and in the rural deanery of Henley and archdeaconry and diocese of Oxford.

...The Church of St Paul is a small building of stone and flint in the Early English style, from designs by Mr Joseph Morris, architect of Reading, consisting of chancel and nave, and a western turret containing one bell and was erected, together with the parsonage house, solely at the expense of the Rev Joseph Smith BD, a previous Vicar of this parish and was opened in 1859; there are 170 sittings, all free. The registrar dates from the year 1860. The living is a Vicarage, tithe rent charge £47, gross yearly value £88 with residence, in the gift of the rector of Rotherfield Greys and held since 1878 by Revd Thomas Henry Lee-Warner MA of St Peter's College, Cambridge."

Frank Baldwin told me that his father, Charles Baldwin, "came to Highmoor in 1878, as a sort of 'General Factotum' to Rev Thomas Henry Lee-Warner, Vicar of Highmoor. It was there that he met and married Fanny Green, who lived at the nearby Church Cottages with her mother." (See also the chapter on Shops/POs)

A very large mounted print of this delightful photograph was found in Highmoor Church vestry in the early 1990s. Although there is no legend on the back, it is believed to be of a group of girls at a Charity School which used to stand at Rotherfield Greys, to the rear of the present day Almshouses. In Gardner's Directory of 1852 it was described as "The Parish School on Greys Green, a picturesque little building erected by Rev J R Roberts, the late Rector. It is supported by the subscriptions of the Rector, the inhabitants and the Misses Stapleton of Greys Court. The latter also clothe the children." It was also noted that there was "an average attendance of 40 scholars and the Mistress is Mrs Hannah Lewis."

I am grateful to Catherine Dingwall of the Victoria and Albert Museum for the suggestion, in view of the phrase pointing out that the Misses Stapleton "also clothe the children", that it is possible this picture is of some of the children, depicting their outfits and their benefactors, since the garments seem uniform and similar to those of Barnardo's girls of the late 19th century. This photograph is reproduced by kind permission of Rev Brian Weaver.

After the death of Rev Lee-Warner, there were several changes of Vicar. It might be appropriate here to list the Highmoor Vicars from the time the church was built until the present day:

Vicars of Highmoor Church:

1859 Rev Munro
1877 Rev John M Collard
1878 Rev Thomas Henry Lee-Warner MA
1890 Rev William Edwin Beaumont MA
1894 Rev Francis George Anderson Phillips MA
1894 Rev Francis Russell Harnett MA
1907 Rev Rawdon Marwood Willis MA
1912 Rev Philip Dalby
1913 Rev John Hughes
1929 Rev Clifford J Offer MA, F R Hist Soc
1941 Rev J Wilkie
1947 Rev Frank Weston
1954 Rev John Martin
1963 Rev Kenneth Martin
1970 Rev Stanley Dakin
1982 Rev Brian Weaver
1999 Rev Brendan Bailey

In 1890 Rev William Edwin Beaumont MA of Downing College, Cambridge, was the incumbent, with a tithe rent charge of £52 and a gross yearly value of £94, plus residence.

In 1894 Rev Francis George Anderson Phillips MA of Christ Church, Oxford, was there for less than a year before Rev Francis Russell Harnett MA of St John's College, Cambridge, took over and left in 1907 for Hinksey, Oxford.

Rev Rawdon Marwood Willis MA of St John's College, Oxford, came in 1907 and stayed until 24 May 1912, when he left for Holy Trinity Church, Henley.

Rev Philip Dalby filled in for about a year, before Rev John Hughes commenced as Vicar of Highmoor in the summer of 1913. George Stevens told me: "the Hughes had two children, Rhona and Michael. Rev Hughes was always known as 'Bravvy', but no-one seemed to know why!"

In another of the Highmoor Memories, it was recalled that "Rev Hughes was Vicar, before the First World War. His wife helped to organise a play or pageant in the summer and a Nativity at Christmas. She also played an orchestral sized harp most beautifully, accompanied by Mrs Beatrice Baker on the piano."

George Stevens pointed out: "how difficult it is to imagine today, when the School has long been closed and the Church is so ill-attended, to realise to what extent the Church dominated the village in the 1920s and 1930s. At that time the Vicar and his wife, together with Mr and Mrs Denham, more or less ran the village."

Alistair MacIntyre, who grew up at Highmoor Hall, recalled: "Rev Hughes was inclined to be High Church and would have liked to have been addressed as 'Father Hughes' but my parents would not have it, as they had been Prestbyterians." Although Rev Hughes and his wife left Highmoor in 1929, they are buried in Highmoor Churchyard.

A wedding at St Paul's Church, Highmoor, in about 1900. Unfortunately, none of the names of the people in the picture are known. Taken from a glass plate negative by kind permission of Mrs Louisa Stevens (nee Wells).

Guild of the Holy Child

Object.

To encourage and assist the children of the parish to keep their Baptismal vows, and to fight manfully under CHRIST's banner as faithful members of His Church.

Rules.

1. To say Prayers every morning and every evening.

2. To try "to follow the example of our Saviour JESUS CHRIST" at home, at work, at play.

3. To especially give up all bad talk, untruthfulness, rough behaviour out of doors, and staying out late in the evenings.

4. To promise to look forward to receiving the Sacrament of Confirmation.

Prayer to be said daily.

O MERCIFUL GOD, vouchsafe, we beseech Thee, to bless and prosper the work of our Guild. Grant that all its members may do that which is well-pleasing in Thy sight. Bless us in our own souls, and make us a blessing to the souls of others, and bring us at last to Thy heavenly kingdom; through JESUS CHRIST our LORD. Amen.

"Jesus Himself is that Little Child, like Whom we must especially become if we would be ever really fit for the Kingdom of Heaven."—*Keble.*

"Jesus increased in wisdom and stature, and in favour with GOD and man."

Member's Name

Admitted by J Hughes *Vicar*

Mowbrays R 13

Miss Marie Meheux told me that during Rev Hughes' time there was a 'Guild of the Holy Child' at Highmoor Church. This was a little social club (probably only for girls). They performed plays and went on outings etc, although the Meheux girls lived up at Newnham Hill and were always kept busy, so they were not often able to go to the Guild. The gates at the front and the stone font were made by their father, George Meheux, carpenter and builder, probably in the 1920s.

Highmoor Church in about 1905. The scene looks very rural, largely because there is a hedge around the graveyard where there is now a wall. By kind permission of Cecil Lambourne.

Rev Clifford Jesse Offer MA of Corpus Christi College, Cambridge, was Vicar of Highmoor Church 1929 - 1941 and during this time he was Hon Treasurer of the Diocesan Sunday Schools' Association and a Diocesan Inspector of Schools. Rev Offer was usually known to his friends as 'Jack' and left in November 1941 to become Rector of Ightham, near Rochester, Kent.

Rev J Wilkie was Vicar of Highmoor during the years of the Second World War and lived at the Vicarage there. Unfortunately, little is known about him.

In 1947 Rev Frank Weston became Vicar of Highmoor and was the last incumbent to live in the Vicarage at the rear of the church. When he left in 1954, the house was sold as a private dwelling. Mrs Shirley Mills (nee Holdish) showed me four Sunday School stamps given to her between 1947 and 1954 at Sunday School by the Rev Weston and told me that his wife used to come once every six weeks and tell the children stories about when the Westons were missionaries. Shirley also received a little book *Holy Communion Epistles and Gospels* for attending Sunday School for the whole year of 1952, without fail.

Rev John Martin took Highmoor under his wing from 1954 to 1963 until the arrival of his successor who, curiously enough, had the same surname. Rev Kenneth Martin, also Vicar of Rotherfield Greys, had Highmoor in his charge from 1963 to 1970 and then, for the following eight years, Rev John Kemp served both churches.

In 1978 Highmoor became part of the Nettlebed, Bix and Pishill group of churches, under Rev Stanley Dakin, who stayed until 1982, when he and his wife went out to do missionary work in East Africa.

Rev Brian Weaver, a former RAF and airline pilot, became Rector of Nettlebed in 1982. He and his wife, Jacquie, retired in 1998. Rev Brendan Bailey took up this post in May 1999. Aged 37, he had been a curate at Purley-on-Thames for four years.

The Vicars of Highmoor in recent years have been very ably supported by their Churchwardens, especially Eric Summers and, until her retirement to Devon in 1994, Miss Barbara Meade. At the present time Roy Stone, David Juster, Peter Lloyd and Karen Schmidt care for this pretty little church.

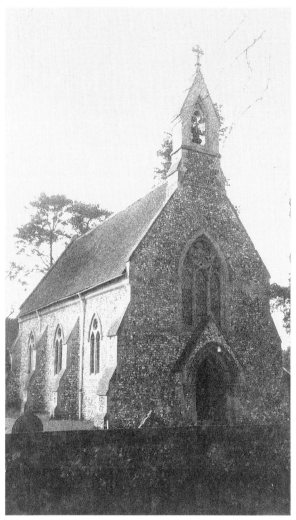

The exterior and interior of St Paul's church, Highmoor today.

6.   Life at the Chapel

The Secretary, Bob Spencer-Harper, opens the doors of the Stoke Row Chapel.
Photograph by the author, 1999.

It surprises many people to learn that the history of the Chapel is longer than that of the Church in Stoke Row. To find out why, we need to go back to 1662.

The Dissenters

In 1662, the Act of Uniformity led to a massive purge of clergy, one fifth of whom were deprived of their livings and the 1664 Conventicle Act barred Dissenters from holding separate church services. But it was the Five Mile Act of 1665 that prohibited dispossessed Ministers from even visiting their former congregations. They were obliged not to practise within five miles of an Anglican Church.

Dissenters had to be registered. Thus we find in the Oxfordshire Archives a note dated 1691, "The dwelling of Richard Blackhall of Stoke Row is recorded as a Meeting House for Congregational Protestant Dissenters." This was almost certainly 'The Old Farm House', Cox's Lane, Stoke Row.

One answer to the 1808 and 1811 Bishop's Visitation (a questionnaire) sent to the Vicar of Ipsden Parish Church states: "About 6 families of dissenters, sect unknown... There is a Licensed Cottage in the Parish attended every Sunday by a licensed preacher from a nearby town."

The numbers of the Dissenters grew in the whole area after that date. Bill George recalled, "At the top of Stoke Row Hill, on the north side, were the stables to 'Binksholme', the house across the road. These stood in an orchard and consisted of a couple of old sheds and a big barn. As a young lad, I went into this barn, which had a level floor and all that was in there were the old oil lamps and a pulpit in one corner, for this had been the later meeting place of the Dissenters, before the Chapel was built in 1815.

This barn would have held about 40 people and presumably they met there when they grew too many in number to continue meeting in the panelled Drawing-room of 'The Old Farmhouse' in Cox's Lane. As the Chapel was built in 1815, and I went into the old barn in about 1915, it means that the barn was not used as a meeting place for at least one hundred years and yet, save for the seats, it was all exactly as if time had stood still there for all that century!"

The Building of the new Chapel

"The foundations of the Chapel were four feet deep and three feet wide. The women collected stones from the fields and the farmers took them to the site with horse and cart. Lime mortar bound them together." These words were brought to mind by Bill George as having been taught to him by his aunt, Mrs Edith Lottie Lester, who died in 1977, aged 98.

On 20 July 1815, a Conveyance was signed, between:

James Toovey of Witheridge Hill, Builder and

Reverend William Harris of Wallingford, Dissenting Minister
Thomas Dodd of English Farm, Newnham, Oxon, Gentleman
Thomas Deane of Newbury, Berks, Shopkeeper
William Dodd of Bottom Farm, Checkendon, Gentleman
John Olding Allanson of Witheridge Hill, Gentleman
William Willmot of Henley-on-Thames, Dissenting Minister
William Giles of Stoke Row, Builder
James Blackall of Stoke Row, Miller
Samuel Whittick of Stoke Row, Miller

for the sale of a parcel of land in Stoke Row for the erection of a Meeting House.

This document also lays out details of the Board of Trustees who were responsible for all aspects of Chapel life then, not to be confused with the later 'Brazil Trustees'.

Marks made in a brick in the east wall of the Chapel read 'W G 1815' – almost certainly this was William Giles of Stoke Row, one of the founder members.

In his 1905 *History of the Berkshire, South Bucks and South Oxon Congregational Churches*, W H Summers lists:

"Stoke Row. The chapel here was opened on 6 August 1816. Previous to that time, services had been carried on in a *room holding about 130 persons, while another not less than 70 were sometimes gathered together about the doors and windows. The services had been commenced by 'itinerants', but a Mr Wilmot was at this time in charge.

A piece of freehold ground was given for the erection of a chapel, which was built at a cost of £350. To raise this amount an appeal was made to the denomination at large... The Rev James Macauley was Minister there for some years, and after his removal the Rev I Caterer of Peppard took the oversight of the church." (*This may have related to the barn described by Bill George).

The Chapel Trustees

The 1904 Deed of Appointment names Trustees of the Chapel as:

Thomas Brazil	William Brazil (Retired)
James Cox	John Pitman King
Frederick Neate	Henry Monk
George Page	William Charles Dodd
William Brazil	Albert Cox
William Smallbone	

A fresh Deed of Appointment of 'new Trustees', made on 14 July 1923 names them as being:

George Page	Walter T Wells
Mr W Wixen	William Brazil
Henry Momer	Ernest Samuel Bushe
A Smallbone	William Brazil (retired)
Albert Cox	Arthur Pither
J A Heath	Frank Harding Burgis
Frederick Neate	

In 1927 a new Committee was formed. This was the first of a long series of Chapel Councils which continues to this day and is responsible for all the day-to-day affairs of the Chapel, though most of the arrangements for the general maintenance today are handled by the Secretary. This voluntary work includes organising contractors to mow lawns, cut hedges, repair and decorate the interior of Church House, the Chapel, the schoolroom, kitchen etc as well as attending to the paperwork normally associated with this role.

The Burial Ground

The 1861 Inclosure Map, in the Bodleian Library, shows that: "A parcel of land (9b) containing one rood, held by them, their heirs and assigns in trust as a Burial Ground for the Independent Chapel now existing on the western side of said allotment, numbered 9b, etc ...fences maintained ...land was sold on 10 October 1861 to:

George Dean of English Farm, Newnham Murren, John Pittman King of North Stoke, William Cox of Mongewell and Philip Charles Dodd of Ipsden."

On 26 January 1926, it was proposed by Mr George Page that Messrs Brakspear and Sons be approached for a strip of land at the west side of the Chapel. Mr A Cox was asked to inspect the land and report on the same, but nothing further appears to have happened as Mr Cox resigned in the September. However, in the will of the same Mr Page of Stonehouse Farm, Highmoor in 1929, instructions were given for the "Purchase of piece of land at Stoke Row from W H Brakspear & Sons and given by the Beneficiaries as an addition to the Stoke Row Chapel." The shed, which stood in the north-east corner of the graveyard to house the visiting preacher's pony and trap, was sold in 1935 to the local blacksmith. A Copper Beech tree was then planted in that corner by Mr Frederick Neate to commemorate the Silver Jubilee of King George V in November 1935. It still stands there today, looking majestic, and sometimes provides the flower arrangers with colourful extra foliage!

A letter from Simmons & Sons, Henley, dated 17 November 1966 informed the Chapel Council about the availability of a piece of land adjoining the Chapel. It was thought this might be suitable for additional burial ground, being approx 60ft wide, 184ft long, was for sale by Brakspears at £2000 and appeared to be part of the plan to develop land at the side of The Cherry Tree. Only part of the land was bought.

The Sunday School

Bill George's aunt, Mrs Lester, also told him that the "The first Sunday School was created in 1823 and a Mother's Union was started for mothers and their children."

Alas, very little survives in the way of written history for the Chapel before the turn of the century, but it seems that the Schoolroom at the rear was built in the early 1880s.

However, I discovered among the few old papers that were passed to my husband when he became Secretary, three beautifully printed Programmes for Amateur Concerts in the years 1884, 1885 and 1886. There was also a letter showing how they came to be there. Dated 8 September 1946, it was from Dorothy S Gunston of 'Culpenrose', Sonning Common, to 'Ada', enclosing several concert programmes. She speaks of "selling the house... Vera and I are turning out... Father just kept everything!" Fortunately for us he did, or we should not have these delightful Programmes hanging on the wall of the Schoolroom today!

New School Room, Stoke Row.
ADJOINING THE CONGREGATIONAL CHAPEL.

AMATEUR CONCERT

WEDNESDAY, MAY 7th, 1884.

PROGRAMME.

PART SONG	... "Dawn of Day" ...	...	Reay
SONG	"Old Timbertoes" ...	...	C. Torry
	Mr. R. GUNSTON.		
SONG	"Anchored" ...	...	M. Watson
	Mrs. READ.		
HUMOROUS SONG	... ...	...	
	Mr. MORRIS.		
DUETT	... "Come o'er the Moon-lit Sea"	...	L. Devereaux
	Miss and Mr. BRAZIL.		
SONG	... ...		
	Mr. J. GUNSTON.		
PIANOFORTE SOLO	... "Tarntella" ...	...	B. Richards
	Miss GUNSTON.		
SONG	"Ring out, sweet Angelus"	...	Gounod
	Miss GUNSTON.		
DUETT	"The Syren and Friar" ...	...	S. Emstead
	Mrs. READ and Mr. R. GUNSTON.		
HUMOROUS SONG	... ...	...	
	Mr. MOAB.		
SONG	"The Road to the Fair" ...	W. M. Hutchison	
	Miss COSTELLO.		
SONG	"Never to Know" ...	Thos. Marsick	
	Mr. BRAZIL.		
PART SONG	"Gipsy Life" ...	...	Schumann

✶ INTERVAL. ✶

PART SONG	"Away to the Meadows" ...	...	
PIANOFORTE DUETT	{ "The Danish National Song and Hymn," }	Franz Nava	
	Miss and Mr. J. GUNSTON.		
SONG	"The King's Jester" ...	...	A. Collier
	Mr. R. GUNSTON.		
SONG	"The Devoted Apple" ...	J. L. Roeckel	
	Mrs. READ.		
SONG	"Across the River" ...	...	H. Parker
	Miss GUNSTON.		
SONG	... ...	...	S. Adams
	Mr. MORRIS.		
SONG	"Ehren on the Rhine" ...	W. M. Hutchison	
	Miss BRAZIL.		
SONG	... ...		
	Mr. J. GUNSTON.		
DUETT	"Broom Girls" ...	...	Luigi Bordese
	Miss GUNSTON and Mrs. READ.		
HUMOROUS SONG	... ...		
	Mr. MOASE.		
PART SONG	... "Serenade" ...	...	J. Greenwood

"GOD SAVE THE QUEEN."

The programme for an Amateur Concert, held in the 'New School Room' of the Chapel on 7 May 1884. By kind permission of Bernard Brazil.

From the 1902 - 1957 Accounts Book we find that much appears to have happened at Easter, particularly towards the end of the 1920s, probably in the Sunday School, as 12/9d was paid for prizes, 4/- for buns and 6/- for oranges. Also 1/2d for half a lb of tea. Bill George confirmed this, saying: "there was always a Service on Good Friday afternoons, followed by recitations by the children and a 'sit-down' tea, including hot-cross buns baked by Mr Lambourne, whose bakery was on the Village Green. Oranges were a treat for the children at that time as they were at Christmas."

A lady who visited the Local History Day at Highmoor in 1993 told me she recalled being taught at the Chapel Sunday School by Mrs Brazier, who wore a long skirt and *bloomers* underneath, when she was Superintendent of the Sunday School in the 1920s. Mrs Florence Elizabeth Lester, wife of the Secretary, Bill Lester, also taught in the Sunday School.

In the 1930s the oft-recalled Sunday School Outings began. The first entry is for 5 August 1930: "Children's Summer Outing to Burnham Beeches, in a charabanc. About 50 went, good tea provided, each child received 6d." Another, for 5 August 1931, reveals:: "57 children and 24 adults were conveyed by Motor Coach to California near Wokingham. Tea was provided and children received money to enjoy themselves as they pleased. Each child, on returning home, received a bag of sweets. Eileen Saunders, who had been in hospital was unable to go, received a doll, cost 5/-."

Forms (benches) for the Sunday School cost 10/- in March 1934 though, sadly, the entry in the Accounts Book did not state how many were purchased.

It also appears that oranges were still given to children on Good Friday as well as prizes, usually bibles, and a tea, certainly up to the late 1930s. In the August of that year the Sunday School Outing was "to Longmoor Lake again." A trip to Oxford Zoo in 1935 must have been quite a revelation to some of the children, who had probably never seen foreign wild animals before.

A really memorable date though, was in August 1936, when the children were taken to a seaside resort for the first time. They went to Littlehampton. "Each child was given 6d to spend at the Fair on the sea front." A similar entry was made for 1937.

Stoke Row and Reading Sunday Schools, outside the Chapel, c 1945.
By kind permission of Mrs Pauline Mann (nee Ruddle).

Nativity Play, Christmas 1990. Standing, left: Blake Piper (American), Donna-Marie Dyer,
Daniel Tee, Peter Slack. Seated: Lucy Hemphill, Alison Hawkins, Victoria Tee, Ian Slack.
Standing, right: Stephen Carter, Helen Fisher, Toni Slack and Jess Hemphill.

In August 1942, "The children went on a river trip to Reading" – going further afield being impossible in wartime. There was no further mention of Outings during the war years but in August 1945 there was a "Sunday School Outing to Beaconsfield" – probably to the Model Village.

By 1962 the Sunday School had 17 - 20 pupils and retained the Reading Shield. One scholar won the National Prize for Scripture and by April 1963 there were "two Sunday School children in the Reading Scripture Festival and the School represented by exhibits in the Festival Exhibition."

At the Sunday School Anniversary party on 23 June 1967, Rev Philip Schofield, Padre at RAF Benson, entertained the children with his ventriloquist doll. In July 1967, the Sunday School went once again to the seaside, this time to the Isle of Wight.

As Stoke Row Chapel was the last member of the Reading and District Sunday School Union to be awarded the Scripture Examination Trophy, the Chapel retains it to this day, having won it three times in the years prior to 1972. Much of this success was due to the work of Miss Phillis Wells, who was Superintendent of the Sunday School for many years, as her mother had been before her.

Bill Morris was appointed Sunday School and Junior Church Leader by Padre Bax in 1982. The Sunday School was growing fast, but the 'Outings' had come full circle. It was decided, since by then almost all the children were accustomed to regular holidays, usually abroad, that the annual celebration should take the form of a Family Summer Picnic on Christmas Common, always good fun! Bill and his wife retired to Devon in 1984 and Stephen Fisher became Sunday School Leader from 1984 until 1992.

Today the Junior Church and Sunday School are in the capable hands of Mrs Maureen Hay. Recent projects have included the creation of a huge collage of the Noah's Ark and the raising of £100 for a 'Clean Water for the Third World' project. The children have also enjoyed several summer camping weekends. The Christmas Party has changed considerably, too – in 1994 the boys and girls went ten pin bowling, and this was followed by a supper in the schoolroom. All the children stay in the Chapel for the first twenty minutes of the Sunday worship, when stories, readings and hymns are designed to appeal to them. The older ones also participate, by collecting the offertory and handing out hymn books. At Christmas and on the Sunday School Anniversary they make their own special presentation to the congregation.

Today's Sunday school teaching is up to date with videos and computers.

The Sisterhood

It is thought that the Sisterhood was formed in the early 1920s, perhaps to give the women of the village some sort of social life in the afternoons and to enable them to hear speakers and go on outings. Certainly they enjoyed many happy times together, especially in the pre-war days, before the Stoke Row Women's Institute was founded. In the *Stoke Row News* of December 1968, in the series 'Old Timer's Tales', the following story was written by 'M H' (probably Maud Howells):

"This concerns the Chapel Sisterhood and our first charabanc outing about 45 years ago (ie about 1923). We started at 6.00 am one morning in the beginning of September to go to Bournemouth with Mr Callis, who had an open charabanc which was quite high off the ground. It was a lovely sunny day and we did enjoy ourselves. Mr Callis was driving, of course. He came from 'Peppard Garage'.

We arrived at Bournemouth at 12.30, after having a few stops on the road; the driver saying 'Well, my dears, we must let 'the old girl' cool down a bit!' So we made tea with a spirit lamp in the back. After drinking our tea and letting 'the old girl' cool down, off we started again.

We had not gone far when the sun seemed to be getting too hot for us. So 'the old girl' was stopped again and the hood drawn over us. I can remember quite well a few of our passengers who are still with us: Mrs G Lester, Mrs G Slade of the Terrace and several others, including a few men folk.

Coming home, the late old Mrs Slade 'the wood lady', said: 'Oh dear, although I've had a jolly good day, I am tired, that was too fer for me!' We stopped at Reading on the way home and raided the Fish and Chip shop. We did this on most of our Sisterhood outings.

When we got to the bottom of the wood, approaching Stoke Row, we started singing to let them know we had arrived home safe and sound. They stood waiting for us at the Chapel and what a grand day that was, for our faces and arms were all burnt with the sun.

I wonder where 'the old girl' is now, and her driver, for I know it was a day that we who are still here will never forget. I am wondering how the 'old girl' would look amongst today's traffic. She'd put a stop to some of them!

Several years later, when the last war broke out, we had been to Bournemouth and were all singing at the tops of our voices as we got near the Fish Shop once more. It was *There'll always be an England*, when some old men outside the shop said 'another bloomin' lot from London I suppose!'"

The Sisterhood continued quite strongly until the Second World War. Then, as women began to go to work in the local factories, it declined somewhat. After the war it was revived and became quite active but again, with the increasing changes in women's lives, it was only the older ones who could come in the afternoons. This club, which had given so much pleasure and friendship to Stoke Row women for nearly 70 years, closed down in 1987.

Chapel Members

Although few written records for the Chapel have been found for the period before 1900; in 1854 the replies of the Vicar of Stoke Row, Rev J Arrowsmith, to the Bishop's Visitation (questionnaire) complained: "The place is overrun by Dissent."

1902 appears to have been an important year for the Chapel, when a new Accounts Book was started. In March a number of people signed a Declaration, and a register of the attendance of those people at monthly meetings was begun. This register was continued until 1907 but sadly no further entries were made until 1923.

A group of members outside the Chapel, c 1908.
From an original postcard found in the Chapel.

On 12 March 1902, an important statement was made in the Accounts book, which seems to have doubled up as a Minutes book:

"At a meeting held at the Congregational Chapel at Stoke Row this day under the presidency of Rev Sydney Tucker of Henley-on-Thames, the following was agreed to, signed by those whose names follow:

'We, the undersigned, believing in and loving the Lord Jesus Christ and being desirous to serve Him together in this place, do hereby consolidate ourselves into a Christian Church of the Independent or Congregational Church and Order, solemnly promising, by His help, to fulfil all our duties in His name and Spirit.'

James Cox	David Earl
Eliza Cox	Harriet Earl
Rose Cox	Helena Neate
Thomas Brazil	Frederick Neate
Helena Francis	William Brazil
Phillis Brazil	Jane Susannah Brazil
Matilda Nagers	William Smallbone
	Sarah Horwood."

It was in this year that the upright piano, which has been used for many, many years in the Chapel, was purchased. It was registered as having been made by Richard Lipp and Sohn of Stuttgart and sold by James Russell and Co of Oxford. The serial number is 22002, the front is ornamented with marquetry and it has brackets for candle-holders on each side. It is regularly tuned and works well.

In the years of the Great Depression, life was hard in Stoke Row, even by the standards of the time. In 1932: "Collections were still rather irregular and generally averaged a total of £1. Donations were also received from certain people and money given by the Sisterhood etc." In February of 1936, perhaps to make donating a little easier "the Committee decided to take collections weekly instead of monthly."

The Chapel had become inclined to the Congregational Church but the original Deed stated that it should always remain completely independent. In February 1943 and for several months to come, discussions continued as to whether the Chapel should formally join with the Congregational Church.

"After much discussion, the Chapel was joined to the Congregational Church County Union in April. William Brazil objected, revealing that he would be leaving a legacy to the Chapel. His will stipulated that the Chapel should not be joined to any other church organisation."

The Chapel Committee then cancelled their annexation to the Congregational Church, thus upholding the original Trust Deed which stipulated the Chapel's complete independence.

Memorial Tablets

There are several very interesting memorial tablets on the interior walls of the Chapel which reveal the faithfulness and long service of some of its members. In 1819, the wife of one of the original trustees, Thomas Deane, died and the first tablet to be placed inside the Chapel reads:

> *Sacred to the Memory of Harriet, wife of Thomas Deane*
> *who departed this life in peace. 25th January 1819*
> *'The memory of the just is blessed'*

Forty years later her husband joined her and his name was inscribed below hers on the same tablet:

> *and to the memory of Thomas Deane*
> *who died September 1859, 80 years*

Another tablet was erected :

> *In memory of John William Allanson*
> *who in the hand of God*
> *was a willing and efficient instrument*
> *of this Chapel.*
> *He died 4th November 1831, aged 86*

This was almost certainly the John William Allanson of Witheridge Hill, gentleman, who was a founder member of the Chapel.

A third tablet is dedicated to:

> *James Cox, died 1912, aged 81 years*
> *A man of God, who was for many years*
> *a faithful and devoted worker in this place*
> *'Well done thou good and faithful servant'*

Mrs Edith Lottie Lester recalled that, whoever the visiting preacher was, James Cox would announce the last hymn at 12 noon to draw the service to a conclusion. The service started at 10.30 am. He thought an hour and a half was quite enough and preachers gradually learned to curb the length of their sermons!

As in St John's Church, there is a brass memorial in the Chapel to the men of Stoke Row who fell in the First World War. On the opposite wall is a smaller, bronze plaque, dedicated to the men who died during the Second World War. The details of these men and their service to their country, are covered in the chapter on the Wars.

The Chapel owes much to William Brazil, who left the Alma Green land to the Chapel. The sale of it provided money to build Church House and set up a Trust Fund which helps to maintain both the Chapel and Church House. Perhaps somewhat belatedly, a tablet was recently erected and unveiled by Bernard Brazil, his son Jeremy and his baby son, also called William Brazil, in the presence of other members of the Brazil family during morning worship in November 1994. It reads simply:

> ### IN MEMORY OF
> ### WILLIAM BRAZIL
> ### 1858 - 1955
>
> Through whose Interest and Generosity
> this Chapel continues to Prosper
> In the Love and Service of God

Maintenance

The Chapel was originally lit by oil lamps, but the arrival in 1934 of mains electricity in the village made better lighting a possibility. The proposed improvement had to be debated after a gift of £5 was received for the Electric Light Fund, and just before Christmas a vote was taken. Votes for this were 3 for, 3 neutral, 1 against. Obviously the motion was passed, for in April of the following year the Treasurer wrote: "Wessex Electricity Lighting Installation – £9.5.0d." The oil lamps and glasses were subsequently sold off. The cost of the electricity was 2/- a quarter year.

On 20 October 1934, a new Stove was purchased from Mr Drew at the cost of £8.19.10d. All this meant less work in cleaning and lighting the lamps, so in the Accounts book in December 1935, we find "Mr Brind's salary for cleaning reduced to £2.12.0d from now on." For the first time mention was made in June 1936 of wages being paid to someone for doing work that was often otherwise done voluntarily: "16/3d to Mr Busby for hedge trimming." This may also have been to help a family in times of unemployment.

Weed killer was purchased in 1937 at a cost of 2/-. Presumably this was to keep gravel paths clear of weeds and continued for many years. Also "soap, powder and black lead (for the stoves) 1s 2d. Chimneys swept 2/-." Jeyes Disinfectant was often mentioned at 7d, probably for use in the outside bucket type closet.

The Chapel during the Second World War

The first sign of the effects of the outbreak of War on the Chapel was on 28 August 1939, when "it was agreed by the Committee that the Harvest Festival be held on 1 October, but owing to lighting restrictions the service would be held in the afternoon to commence at 2.45 pm. It was also decided that the evening service would not be held during the winter months, but would be at 2.45 pm instead." Later that year "it was decided to discontinue the afternoon service during November." An estimate of blackout material for Chapel windows in 1940 was £6, so it was decided to use the Schoolroom instead during the winter, perhaps because it had only two windows to cover and, being smaller, was easier to heat.

A local builder, Walter T Wells, became Chapel Secretary in April 1942. We still bless his memory for he did much to set the records in order, including getting the Chapel registered and drawing up a hand-coloured plan of the graveyard which is invaluable to this day.

It seems that the Chapel Schoolroom was also used by the ARP (Air Raid Precautions) First Aid Party, because on 28 May 1942 they paid their share of the fuel, exactly 3s. 4.1/2d.

The Chapel building was registered as a place for Religious Worship on 18 July 1942, a full 127 years after the foundation stone was laid! Certificate No 60197 was issued by the Registrar General, Somerset House, London.

The Chapel was also registered for solemnizing marriages on 21 October 1942. Certificate No. 28528 was issued by the Superintendent Registrar, Henley and registered at Somerset House, London. The first wedding to take place at the Chapel was between George Patrick Dyer and Kathleen Maud Howells on 22 May 1943.

A Day of National Prayer was declared on 3 September 1942 when the collection was 4/-. Offertories varied between 3/9d and 17/6, but were often around 10/-. A donation of 4/- was made to the Red Cross. The Royal Insurance was paid an extra 10/- for War Damage Insurance, the normal Fire Insurance being 14/9d. The insured value was declared at £938.

In the early autumn of 1942 a 'light trap' was fitted to the inside of the entrance door to the Schoolroom, the seating was rearranged and the pulpit put on west side. This work obviated the need for costly blackout curtaining in the Chapel.

The brass commemorative plaque was stolen from beneath the Copper Beech tree in October 1942. The Committee agreed to replace this "when conditions allow the use of metal for this purpose..." (in fact, it never was replaced). Thefts must have been prevalent at the time because the Committee decided "to put a lock on the Schoolroom door against petty mischief and theft." Several people had keys, including the Caretaker and the Secretary and one was cut "for an emergency."

Early in 1943, the sum of 10/- was donated to St Dunstan's Fund for the War Blinded. The Harvest Festival sale proceeds were sent to the Red Cross Prisoners of War Fund.

By October 1945 the war was over at last and the Chapel Committee, always careful with the congregation's money, saw to it that "the blackout curtains removed from the Schoolroom windows were sold."

Post-War Improvements to the Chapel

Mr William Brazil, of Kidmore Game Farm, who had been a long-serving and very faithful member of the Chapel, died on 8 July 1955 at the grand old age of 97. In his will he left a bequest to the Chapel of a piece of land on which Alma Green was built and also a residence for a permanent Minister.

He also left a sum of money, the income from which was to provide an Annual Treat or Summer Outing for the children of the Sunday School, in memory of his mother who, with the help of the late James Cox first started the Sunday School which both families attended.

In July, 1958 the Chapel Council debated the problem of "preventing the Chapel from falling into complete decay", but in 1965 money at last came in from the sale of the Alma Green land. Early in 1966 plans of a proposed house for the Minister at the side of the Alma Green site were drawn up and in August 1968 "Plans for the Proposed Alterations, including the provision of a platform and panelling, to Stoke Row Chapel were prepared by Langton T Foster, ARIBA, Chartered Architect, Wallingford."

In 1969, Geoff Boyson of Stoke Row, a wood turner and skilled craftsman, made a wooden cross of local cherry wood, affixed to the wall behind the communion table, the oak table itself and three Glastonbury chairs, all dedicated to the memory of William Brazil. In January 1970, a wooden lectern was donated by Rev John Potts in memory of his wife. In 1971 an "Oak book rest was made by Geoff Boyson and given by Mrs Jago." A Victorian Casson pipe organ was acquired in 1978 by Padre Bax from the United Reformed Church at East Hagbourne, Oxfordshire and dedicated to the memory of the faithfulness of Mrs Edie Lottie Lester. Mrs Mabel Cox continued to play the organ in the Chapel until she retired in 1981, after 72 years' service.

Mrs Mabel Cox who will be 105 years old in June 1999. By kind permission of the Henley Standard.

Improvements have continued, and in 1987 windows in the Schoolroom were replaced with double-glazed sealed units in the correct Georgian style. In 1988, new lightweight tables were purchased for the schoolroom. This room was also panelled with wood to dado height and carpet tiles laid. The verge outside the Chapel was hardened in 1993, with perforated concrete blocks to drain this strip and make it suitable for car parking. A year later the two front windows of the Chapel were double-glazed to keep out the south-west wind.

Preachers and Ministers

In 1923 a new Accounts book started with the words, "Preacher's Entertainment Account", from which it would appear that visiting preachers were entertained to Dinner and Tea. The cost was split between:

Mr A Cox	Mr W T Wells
Mr P Cox	Mr Clayton
Mr J A Heath	Mr George Page
Mr W Wixen	

This arrangement seems to have continued until 1926, when an Entertainment Fund appears to have been started for the purpose of giving Dinner and Tea to the visiting preacher. Sometimes this included hire of a pony and trap, car or the cost of bus fare or bicycle. All the preachers' names were given with dates of visits and this went on for many years to come. In January 1928 there was: "No preacher, owing to rough weather."

Now we take a big leap forward to 1950, since the 1930s was a quiet period and the war years are covered in another section. The 1950s were extremely active times in the Chapel. We read in the Accounts book in January 1950 that £7.00.00 was paid to "Chinese Missions: Miss Gladys Aylward." Miss Aylward was a famous missionary, about whom the book *The Inn of the Sixth Happiness* was written. A film was also made of this book – a very moving and inspiring story of great courage.

She came to the Chapel on Good Friday 1950, when a big revival meeting was held in a marquee erected on the Village Green. In February 1956, another donation was made "to Gladys Aylward for work amongst Chinese Seamen, £1.14.00."

On 14 October 1951 a new Register of Members was started and in early May 1959 the Council asked Rev Dickerson to be their permanent Minister, "rather than rely on lay or local preachers."

The *Henley Standard* reported in late May 1959: "Induction Service: The induction service for Pastor Dickerson was held at the Stoke Row Chapel on Wednesday of last week. The Chairman of the Trustees was Mr John Cumber of Theale, the charge to Pastor Dickerson was given by Rev Arthur Nye of Earley and the charge to the church by Pastor Eeles of Caversham Hill."

On 17 March 1965 Pastor Dickerson left the Chapel after six years service and was given a leather briefcase. Thereafter followed a period of interregnum until 13 March 1967, when Rev John Potts, CBE, a retired Chaplin-in-Chief to the Royal Air Force at Benson, was invited to become Minister of the Chapel. Mrs Yvonne Bax recalled: "He was greatly loved and did much to bring new life to the Chapel." He continued as Minister for five years. Sadly, in 1972, he died whilst in Bahrain visiting his daughter.

From 1973 Rev Arthur Tilling became Minister but he left two years later. Again, there followed a long period of interregnum.

The Bishop of Oxford visited Stoke Row Chapel in January 1980. Left to right: Padre Bax, Minister of Stoke Row Chapel, Rev David Salt, Rector of St John's Church, Stoke Row, the Right Rev P C Rodger, Bishop of Oxford, and the Bishop's Chaplain. By kind permission of the Henley Standard.

Early in 1977, Padre Bernard Railton Bax took office as Minister to the Stoke Row Chapel. He renamed it 'The Chapel of Christian Unity', as he was a great champion of ecumenicism. An Annual Thanksgiving Gift Day was held on the first Sunday in Advent. This reflected the growing prosperity and changing life-style of the congregation, where some women went out to work and were more able to give money to give than the time necessary for organising fund-raising events.

The 1979 AGM report showed a growth in the congregation. There had been visits from the Salvation Army, Checkendon Choir and the Rural Dean, Rev David Salt. The following year the Bishop of Oxford also visited the Chapel.

Ecumenical visits and exchanges with other churches were the order of the day. Padre Bax endeavoured to involve everyone in the life of the Chapel. The choir was a particularly strong feature too, as Rev Bax was very musically minded and himself played his old Salvation Army squeeze-box with great gusto!

By 1987 Padre and Mrs Bax had been ten years with the Chapel. The same officers were re-appointed at the AGM – it was a period of great stability. The buildings and grounds were also reported to be in very good condition. Padre Bax died on 23 February 1990, having been ordained for 52 years. His death was a great loss, after 13 years at the Chapel. Mrs Yvonne Bax was very helpful to the Council during the period of interregnum that followed.

Church House, Reading Road, Stoke Row, the house built for the Chapel Minister in the late 1960s, with money realised from the sale of the Alma Green land which was left to the Chapel by Mr William Brazil. This photograph was taken by the author in 1994.

The interior of the Chapel, c 1900. From a postcard found in the Chapel.

The Chapel in 1992 with Rev John Harrington at the lectern.
Note the changes, carried out in the late 1960s. Photograph by the author.

The Chapel Today

I am glad to report that the Chapel is still thriving. It usually has a congregation of about 30, this being doubled on high days and holidays. Members come from as far afield as High Wycombe, Marlow, Henley, Woodley, Gallowstree Common, etc as well as from Stoke Row and the neighbouring villages of Highmoor, Checkendon, Sonning Common and Woodcote.

We are blessed with a wonderful Organist/Choir Master, Mrs Wendy Hawkins, who also teaches in a school in Henley. In addition, we have a Deputy Organist and a choir of about ten.

The Sunday school has a roll of about fifteen children and, as the Secretary, Bob Spencer-Harper, said in his report to the AGM in 1995: "The children bring much life and joy to our family worship each Sunday. The stories told to the children are enjoyed by everyone, young and old, and the children's reactions are, at times, both touching and amusing."

Once a month a visiting preacher relieves Rev John Harrington and refreshments after worship ensure that everyone enjoys a social event on a regular basis. Members also go out together from time to time, on picnics, to the theatre, etc.

Thanks to a Covenanting scheme introduced in 1995, the finances of the Chapel are in a healthy state, assisted by grants from the Brazil Trust. A set of rotas ensures that the interior is cleaned, flowers arranged and a cheerful Steward welcomes everyone, especially newcomers.

Chapel members on a picnic at Wellington Park in 1998. Photograph by Ken Lyndon.

7. School Days at Stoke Row

Introduction

Whereas most of the other chapters are based on the memories of the older generation, either as related to me or as previously written, the history of Stoke Row and Highmoor schools is largely based on four log books that are safely kept in the Oxfordshire Archives. As the three Stoke Row log books cover 68 years and the one Highmoor log book spans 92 years, the amount of material available to me was daunting. Even more so was the challenge of what to do with it all.

These chapters are the result of sieving my new found knowledge into sub-headings, to make it more readable, which was suggested by both Tony Hall and Stuart Copeman. Fortunately, Tom Kumsang, Headteacher of Stoke Row Primary School has kindly agreed to keep the full version of the results of my investigations in the school files for anyone who would like to study the matter in more detail.

I found the log books fascinating, not only for the details of the school life, but for giving a picture of each master and mistress, as they took over the school, usually with optimism and the best of intentions. Sometimes the circumstances under which they left were not so happy. Another of the sad revelations was that, although there was a great deal of written material, until the early part of the 20th century, very few photographs were taken.

In order to assist the reader, I have devised a set of tables, showing the head teachers, the numbers of pupils and the major events mentioned. These will be found at the end of the chapter.

The First Schools

Although there was a small private school for young children in Ipsden (which then included Stoke Row) early in the 19th century, it was probably held in a private house and may have been a 'dame school'. Professor Hassell's notes for the Victoria County History, now in the Bodleian Library, also include reference to: "Ipsden – two daily schools, one for 33 females, supported by John Reade of Ipsden, commenced 1831 and the other for 11 males, supported by private contributions."

School Buildings

Following the erection of St John the Evangelist in 1846, the Church of England School was founded in 1853 "for the labouring, manufacturing or other poorer classes in Stoke Row, with residence for school master or mistress."

The church schools of Ipsden and Stoke Row were administered under the Ipsden Union of Schools. Professor Hassell observed that "in 1867 there was an average attendance of 31 and a grant was made in the sum of £14.5.8d."

In 1863, the dimensions of the single School Room were given as:

Length: 28 ft 6 inches. Breadth: 16 ft 3 inches. Height 14 ft.
(This room was at the western end of the present school).

In 1877, HMI (Her Majesty's Inspector of Schools) stated in his report: "Better desks and a gallery …are essentials." The school was closed for a week for cleaning and repairs in 1878, but no 'gallery' was constructed.

Although 'separate toilets' had been provided in 1870, the Inspector noted in 1878 that they were "roofless" and "should be at once put into a thorough state of repair."

There were 92 children on the register by 1887 and the Inspector called for:

"…a classroom required to accommodate the number of children who ought to be in attendance at the school and I am to enquire whether the Managers are to provide one. Otherwise their Lordships will have to publish notices under Section 9 of the Elementary Education Act of 1870, with a view to the provision of the required accommodation…"

After ten years, the words of the Inspectorate were at last to have some effect. On 7 October 1887: "Rev J Arrowsmith, with the Architect and Messrs Morris and Voss, came through the School with a view to selecting a site for a Classroom." (This was probably Mr Morris of Reading, the architect who designed Highmoor Vicarage).

Finally, progress was made. On 23 November 1888, the School was "closed for a week to enable the workmen to make alterations in the wall for a new Classroom." In the event, an extra week had to be added to the Christmas holidays, "in order that the workmen may complete the new drainage."

Kelly's Directory for 1889 gave, not only the size of the original 'Mixed Room', but also the new one: "Infants' Room: 30 ft long, 15 ft wide and 14 ft high."

HMI was very pleased with this work. In July 1889 he stated: "The extension of the premises is a great boon to teachers and children and thanks are due to the Managers for their successful exertions. The building operations must have caused temporary inconvenience; nevertheless, the School shows some improvement…"

Alterations to the windows took place in December 1896, one of the coldest months of the year. As a consequence: "School was not held this afternoon, owing to the work of taking out school windows for alteration to same having commenced."

The first time the temperature of the rooms was recorded was on 5 September 1898, when Mr Willimont noted: "The heat is affecting the children, it being 76 degrees in each room. This afternoon the thermometer indicates 80 degrees and it is impossible to work comfortably."

And a day later: "The heat is causing the children to be in a state of collapse – work being out of the question. Thermometer 82 degrees."

By 8 September, he had "…given up all attempts to work this afternoon, the temperature being 85 degrees and the children entirely unfit to do anything."

Only six months after this, on 22 March 1899, he wrote: "It is very cold in the Mixed Schoolroom, owing to the uselessness of the stove, which gives out hardly any heat. The temperature at 11.00 am was 38 degrees. This became a common type of entry in the log book.

The following autumn everything was not as it should have been. "19 September: The offices (toilets) are smelling very badly this morning, owing to the high wind blowing the stench straight into the school." In order to cure the problem, but not until the following May(!): "The children's out-offices have now been made clean and tidy and free from offensive smell; with the use of a little lime as a deodoriser, it is hoped they may be kept so in future."

Under the auspices of Mr and Mrs Sutherland (1900-1908) many improvements were made to the school. In September 1900: "A School museum has been provided and placed in the Mixed Department. Two new suitable stoves have also been purchased and put up in either room. During the holidays the School has been thoroughly cleansed, the walls swept down and the desks, benches, etc, well scrubbed. The bricks outside the back door flooring have been put right and material provided for making the interior of the School House a more fit and decent habitation than was formerly the case."

Stoke Row School, 19 March 1907. This photograph, which shows the School Room viewed from the east, was taken by Mr P Elford, Secretary of the Oxfordshire Education Committee. Reproduced by kind permission of the Oxfordshire Photographic Archive.

This photograph, also by Mr Elford was taken from the north. It depicts the School House, the extension and the outside toilets. Kindly lent by the Oxfordshire Photographic Archive.

Improvements to the playground were undertaken in March 1909, in accordance with the Medical Report, which was probably also responsible for an entry later that month, which reads: "The lavatories have been cleaned throughout – walls scrubbed with solution of ammonia."

The school was obviously not at all well maintained in the early part of the 20th century. On 3 April 1911: "The stonework of the Infant Room fireplace fell down before school commenced. The Vicar called this morning respecting it." It was replaced ten days later and "a new stove put in the old room in place of the broken one."

However, it was not until 23 May 1912 that "water was laid on for school use." One benefit of this was probably the "new lavatories to be built in the coming holidays." In fact, they were not constructed until the Christmas holidays.

HMI had been complaining for some time about overcrowding at Stoke Row School. "9 September 1913: The inadequacy of the accommodation for the Infants is now more pronounced than in the earlier part of the year, when this defect was reported upon."

Trouble with the heating persisted, though. On 13 December 1914, the following entry was made by Mr Dakin in red ink, perhaps to give emphasis. "For some time now I have reported upon the condition of the stove in the Infants' Room. This morning the smoke was so bad that the room was absolutely untenable, especially with the thermometer at 32 degrees F."

Stoke Row School, c 1930. The lady with the two visitors is thought to have been Miss Turner. Rev Wood, the Vicar, is standing further away and the two teachers are probably organising a game. By kind permission of the Rural History Centre at Reading University.

School Staff

The first person in charge of the Stoke Row Church of England School was William Crews who, with his wife, were registered as "Parochial Schoolmaster and Mistress" in 1853.

In 1854, the *Post Office Directory* listed: "Miss Sarah Needle – National Schoolmistress and Postmistress." She was probably one of the few literate people in the village at the time and therefore qualified for both jobs.

Dutton Allen's Directory of 1863 listed "Jane Mahoney, Schoolmistress and E Wilson, Ambulatory Master." As the title suggests, he was one who travelled around a number of schools, giving a day's tuition at each. He appears to have attended Stoke Row School on Fridays until 1868.

On 4 May 1866, Miss Kate Stannard (who had been Assistant for some time) was appointed as Schoolmistress. Apart from the occasional mention of severe weather of some kind, the entries in the log book, day after day, just state: "Ordinary progress." It sounds as if the school life was very boring, not only for the mistress but probably also for her pupils! Five years later *Harrods' Directory* mentioned a Mrs Kate Francis as Schoolmistress. She left in 1878, having "had charge of this school for more than eleven years." This was the same lady, who had married during her term in office.

"S A Reynolds" came then, but stayed for less than a year and was replaced on 2 December 1878 by Miss E S Carter, Certificated Mistress. She stayed five years but, judging by the 63 pages of entries she made in the log book, her period at the school was far from happy.

A typical remark, made by Miss Carter on 31 October 1879, read: "Eating beech nuts has transpired very much in school this week. Two boys have persisted in doing so after repeated reproofs and corrections." These were very hard times in the village and the children were probably hungry!

Part of the entry for 5 November states: "Half holiday for there (sic) bonfire." The tone of the whole entry gives the impression that she did not approve of this measure!

Four years later Guy Fawkes Day still seemed to be a problem for Miss Carter. 9 November 1883: "About half the children took a bonfire half-holiday without leave and with rude self will, meaning to secure another the next day which was not given..."

At the end of 1883 Miss Carter left the school. Her tone was much kinder in her parting remarks than it had been throughout her five years there.

The next Headmistress was a Miss C A Duffield, who came straight from Truro Training College and remained at Stoke Row for three years. Her first entry in the log book read: "I entered upon my duties as Mistress of this school on Monday 31 December 1883. There is no assistance whatsoever in the school, which I really seem to stand in need of. The average attendance for the week has been 57.5. The children come in good time and some really are intelligent, but the majority are backward, especially in the lower classes. The girls are well behaved but some of the boys are rude and troublesome. Several of the boys knit very nicely. The children have not been taught anything but Reading, Writing and Arithmetic, with Needlework and Singing."

Miss Duffield's teaching included 'Object Lessons'. The subject was quite often just a simple one such as 'a match', 'the mole', 'rice', 'glass', 'salt', etc.

In July 1886 the Inspector noted: "There has recently been an influx of newcomers, owing to the closure of a private school..." This, perhaps, referred to the school that had been run for several years at Dogmore End by Mr Morris.

A few weeks later, Miss Duffield wrote: "Received my Parchment Certificate from the Government." She appears to have left at this point, but there is no mention of her leaving, even though she had been there for three years.

The school managed with a locum teacher until over a year later, when a permanent Mistress was appointed: "5 December 1887: Commenced duties at this school. (signed) Annie Reid, Head Mistress, with Mary Reid, Assistant." What their relationship was is not stated. Annie Reid set to work at once to remedy the bad state of affairs that she found and in this was helped by the provision of the new schoolroom.

The Vicar, Rev J Arrowsmith, and his wife were very supportive of the school. Mrs Arrowsmith helped with the Needlework lessons and in August 1887: "Mrs Arrowsmith came in on Friday afternoon and gave the whole school a Scramble of Sweets."

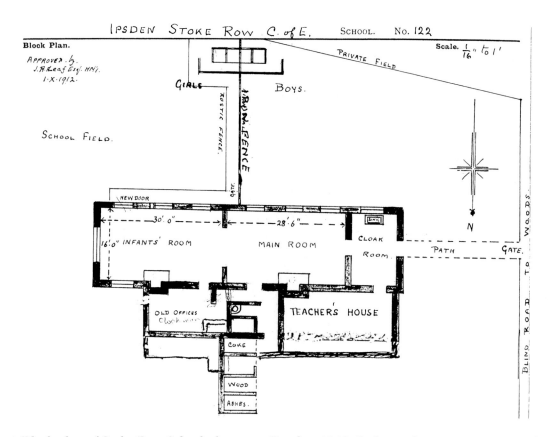

A Block plan of Stoke Row School, drawn in October 1912. It shows the two main rooms, the old and new 'offices' and the teacher's house. By kind permission of the Oxfordshire Archives.

On 4 June 1890, Rev J Arrowsmith, who had been Vicar at St John's for 41 years, died. Miss Reid wrote of him as being "Manager and friend of the school."

After 3.1/2 years of attempting to raise standards in the school, on 28 August 1891, Miss Reid resigned. Her place was taken by a temporary Mistress until, on 22 February 1892, we find the entry:

"I, Elizabeth Partington, 1st Class Certificated Mistress, took charge of this School." By 15 June there were "80 children present." By this time the curriculum was beginning to improve. That October, Miss Partington wrote:

"Began Model Drawing... very fair result." and two days later: "Began bead threading with Infants. The children enjoyed it... The boys tried their hand at drawing the map of Scotland... Taught Infants to march and sing in their room, preparatory to teaching them Musical Drill, as Swedish Drill is too hard for Infants."

Her tone was kind too, and implied that she helped her staff by setting an example. "Decided upon taking the Reading myself this week, to show the little Monitoress how I wanted it done." By the end of April 1893, she had "A good school today of 113 children, admitted three more today from Ipsden." It is amazing that she coped at all, for she only had one Assistant, Jessie Hope, of whom HMI was "unable to approve."

92

However, on 11 September 1893, "Miss C Clements (Article 68) from West Hanney Mixed School came today as Assistant Teacher."

There were no further entries in this, the first of the Stoke Row School log books. Miss Partington appears to have left at this juncture and a new book was started by a temporary Mistress.

From then on there were two locum teachers until, on 27 March 1894, Miss Laura Carter (Certificated 1st Division) was appointed but again, she did not stay long – just one year, in fact. A Master and Mistress were then appointed:

"24 June 1895: I, Charles Rowland, Certificated Master, commenced duties in this school today; Mrs Rowland acting as Assistant. The disorder prevalent in this school is deplorable, there being not the slightest order."

They stayed three years – Mr Rowland's handwriting was small and very neat, in contrast to most of the other Headmasters. He had a very formal tone and was inclined to circumlocution.

Like their predecessors, Rev Richard Isherwood and his wife, who came in 1891, had been very supportive of the school since their arrival. "9 August 1895: Rev Isherwood called during the morning and addressed a few words to the children." Mrs Isherwood often helped with the Needlework lessons. "...she also brought materials in for patchwork."

Sadly, by June 1898, the management situation was becoming rather unpleasant, judging by the entries in the following two pages of the log book:

"6 June: During the time the school has been closed, one new map and one mat have been placed in the school, the Master also finding that one map and one mat had been taken from the school."

There then followed an entry which appears to have been in the handwriting of Rev Isherwood and blacked out, possibly by Mr Rowland. Whatever transpired, the Rowlands left the school at the end of June 1898.

Mr and Mrs Willimont came soon afterwards. On 27 June 1898, the new Master wrote:

"Took charge of this School today, with Mrs Willimont as Assistant. (signed) J Willimont, Certificated Teacher. I find the order good, but the attainments very low. 75 children were present."

Mr and Mrs Willimont stayed for two years and much of this Master's entries in the log book were concerned with absenteeism. Another problem was with children who were not kept clean; no doubt it was difficult for their mothers who had no access to running water.

"11 October 1898: Complaints are continually being made by parents of the filth caught by their children from sitting next to the (named) family... No amount of warning has had any effect on the family.

I have reported the matter to the Managers, but the children are still as dirty as ever, both in their heads and bodies." Later he isolated them from the rest of the class.

Surprisingly, Mr Willimont did not approve of hair in plaits, either: "26 October 1898: A girl came to school this morning with her hair done up in unsightly plaits, which she refused to take down, on the instructions of her mother, who knows that children cannot be allowed to come to school with untidy heads. I sent her home to be tidied but she did not return."

Because of the absenteeism, or perhaps for other reasons, Mr Willimont was clearly dissatisfied. On 28 December 1899 he entered: "Resigned my post as Master of this School..."

9 April 1900 was an auspicious date for the school, with the arrival of a new Master, Mr Sutherland, who was kinder and more personally interested in the children. "I today commenced duties as Master of this school, with Mrs Sutherland as Assistant Mistress and Sewing Mistress, and with the assistance of our daughter as Monitoress. The Vicar, Rev R Isherwood, in a few kindly words, made me known to the children and the usual work was at once resumed."

Mr Sutherland and his wife, teaching at Stoke Row School. Another of Mr Elford's photographs, taken in 1907. By kind permission of the Oxfordshire Photographic Archive.

The entries, even in his first month, show that Mr Sutherland had a more relaxed, but nevertheless, caring attitude:

"My work this week has been devoted to revision chiefly, and in ascertaining the capabilities of the children. As far as I can see at present, Spelling and Arithmetic seem weak, and the Reading lacks intelligence and expression.

By consistent and steady attention to these subjects, I trust to be able to report some slight improvement bye and bye."

Later, Mr Sutherland "Received from the Managers a strongly bound book, for recording instances of Corporal Punishment, as required by 'Instructions-Code 1900'." That book has not survived, but he only mentions corporal punishment once in the log book. He found other and better means of controlling the children, as can be seen by later entries.

They were soon to lose a much-valued friend, though. On 27 July 1900: "Rev R Isherwood, for ten years Vicar of this Parish and Correspondent with the Education Board on behalf of the school, left the Parish on Tuesday last, having been appointed to the Rectory of Meppershall, Beds." (This was the father of Rev Cyril Isherwood who, in 1940, returned to Stoke Row, the village where he spent his youth).

In the middle of February 1901: "Rev H H and Mrs Appleford visited the school. The reverend gentleman has recently been appointed Vicar of the Parish."

One sign of Mr Sutherland's kindliness was shown on 26 March 1901: "Lessons were given to the children of the Upper Standards, bearing on the forthcoming Census-taking. The children were shown how they might be of assistance to their parents in the matter of filling up the required form."

In September 1901: "Daisy Hall commenced duties as an additional Teacher and Ada Hayward commenced work as Monitoress in the Infants' Room, to help with the babies and assist Mrs Sutherland." Altogether the school seemed a lot happier place.

On 6 June 1902: "Yesterday's School Walk proved both pleasant and profitable. The children greatly pleased and interested. Their behaviour, going and returning, was very good. Today they wrote an account, assisted by a few notes, of their outing."

Several other entries in the log book confirm Mr Sutherland's benign manner. For instance, on "11 September 1903: Herbert Wells has left school this week. His conduct has been uniformly exemplary in school and playground and I part from him with regret."

Truancy was still a problem though, but in January 1904, he thought of another idea to encourage regular attendance: "Ten minutes extra playtime will be given to children not absent at all during the week."

There is no doubt that he had a way with children. On 29 April he "admitted a boy on Monday last, described by his mother as 'a very bad boy'. His conduct this week has been very satisfactory."

Ada Hayward gave several Observation Lessons to the children that August, on the subjects of 'Jam', 'Farms', etc. "Materials to illustrate the lesson were to hand and the subject matter was intelligently handled. The class seemed much interested." This young lady was, by then, 20 years of age. She went on to become a qualified Assistant Teacher at Stoke Row School and married Wally Biggs of Stag Farm. She was a great friend of Miss Varley, Head Mistress of Highmoor School and often helped her there.

In March 1908, after a very cold and snowy winter, Mr Sutherland was taken ill with influenza and retired in August 1908.

This photograph may have been taken in 1907. Mr Sutherland is on the right, whilst his wife (wearing a fashionable fur collar) is on the left and behind her is probably Ada Hayward. The names of the children are not known, except that one girl, Ada Greenaway, is wearing her attendance medal. By kind permission of Mrs Sibel Betts (nee Delafield).

Mr Sutherland was succeeded on 5 October 1908 by Percy Richard Latter, who stayed for five years but was quite a different type of man. His wife was an untrained certificated teacher and was helped by Miss Cecily Turner, who stayed as a teacher at Stoke Row School until she retired. There are references to her on the chapter about the Wells.

Mr Latter did not find the school in a satisfactory state and succeeding pages of the log book show that he was extremely keen on attendance figures, probably related to grants. It was during Mr Latter's time at the school that the education authorities introduced gardening for the boys. On 11 January 1912, Mr Latter "received from Oxfordshire Education Committee a 'Special Subject' Register and tools for School Gardening, which it is proposed to take this year."

The village was more self-sufficient in those days and was able to provide for all the school's gardening needs. In the spring, he was able to write: "The wheelbarrow has been made in the village and received this morning. Paths finished off, trees have had branches lopped off and cleared away... Boys cut pea sticks and tied them up, ready for use." Even Rev Hutchinson became involved. "The Vicar assisted in removing branches and lent his tools."

Eventually, the gardens were ready for visitors. "14 June 1909: Mr H Kittle, Assistant Horticultural Inspector, visited the school gardens for judging crops etc."

By July the timetable had been changed "to allow for two separate hours gardening" and on 22 July: "Preparation in the school gardens today for the Flower Show tomorrow." The next day he gave: "half-holiday this afternoon as the gardening children went to Nettlebed Annual Horticultural Show."

Mr Latter resigned from the school in November, 1913, after five years as Head Teacher and, on 26 January 1914, he recorded: "The children kindly presented me with a bookcase and the Juniors gave Mrs Latter a fern stand."

Stoke Row School group, c 1909. The teacher was probably Mrs Latter, wife of the Headmaster. The children at the back are: John Carter, Ivy Johnson, and Lily Chapman.

Standing: Olive Busby and her sister Nellie, Fred Carter and George Johnson (this boy was blinded in one eye in an accident with a penknife). Next to him is Percy Stallwood and his sister, Maggie (wearing a sash). The two Ruddle brothers, Jack and George, are at the end.

Seated: Chris Busby, Lily Johnson, Claire Ruddle, Rose Carter, Uda Ada Stallwood (holding the board), Edie Chapman, her twin sisters and Gladys Chapman.

By kind permission of John Townsend.

Frederick Griffiths Dakin, ACP, commenced duties as Master on 16 February 1914. His wife, an uncertificated teacher, assisted him. Ted Evans remembered Mr Dakin. "He had a club foot and was very harsh." The Dakins left after only two years at Stoke Row.

They were replaced by George Wilson and his wife. Cecily Turner continued as Supplementary Teacher and Ethel M Pitt as Pupil Teacher. Mrs Daisy ('D') Newman (nee Wells) told me: "Mr Wilson used to suffer with migraine and was quite often ill with it" and Mrs Joan Watkins (nee Powell) remembered that "Mr Wilson was very strict and crept silently between the rows of children and would bring the cane down hard, on the desk, sometimes catching a child's finger!" However, Mrs Lily Tayler (nee Johnson) recollected Mrs Wilson as having "natural curly hair and a beautiful skin".

Ted Evans also recalled Mr Wilson and his stout wife, who taught the Infants. "Although Mr Wilson was strict, he was also clever and taught us a great deal. For example, he showed us how to make models from wood.

He also taught us the rudiments of physics and chemistry, making the lessons more interesting. One time he made a 'volcano' out of ground pumice and sand and made the whole thing explode with home-made gunpowder, mixed from saltpetre, charcoal and sulphur. The boys copied this experiment and made their own fireworks, even putting some gunpowder into a bottle. Looking back, it was a miracle that no-one was hurt with those home-made pyrotechnics!"

The third log book ended on 23 May 1921, with these words: "See new log book", but to my knowledge, this has not survived.

Mrs Johnson was Headmistress in the 1920s and early 1930s. Mrs Rose Textor (nee Stallwood) told me that "She had three daughters at the school, Betty, Sheila and Sylvia. Miss Cecily Turner taught the Juniors then and a Miss Jenkins was in charge of the Infants."

Reg Seymour was the first pupil from Stoke Row School to get a scholarship to Henley Grammar School, in 1929. "Mrs Johnson was so elated by the news that she walked down to the Forge in Newlands Lane, where my father was a blacksmith, to give the glad tidings to the family in person!"

Mrs Foreman became Headteacher in 1940 and the story of her time in Stoke Row is set down in the chapter on the Wars.

Miss Bates was Headteacher in the 1950s and former pupils still have kindly memories of her. Mrs Jean Kent (nee Powell) recalled: "She was a brilliant teacher and the forerunner of modern education. She taught us to paint murals, one was of a man who made a journey through the Andes.

We also learned spinning on wooden looms and other crafts. We wove table runners and things like that. For these we collected plants and made our own dyes. One of these projects was a patchwork of the children's handiwork, using some form of their names." (I wonder what became of it?)

Mrs Johnson and Miss Cecily Turner, outside the door of Stoke Row School, c 1930.
Kindly lent by Cecil Lambourne.

Sometime in the early 1950s, the BBC 'Panorama' programme came to Stoke Row School. The interviewer, Robin Day, came to speak to the staff about teachers' salaries. Barbara Hillier told me: "One of the teachers, Miss Valerie Pratt, lodged with my family for about two years at that time."

In 1964, the *Henley Standard* reported: "A new Headteacher for Stoke Row School has been chosen from a short list of five. He is Mr P D Houghton of Leicester, who is married and has a small son."

Mr Houghton wrote regularly for the *Stoke Row News* and in March 1968, reported: "The School, following up its links with The Gambia, sent out there a pack of pictures, drawn by the children of one another. They also sent a graph, showing the maximum and minimum temperatures for the first fortnight of the term and a book about the recent big snowfall, which must have been very interesting for the Gambians, who have probably never seen snow!"

In December 1969, Mr and Mrs Houghton left the school, after five years at Stoke Row. The *Stoke Row News* reported:

"In late December the children had their Christmas Party but, before starting their tea, they presented Mr Houghton and his wife with a bottle of wine, a box of chocolates and eight iced sponges, each with letters that read: GOOD LUCK. On behalf of the parents, Mrs Nina Evans presented Mr Houghton with a silver Parker pen, pencil and ballpoint set, £4 of book tokens and £3 of record tokens."

A new Headteacher, James B Paveley, took over in early 1970. With his wife Pam, he had just come from Crawley New Town, so Stoke Row must have been a remarkable change of scene for them.

In 1975, Stuart Copeman became Headteacher at Stoke Row School and stayed for ten years. He was imaginative, artistic and devoted to the children. During the 1979/80 school year, he was granted a year's secondment to study for a Master's Degree at the University of Bath. As a part of a module on the History of English Education, he wrote a thesis on the state of Rural Education in the 19th century and used the log books of Stoke Row School as exemplification material.

More recent Headteachers have included Mrs Joy Fiddaman (1985 - 1992) and Mrs Jane Bache (1992 - 1996). Both were assisted by Elizabeth Sayer and others and are remembered with affection by former pupils today. Jane helped considerably with the compilation of the *Stoke Row Village Appraisal* in 1995 and wrote of the school:

"The Stoke Row Primary School takes over 60 children from the age of four to eleven years. Being a state school, it delivers a broad, balanced education, based on the National Curriculum. Much emphasis is placed on assessing each child's capabilities and needs, and planning their work around this assessment. The numbers have shown a steady increase over the last few years and, as a result, the school has expanded into three classes. There are two full time teachers, plus two classroom assistants in the Juniors and one full time teacher and a qualified nursery nurse assisting in the Infants' classroom. Of the total 61 children in the school, 29 of these are from Stoke Row and the remaining 32 from surrounding villages."

The present Headteacher is Tom Kumsang, who took up his appointment in April 1996. He has already made many improvements to the school buildings and plans several more. The number of pupils is still rising. Under his headship the school looks forward to a thriving future.

Henry Casley, the Chief Executive of Southern Electric, who lives in Stoke Row, handing the key to Headteacher Jane Bache, as the Stoke Row Primary School receives its Minibus in December 1994. By kind permission of the Henley Standard.

Attendance and Health

Attendance was a great problem for Victorian teachers, largely because numbers were related to grants. Stuart Copeman summed it up clearly: "Each year H M Inspectors of Schools came to the area to test the standard of Reading and Arithmetic and, as this was on a known date, the children were nagged and cajoled into being sure to attend, for the following year's monetary grant was based on the number of passes attained. If they did well, an extra grant was given." Throughout 1880, for example, the pass marks were not good. Gradually matters got worse and worse and there were threats to withdraw the grant altogether.

Absenteeism was due to several factors: lack of money to pay fees, arriving late, extremes of weather, illness of the child or its family and, above all, the employment of children in the fields to help with the family income.

Some families could not even afford to pay the small fee, as some of these excerpts show: "January 1880: Many have been sent home for their arrears in school money. (The actual amount to be paid, probably 3d, was not shown). 17 September 1883: One child lost her father before the holiday and is again sent to school by the Relieving Officer who has paid for her schooling. Four children all absent, playing about in the road. They all owe for more than a year's irregular schooling. November 1883: Three children have again returned to school with promise of paying 2/6, plus weekly fees of 9d to clear up their long arrears. 25 May 1886: One girl came to school with twopence instead of her usual payment of three pence on Tuesday morning; she was sent home for another penny, but has not been to school since. February 1895: One boy has been absent from school for six weeks, owing to great poverty at home."

Whether the children paid or whether they did not, unpunctuality was not tolerated. If they were late, even though they may have walked several miles, they were sent back again. In January 1889, Miss E S Carter wrote: "Several children have had to go home for coming to school after 9 o'clock. 30 November 1883: Three children came at 9.1/4 (9.15 am), so I told them they were better away, so they went away." Miss Carter never minced her words!

There is little doubt that Victorian winters were far colder than those of the late 20th century and heavy snowfalls were common. Heating in the school was inadequate, too, only by means of a 'Tortoise' stove ('Slow, but Sure' was the motto of one manufacturer).

The Inspector's report in July 1879 explained the poor state of the school at that time: "Some of the deficiencies are likewise due to absenteeism... many have been scarce three months out of the six months, on account of the long and exceptionally hard winter from December to March, being almost continuous snowy weather."

As Stuart Copeman pointed out: "...these were the days when a child of 4 or 5 years, with inadequate footwear, would have to walk some 2.1/2 or 3 miles to school (and back home afterwards) in the snow." In December 1888, Miss Reid noted: "Many children have chilled feet, preventing them from putting on their boots."

The winter of 1880 was certainly very bad and the following one even worse. Miss Carter noted on 21 January 1881: "All Wednesday there was a heavy fall of snow, with driving wind, which blocked up the roads, so that no children could come. By Thursday noon footpaths had been cut through the snow which, up to Uxmoor was 5 ft deep and up to the school door 3 ft deep. Friday was so bitterly cold that only three children came in the morning."

This interior view of Stoke Row School was taken by Mr P Elford in 1907.
It is reproduced by kind permission of the Oxfordshire Photographic Archive.

A week later: "28 January 1881: A very hard and bitter frost. The 20 children who came through this week could scarcely gain any heat all day, though seated close around the stove. Today the whole length of the floor was wet with the thaw of the snow drifts, dripping through the roof."

Not surprisingly, Miss Carter's entry a fortnight later read: "In consequence of the continuous snowy weather this winter, colds, coughs, Diarrhea (sic) have been prevalent among the children attending the school."

Not all the absence was due to bad weather or illness. Miss Carter seemed very bitter on the subject. "20 February 1880: The elder children have derived a notion from the Visitor, which accords with their own convenience, that they are not necessitated to attend more than two days a week. Several of them told me so and acted in accordance."

102

On 5 April 1888, Miss Reid noted: "54 in morning school. Many of the children are gone into the woods, with the permission of the owners, to gather sticks for fuel which is still urgently required by the continuance of the severe weather..."

Miss Laura Carter wrote, in February 1895: "There has been some trouble with boys going on the ice and being late for school. Many of the children are suffering with bad feet and are unable to get to school." By April of that year Miss Carter felt the need to justify the poor state of attendance. "Immediately after the last exam we had an epidemic of measles which, though of a mild nature, affected the majority of the children and lasted in its most severe state for three weeks, but really affected the school longer than that."

Not only were Victorian winters often extremely cold but the summers could be very hot, too. On 29 September 1898, Mr Rowland wrote: "Several of the children stay away to fetch water which, owing to the severe drought, has to be carried for miles."

Gradually more attention began to be paid to the health of the children. In February 1902, Mr Sutherland made an entry about an immunisation programme. "Some of the children have been vaccinated and are absent from school from that cause." In the margin he wrote, as if to voice his approval: "Vaccination in vogue."

This photograph shows the children of Stoke Row School doing 'PT' (Physical Training) in May 1909. Their headwear, especially of the girls, who are all wearing pinafores, is very attractive, if somewhat unsuitable for this kind of 'drill'!
By kind permission of the Rural History Centre, Reading University.

During the headship of Mr Percy Latter (1908 - 1914) children who became 'long-term sick', were taken off the register until they recovered. This made the attendance figures look better and is an example of how the important link between funding and attendance could be improved.

By November 1908 regular medical inspections began. "The weighing machine, tape measure, screen, etc. arrived today. Entered particulars on cards at Doctor's wish." A few days later: "Doctor McIntyre commenced inspection of 25 children at 10.00 am and Doctor Evans arrived at 11.30 am. From 11 till 12 the teachers were engaged helping the doctors." The children were also being drilled and the teachers had to learn how to do it, too. "...teachers attended a lecture on Physical Drill, given by Capt Harvey."

Despite these 'physical jerks' as the children often called them, their health did not improve a great deal. There were coughs, colds and other, more dangerous diseases. The fact that they were passed on so easily is not surprising, considering that many of the children slept two or more to a bed.

On 14 December 1910: "The Medical Inspector called this morning and ordered the immediate closing of the school – the majority of the children suffering from whooping-cough." This epidemic continued throughout the winter and into the spring of 1911. Children who had brothers or sisters with whooping-cough also had to be excluded from the school, for this could be a fatal disease.

There were other illnesses, too. On 31 March 1911: "Five children forced to stay away through contagious sickness – ringworm or measles."

Often when the father was out of work, or even died, times were very hard indeed. "13 October 1911: Three children have been admitted to the Henley Union (this was the dreaded 'workhouse') and therefore their names have been removed from the Registers." At the end of that month: "Six children are away attending funerals."

On 3 November 1911, Mr Latter "readmitted a boy who has to lie on his stomach. This boy was soon found to be suffering from tuberculosis of the spine, resulting in spinal curvature and was ordered from school for special treatment."

By 1916, there was little doubt that the injuries and deaths of the men of Stoke Row were already bringing the horrors of war home to the village in a private capacity. When country men enlisted for the army during the First World War, the government were appalled to find how poor their health was, especially their teeth. By 1917, not only were Medical Inspections a regular feature of school life, but dental treatment was also commenced.

Also during the First World War, children were encouraged to pick blackberries, so that nutritious jam and juice could be made for the army; no doubt the money raised from their sale was also useful at home. Local fruits were also gathered for meals made at home; food was very short by the end of the war.

As the Armistice was signed, the health of the nation was at a very low ebb and influenza raged throughout Europe. "1 November 1918: Visit by Nurse. Influenza spreading – 25 children away this afternoon."

A week later: "Mrs Wilson was home all day – very sick." The epidemic lasted all that winter. On 11 November 1918: "Mrs Wilson resumed duties. Mr Day received a note from the Medical Officer to close the school for a fortnight.

And then, almost as an afterthought, was a brief bracketed note: "[Armistice signed today]". Was she too tired to write more than that? No further mention was made of the end of the war.

Once the country began to return to some semblance of normality, it was decided that more physical exercise should be taken at schools. In June 1920, Stoke Row School was "visited by Mr Forder, who took the whole of the school, in three divisions, for physical exercises."

Eventually, in the 1930s, music and dance became popular as a means of physical education. This picture shows 'Spring', a pageant at Stoke Row School in this period. Left to right: Nancy Wixen, Rose Stallwood (later Mrs Rose Textor), Kathleen Howells. 'The Sun' was Sheila Johnson. Seated in front are Joan Wells and Joan Clark. The rest are unknown, except for the girl on the extreme right, Joan Haines, who lived at 'The Haven'. Their dresses were made of coloured muslin. By kind permission of Rose Textor.

Work-related Absenteeism

Some children came to school most of the time, apart from when they were ill, but many had to stay at home in the summer to help with the harvest. This was in spite of the Agricultural Children Act of 1873, which sought to prohibit the employment of children below the age of eight in agriculture and to secure a minimum school attendance for those between the ages of eight and twelve years.

In July 1887, at which time Miss Annie Reid was in charge, Mr S G Treherne inspected the school:

"There were 79 children present out of 92 on the Register. The Inspectors heartily endeavoured to improve the attendance, which has hitherto always been depressing to every Mistress, the average for the year reaching only about 50, so that during the hay-making and fruit-picking season about 40 children would be absent. Very few children obtain 22 weeks instruction during the year, though their names may be on the Register for a longer period. The parents insist on keeping the children at home when they require them, in spite of all the consequences."

Miss Reid wrote soon afterwards: "Attendance very dispiriting. 51 children absent on Wednesday. A Creche would be a great measure to prevent so many staying away and would doubtless be appreciated by Mothers who are obliged to go fruit picking and leave their young children." Again on 10 August 1887: "A poor and unsettled attendance. Hay-making and cherry-gathering. Bank Holiday interferes with the School and the children take advantage of the fact that other schools have commenced holidays." By 30 October 1888 there was: "A very poor school... the children have been busy picking up acorns." These were usually sold to feed local pigs.

Mr Rowland (1895 - 1898) was obsessed by poor attendance. He never mentioned the name of any child and referred only to the numbers of them. The first mention of the Attendance Officer occurred on 15 July 1895, this may have been as a result of new leglislation. "The Attendance Officer called today, having been requested to do so by the Master, in consequence of the very great irregularity of the children, and took the names of the worst examples."

The new Master found this very poor attendance to be extremely frustrating. "May 1896: On asking the cause of a boy's absence this morning, he refused to answer, stating that his father had instructed him to do so. This boy is constantly kept at home to work on his father's farm (the latter two words were underlined) but the father informs the Attendance Officer that such is not the case, which is untrue. It is absolutely impossible to get the parents, who keep their children at home to work, to tell the truth..."

Little assistance was offered by the authorities. "25 July 1899: The Attendance Officer... has written to me stating that leniency is usually shown towards absentees during the fruit season. This compulsory attendance becomes a farce and it is of no use for the teacher to report absentees... One family are all pea-picking at Stoke Row Farm." Eventually, Mr Rowland stopped making Attendance Returns altogether.

One child who attended Stoke Row School in 1879 and 1880, when Miss E S Carter was Head Mistress, was Clarinda W R Clinch, who came from Tewkesbury and whose Child's School Book has survived. This was an official document, which accompanied the child around the country and was especially useful when parents moved from place to place to find work. Reproduced by kind permission of the Oxfordshire Archives.

Mr Willimont became Headmaster in 1898 and on 23 February 1900 he listed nine children who were continually absent and the reasons for their non-attendance. The chief one was 'baby-minding'. Some of the children were as young as eight, and one or two of those who were 'working for father' were only eleven.

However, changes were beginning to take place. Perhaps it was the turn of the century or the death of Queen Victoria, but certainly constant visits and, in some cases summonses, by the Attendance Officers were starting to have a real effect. This, combined with better tuition and kinder attitudes, warmer rooms and more staff were, at last, making life at schools better for everyone.

Mr Sutherland, who had a more positive outlook, set up a Roll of Honour in April 1903. "The following children have not missed one attendance from 1 April 1902 to 31 March 1903: Albert Greenaway, William Greenaway, Ada Greenaway, Dennis Greenaway, Isabel Sutherland, Wallace Sutherland and Aubrey Sutherland." (The latter three were probably his own children).

Early in 1907, Mr Sutherland noted, with pride and sorrow: "Ada Greenaway, who has an unbroken record of attendances for a period of more than seven consecutive years, left school this week. The family are noted for their regularity and punctual attendance at school." A little later, she received a silver watch from the County Education Committee "as a reward for regular attendance for five years and upward." In a photograph displayed earlier in this chapter, Ada is seen wearing her attendance medal.

By the 1930s, with stricter legislation, more farm machinery and better conditions all round, attendance had improved enormously for the most part and photographs of the time show the children looking healthier and happier.

In September 1930, the new Senior School opened at Rotherfield Peppard and children over the age of eleven were transferred to it, unless they passed into the Henley Grammar School. Many adults today have happy memories of the Rotherfield School and a section on it will be found in the chapter on Highmoor School.

Religious Education

Religious teaching played an important part of the curriculum of both Stoke Row and Highmoor, especially in the early days, for both were Church of England schools. The work was largely catechismic and much was learned by rote. Each year there was a Diocesan Examination and prizes were awarded.

These are typical entries relating to visits by the Diocesan Inspector:

"24 May 1883: The 1st class, consisting of 4th and 5th standards wrote an account of Job (the prophet) on paper. The 2nd class, comprising the 2nd and 3rd wrote Catechism on slates, whilst the Infants were questioned by the governess and then dismissed. The 1st and 2nd standards, after writing the Lord's Prayer, were examined.

Edith Godwin answered nearly all the questions, the others [being bad attendants] scarce any..."

However, the July 1903 report was much kinder: "The Infants and Standard 1 said their Repetition nicely and answered easy questions well. In the Upper Division many good answers were received from the children who were commended. The younger children will need to be encouraged to take their share of the answering."

These visits and similar reports were made every year and are recorded in the log books right up to the end of the last one, which finished in 1921.

An exterior view of the eastern end of Stoke Row School, taken by Mr P Elford in 1907. By kind permission of the Oxfordshire Photographic Archive.

The Lighter side of School Life

On various dates in the spring and summer of 1868, and from time to time throughout the school log books, there were notes like this: "Small attendance due to various clubs which are held in the neighbourhood." These may have been outings or social events to which people contributed small sums of money throughout the year.

On 18 March 1881: "Friday afternoon had school from 1 o'clock to 3 o'clock, on account of a lecture on Figi (sic) being given for our entertainment in the evening by Capt Meade, RN." This item is of particular interest at the moment, as Tom Kumsang, the Headteacher of Stoke Row Primary School, appointed in 1996, was born in Fiji, although he has lived most of his life in England.

Monday, 15 May 1882, was very special. "This day was kept as a Fete Day by the school. A Tea and Gifts being given to the children and the poor by the Maharajah of Benares, in remembrance of the Queen being saved from assassination." (See the chapter on the Wells).

At the end of July 1882, the school was granted "a whole day's holiday, on account of the Flower Show being held at Stoke Row and the room being required in the morning for the children to make up their wild flower nosegays."

That year seemed to finish well, too. "22 December: The boys and girls, big and little, produced finished needlework: herringbone, knitting, crochet and netting. Fred Busby and Frank Hillier finished excellently a printing book."

In January 1883, when the one room was being used for over 60 children: "The school Visitor came in the dinner hour, there being a half-holiday in consequence of preparing the room for the Concert..."

Queen Victoria's Golden Jubilee was celebrated in June 1887: "Three Committee meetings have been held in the Schoolroom after school and it has been decided to celebrate the Queen's Jubilee by giving a Dinner to all in Stoke Row over 16 years of age and a Tea to all under that age. Towards this, the Maharajah of Benares has kindly sent £40, the rest has been collected from friends interested in the Parish."

On 21 June 1887, there was "a whole holiday for the festivities, when lovely weather enhanced the enjoyment of all. The 90 schoolchildren assembled in their playground at 4 o'clock and, with banners and music, marched to the Well Field, had tea and each received a medal and spent a happy evening."

Ten years later, on 22 June 1897: "Being the day appointed for the celebration of Her Majesty's Diamond Jubilee, the school will be closed during the whole day."

On 22 February 1900, Mr Sutherland noted: "Tuesday's (Shrove Tuesday) attendance was the worst. A number of children went with a party 'Shroving', some old local function." This custom was much practised in other parts of England, but I could find no reference in the Centre for Oxfordshire Studies of its happening in Oxfordshire. It usually involved begging at doors for ingredients with which to make pancakes and a last chance for frolics before Lent.

"News was received in the Village of the Relief of Mafeking" on 19 May 1900. This related to the Boer War, which was being waged in South Africa at that time. Mafeking had been under siege for five months and the breakthrough of the British troops was the cause of great rejoicing, nationwide.

A few days later, on 24 May 1900: "Today being the Queen's Birthday, the National Anthem was sung at the opening of the school session and a short and appropriate address, relating to the Glorious Reign of Her Majesty Queen Victoria, was spoken to the children of the Upper Class by the Vicar."

Christmas of that year was also marked. "19 December 1900: The latter part of this afternoon was given up to games... Books, magazines and other little presents were distributed among the children. Efforts are being made to provide them with a Tea and Amusements on New Year's Day."

However, the entry for 1 February 1901 was heavily edged in black: "A special funeral service will be held in the Parish Church tomorrow (Saturday) at 5 o'clock, in memory of the late Most Gracious Queen Victoria."

Rev H H Appleford and his wife took a considerable interest in the children. On 16 June 1901, following the Examination by the Diocesan Inspector, "The Vicar announced that a Day School Treat would, by the kindness of two ladies in the neighbourhood, be given to children attending these schools (ie the Day and Sunday Schools), a half-holiday being given for this purpose."

The Sutherlands were finding means of giving more pleasure to the children, too. "The children attending here are going to give an Entertainment (organised by the teachers) in the Schoolroom on Mon and Tues next, on behalf of School Funds." This took place on 18 November 1901: "Children's Happy Evening, 6.00 to 8.00 pm. By kindness of Mrs Appleford and friends, children attending both Day and Sunday Schools were entertained in the Schoolroom to games, refreshments and sweets."

Stoke Row School group, c 1918.
Back row: Harry Webb, George Shaw, Johnnie Britnell, Reg Cox, Cyril Tilby.
Middle row: - ? -, Rose Carter, Roland Page, Jim Evans, ? Eley or ? Lambourne,
Ted Evans, Chris Busby, ? Lambourne.
Front row: Kathleen Evans, Gladys Chapman, Lily Johnson, Daisy Green, Doris Webb
and Charles Godwin.
By kind permission of Mrs Lily Tayler (nee Johnson).

111

In the summer of 1902, there was an entry that revealed the joyous state of the nation that year. "9 August: The usual period of four weeks holiday is supplemented by an extra week, to commemorate the Coronation of His Majesty Edward VII."

When the children returned, those "of the Upper 2 Divisions taken for a School Walk by the Head Teacher, with the object of Nature Study, with special reference to the changes in the foliage etc in the autumn. The children were eager to learn and discover for themselves, the fresh beauties in their surroundings."

A similar treat was in store for the children the following year: "14 May 1903: A bright morning. Children taken for a School Walk. Instead of History, the children were allowed a Conversational Lesson on the subject of this morning's Walk."

There was an interesting entry for "13 October 1905: ...considerable interest was evinced in some pictorial postcards, illustrative of scenery and employment in Canada. ...received by courtesy of the Commissioner for Emigration. These were afterwards distributed among the children concerned..."

In May 1908: "Special lessons on 'The British Empire' were taken in the afternoon." and in August: "Rev Mayle called this afternoon and gave the senior children an interesting account of Newfoundland."

At Christmas, however, more interesting attractions than school depleted the classes. "21 December 1909: The attendance has been poor this week – parents take their children to see the Reading Bazaars." The 'bazaars' in this case were probably the stores in Reading, 'Heelas', for instance.

More celebrations began on 21 June 1911: "School closes today for one week's holiday in honour of the Coronation of King George V and Queen Mary, reassembling Thursday 29 June. The school during this week has been decorated with the national colours and lessons have been taken on patriotic lines."

In July 1911, there was a great thrill: "The school will be closed tomorrow for the Summer Outing to Portsmouth and Southsea." It would be hard for us today to capture the feeling of excitement that such a simple outing would have produced throughout the school – a once a year chance to paddle in the sea and to enjoy all the treats that went with such an event – the journey, picnics, ice-cream, sand-castles, Punch and Judy shows, etc.

The boys were already having gardening lessons when, on 3 February 1913, Mr Latter "received notice from County Education Secretary that girls over the age of 11 years will attend Nettlebed Centre for Cookery Lessons." A few days later he "received forms for gardening for girls in addition to those for boys. Have altered timetable to allow of this innovation." Unfortunately, all did not go according to plan. "The girls were present at 1.30 pm for Cookery Lessons, as the trap had been promised to convey them to Nettlebed, but no conveyance arrived."

New ideas were coming in thick and fast from the Board of Education by February 1913, when Mr Latter "attended private cinematograph exhibition and arrangements were made with HMI for upper classes to attend once weekly at Nettlebed Village Hall."

A little while later, "30 children, with two teachers visited Nettlebed for the Cinema Educational films." This would have been the first time that Stoke Row children would have seen moving pictures. Not all the parents agreed with the novelty, however. "4 June 1913: A number of children stayed away from the Cinema this afternoon, at parents' wish." On 9 July, the following entry was made into the log book: "The Managers wish the Cinema visits to cease." After this no further pleasures were recorded, though no doubt, some took place.

Were it possible for Victorian and Edwardian teachers and their pupils to visit Stoke Row School during successive years and especially today, they would certainly be amazed at the improvements in the buildings, educational standards, and indeed, improvements in the health and well-being of the children themselves, as the following photographs show:

Stoke Row School group, c 1960.

Back row: Sandra Green, Elaine Earle, Carol Clark, Brenda Hayes, Brenda Wixen, Josephine Wixen and Gillian Sparks.

Middle row: Martin Asquith, Robert Pitcher, Elizabeth Hryczanek, Christine Kosakiewicz, Heather Townsend, Neil Arundel and John Peters.

Front row: Christopher Hicks, John Textor, Geoffrey Bennett and Paul Woodley.

By kind permission of Mrs Phyllis Townsend.

Stoke Row School group, 1970. Back row: Andrew Hayes, Nigel Greenaway, Neil Wooldridge, Tony Ball, Tony Searby, David Hughes, Colin Langham and Nicholas Cox. Centre row: David Evans, Sharon Clisby, Susan George, Norma Wixen, Tracey Martin and James Dunne. Front row: Richard Slade, Peter Chaffey, Paul George, David McNaughton, Gary Saady and Colin Woodward. Kindly lent by Arthur Wixen.

'Picnic Time for Teddy Bears' was the title given to this photograph taken in April 1995. Mrs Rachel Fleming sits behind her Infants class. By kind permission of the Henley Standard. Some readers may be interested to compare this happy picture with the one of the pinched and frightened children in the earlier group photograph, dated 1909.

114

Teachers at Stoke Row School

Date	Headteacher	Assistant(s)	Pupil numbers (where given)
1853	William Crews	Mary Crews	
1854	Miss Sarah Needle		30
1863	Jane Mahoney	E Wilson (Ambulatory)	
1866	Miss Kate Stannard		31
1871	Mrs Kate Francis		
1878	S A Reynolds		
1878	Miss E S Carter		
1884	Miss C A Duffield		75
1887	Annie Reid	Mary Reid	
1892	Eliz. Partington	Jessie Hope	113
1894	Laura Carter		
1895	Charles Rowland	Mrs Rowland	
1898	J Willimont	Mrs Willimont	84
1900	A W Sutherland	Mrs Sutherland & Ada Hayward	75
1908	P R Latter	Mrs Latter & Cecily Turner	
1914	F G Dakin	Mrs Dakin & Cecily Turner	
1916	George Wilson	Mrs Wilson & Cecily Turner	47
1920/30s	Mrs Johnson	Miss Jenkins & Cecily Turner	
1940/5	Mrs Foreman	Cecily Turner/ Mrs Ada Biggs	
1950s	Miss Bates	Cecily Turner/ Mary Blower	
1964	P D Houghton	Mr Claude Smith and students from Culham	
1970	James B Pavely	Mrs Pam Pavely	
1975	Stuart Copeman	Eileen Simmonds, Elizabeth Sayer	
1985	Mrs Joy Fiddaman	Tricia Foden, Elizabeth Sayer	
1992	Mrs Jane Bache	Rachel Fleming, Rachel Taylor	50
1996	Tom Kumsang	Rachel Fleming, Kathleen Putman	75

Notes from Stoke Row School Log Books, 1853 - 1920

Decade	Buildings	Attendance	Health
1853/60	Single Schoolroom		
1861/70	Overcrowding		
1871/80	Insufficient space	Some couldn't pay Unpunctuality Agric. Children Act, 1873	
1881/90	New Infant Room	Hard winters Gathering wood Boys ice-skating 40 absent, working	Coughs & colds Chilblains
1891/00	Window alterations Very hot/cold Stove useless Toilets smelling	Attendance Officers appointed Fruit/pea picking Baby-minding	Measles Head lice
1901/10	Museum provided New stoves House improved Playground better	Roll of Honour Silver watches won Reading 'Bazaars'	Vaccinations Medical inspections
1911/20	Fireplace collapsed Water laid on Infant stove smoked Cess pit problems New toilets built	Attending funerals Less absenteeism	Scarlet fever Whooping cough Ringworm Tuberculosis Influenza Dentistry Physical training

Curriculum and the Lighter Side of School and Village Life

1853/60	No details given
1861/70	Club Outings & Village Sports Days
1871/80	No details given
1881/90	Lecture on Fiji, 1881
	Maharajah's Tea Party, 1882
	Stoke Row Flower Show, 1882
	Knitting, crocheting, netting,
	herring-boning & book printing, 1882
	School Concert, 1883
	Guy Fawkes celebrated, 1883
	Bead threading and Object lessons, 1883
1891/00	Map and Model drawing, 1892
	Swedish & Musical Drill, 1892
	Queen Victoria's Golden Jubilee, 1887
	Queen Victoria's Diamond Jubilee, 1897
	Children went 'Shroving', 1900
	Mafeking celebrations, 1900
	Queen Victoria's Birthday celebrations, 1900
	Day and Sunday Schools Treat, 1900
	Christmas party and gifts, 1900
1901/10	'Happy Evening' for School Funds, 1901
	New Year's Day Tea, 1901
	Needlework and patchwork
	Queen Victoria's funeral, 1901
	King Edward VII Coronation celebrations, 1902
	Nature Walks, Reports and Conversation, 1903
	Observation lessons, 1904
	Talk by Canada Commissioner for Emigration, 1905
	Official Photographs taken of the School, 1907
	Talks on British Empire and Newfoundland, 1908
	Children taken to Reading 'Bazaars', Christmas 1909
1911/20	King George V Coronation celebrations, 1911
	First School Outing, to Portsmouth, 1911
	Gardening begun for boys, 1912
	Nettlebed Annual Horticultural Show, 1912
	Cinematograph sessions at Nettlebed, 1913
	Cookery lessons for girls, 1913
	Basic Physics and Chemistry, 1916
1920/30	First Scholarship to Henley Grammar School, 1929.

8. School Days at Highmoor

The Dame School

The first school at Highmoor was started by Rev Joseph Smith, the Vicar of Rotherfield Greys, a wealthy and generous man, who also contributed substantially to the building of the Church and the Vicarage. In 1927 Mr Richard Slade, senior, told Mr J H Baker that "there was a Dame School, held in the old cottage between The Rising Sun Inn and the present village school. Old Mrs Jarratt ran it and her daughter helped her teach." *Gardner's Directory* for 1852 states: The school on Witheridge Hill receives a subscription from Trinity College, Oxford."

Mr Frank Baldwin remembered that his mother, Fanny Baldwin, the Postmistress, was "one of the few people in Highmoor who had received an education, at a Dame School, for which her mother sacrificed 3d a week. This school was held in the long room at the back of the then Manor House (today known as 'Witheridge Hill Cottage'). Mrs Jarratt was the mistress and her daughter, who became Mrs Baylis, was the organist and pianist. It was she who taught Mrs Mabel Cox of Stoke Row how to play the organ." Mrs Cox will be celebrating her 105th birthday in June 1999 and is mentioned in the chapter on Interesting Inhabitants.

The National School

Eventually a National School was built on Witheridge Hill in 1862. Unlike Stoke Row School, no details of life at this one before 1901 have come down to us. The Highmore School Log Book for 1901 to 1954 has survived, however, and is now in the Oxfordshire Archives. (Until the mid-1950s Highmoor was spelled in this way).

The Buildings

The book opens with the measurements of the two rooms:
   Main Room: 25' x 16', 50 children.
   Infants' Room: 21' x 12', 32 children.
The School building was 40 years old by 12 February 1902, when the HMI wrote: "Infants' desks and gallery must be condemned. The Boys and Girls offices (toilets) should be effectively separated. Enlargement of the South windows in both rooms is much to be desired."

The same problems of heating the building occurred at Highmoor as at Stoke Row. "16 January 1903: The weather this week has been intensely cold and the children have been too cold to write or to do ordinary lessons. It was necessary to give them marching and drill every few minutes to keep them warm." One elderly lady told me that the ink used to freeze in the inkwells overnight!

Mr Alfred Spilling and his wife, outside the newly built school on Witheridge Hill at Highmoor, c 1870. By kind permission of Mrs Ada Britnell (nee Wells).

The School was refurbished in June, 1905: "The School has undergone a thorough repair. Walls inside recoloured and woodwork painted; outside spouting and doors painted and the girls' lavatory effectively separated from the teachers'."

On 21 December 1910, when the school closed for the Christmas holidays, it was "to be in the hands of the decorators."

A new school piano, purchased in January 1911, proved "to be a useful addition to the school. The cost £16 met by a grant of £7 from Oxfordshire Education Committee and rest by School Concerts and subscriptions. 10 year guarantee given by the makers, Morton & Co of London."

One of the entries in the February of that year showed that the numbers had again increased: "Revised accommodation: Main Room: 39, Infants: 31."

Some improvements to the storage were necessary in early 1913: "The Vicar is making application for increased cupboard accommodation... The Committee are willing to provide the material to build a tool-shed for the garden tools..." By June of that year Mr Baker was able to enter: "The new cupboard, supplied for the school library and other books, proves to be a valuable acquisition."

Mr A Butler, the HMI, inspected the school buildings at the end of January 1914, "with a view to having them redecorated; and other small repairs attended to. Master has applied to the Managers for permission to have the Garden Tool Shed erected on the space between the Infants School and the coal-shed and offices (toilets).

This site would be most convenient for the school and be a permanency... The Education Committee will make a grant of £3 towards the cost of the shed and 10/- towards digging the new school gardens, situated on the Allotment."

More suggestions came that May: "Mr Butler, the HMI, to enquire as to the Cloakroom accommodation... the small, inadequate porch, formerly used by the Infants, not now used – they share the cloakroom used by the older children."

In contrast to the previous winter and spring, Mr Baker was able to write, in the June of 1916: "The weather has been very summer-like, a heatwave having passed over the country recently." Perhaps it was due to this heat that on 14 July: "The Vicar and Mr MacIntyre visited to see the effects of the fire, which was discovered in the school premises on Thursday at 4.00 am. Neighbours assisted the Master to extinguish the fire." A week later "The Vicar and Mr Butler inspected the school premises during the week. Considerable damage has been done but is covered by insurance."

In a report by the HMI, Mr C B Hunt, in December 1919, he noted: "The main room is cramped and the children sit crowded together at their desks, a condition unfavourable to independent work. Premises: 1) The Cloakroom is cramped, dark and stuffy. It provides inadequate accommodation. 2) The Infants' Room is not adequately heated."

However, no mention was made of what steps, if any, were taken to rectify this situation. In fact no mention that was made of the buildings until much, much later, in June 1951, when, on 23 November: "the School Architect called." There seems to have been some investigation into alterations to the school building again in 1952, for on 29 October: "Mrs Moorhouse called re lighting improvements and new windows." and on 13 January 1953: "New tables and chairs arrived."

There were more thoughts about improvements to the school building in 1954, when, on 17 February: "Director of Education and the School Architect called to inspect the buildings and Miss Ankland called with reference to the Canteen."

No further improvements were made to the school – perhaps it was decided even then that such works would not be viable.

School Staff

Mr Alfred Spilling was the first Headmaster, 1862, assisted by his wife. In 1887 the Post Office Directory notes the average attendance as being 60. Mr Spilling may have died soon after this, because by 1891 his wife, Mrs Charlotte Spilling was in charge. The *Post Office Directory* lists Mrs Charles Hughes as Mistress in 1895.

The name of the Master is not given in the log book when it was opened, but the *Post Office Directory* lists Mr Thomas Hughes. Mrs Earle assisted with the sewing and May Delafield was Monitoress.

On 6 January, 1902: "Mr A T and Mrs M M Pooley took charge as Master and Mistress. Mr and Mrs Talfourd Inman visited the school in June 1902 and were "pleased with tidiness of the children and way in which the school was conducted by

Mr and Mrs Pooley. However, in the February, Rev Harnett wrote: "Neither Mr nor Mrs Pooley in attendance. Mrs Pooley had no permission from the Managers to absent herself. Wrote to H M Inspector. Found some of the younger boys cannot read at all, otherwise pleased with the state of the school."

Mrs Kathleen Kucor kindly donated several of her aunt's Highmoor School Group photographs to my collection, but unfortunately, only this one was dated, by the blackboard held in the centre. Each photograph shows a different set of teachers, but sadly, neither their names nor those of the children are recorded on the reverse.

Robert Clears Lucas took charge as Master at the end of March, 1902, with his wife teaching the Infants and Miss Baylis (whose mother had run the Dame School) as Helper. Revd F R Harnett was still teaching Science and Scripture, but by 30 September 1904 things had changed: "The Vicar ceased his Science lessons. I have taken over Elementary Science of the Upper Division. I propose taking lessons on the Animal Kingdom and Elementary Physiography."

School broke up early for the Christmas holidays in 1905, on 14 December. The reason was noted: "Robert and Alice Lucas cease their duties as Master and Infant Mistress today."

The new Master wrote in a beautiful copperplate hand on 1 January 1906: "I, William Chatterley, took charge of the School as Master, with Jane Chatterley as Assistant. The work of the Upper School was carried on as to timetable, but the Infants did not commence, owing to the new lighting scheme not being completed."

At least seven official photographs of the interior and exterior of the School were taken during 1905 and yet no mention is made of this in the very detailed School Log Book. This one shows the Main Room, with its 'Tortoise' stove, one oil lamp, half-empty cupboard and blackboard, neatly written up for the occasion! Both photographs are reproduced by kind permission of theOxfordshire Photographic Archive.

This picture shows the Infants Room, which had the benefit of a large window, couple of pictures and two hot pipes. The fire was probably not often lit, though there is a fireguard. The white blobs in the fireplace may have been paper flowers. The easel has no blackboard and just seems to be a useful prop for the Mistress's bicycle!

Mr Chatterley was, apparently, very strict and wanted to be seen so, for on "26 January: Five boys (named) punished before the Vicar, four strokes each, for very bad behaviour in the street." The girls fared better. "16 February: "The girls still maintain their splendid record of no absentees. It has now been so for seven weeks."

Later on matters were getting better all round: "Recitation has greatly improved, the monotonous style having nearly disappeared… Needlework improves slowly, but strongly based." This Master wrote of the 'Mixed Dept', the 'Infant Dept Proper' and the 'Under Fives'.

Again, the new Master did not stay long. On 27 September 1907: "I, William Chatterley, ACP, finish duty today. A cheque has been sent this day to the amount of one pound four shillings and a half-penny, for goods made up and sold in the Needlework Dept." There was no indication as to why he left. A few days later: "I, Jane Chatterley, took charge today. Miss Delafield in charge of the Infants."

Then the school closed for two weeks until "18 November 1907: I, John Harold Baker, took charge of this school, with Beatrice Annie Baker as Infants' Mistress and Hilda Baker as Monitoress. The Vicar, Rev Randon M Willis visited the school."

Later that month: "An Evening School, under Government Inspection, was announced this week – two evenings a week, 7.00 - 9.00 pm. 16 youths and men enrolled. Arithmetic, English Composition, Drawing and Choral Music." This Evening School continued up to the First World War and was no doubt very much appreciated by those whose education had been very poor under previous teachers.

The HMI's Report for 1910 was very lengthy, with detailed criticisms and constructive suggestions on subjects such as gardening, nature study, home-mending, needlework, drawing, voice-training and handwriting. Education generally was beginning to supply the children with more than just the three R's.

The Evening Continuation School commenced again in October 1910, "with 22 pupils, the classes are mixed. Subjects include: Part Singing, Arithmetic, Writing/Composition and Rural Science."

In March 1912: "Owing to the high price of coal, due to the miners' strike, Oxfordshire Education Committee suggested using less coal and more physical exercises if the rooms are not warm enough." Perhaps one way to keep the children warm was to encourage them to do gardening: "Mr S Heaton, Horticultural Inspector to the OEC, proposed that school gardening should be commenced on ground already available and a larger plot secured when allotments are obtained." Eleven boys were later enrolled on the Gardening Register.

A rather unusual entry was made on 17 July 1912: "Four boys in the Upper Group severely punished for lying, stealing and insulting the Headmaster behind his back. Each boy acknowledged his guilt and received 12 strokes with the cane."

Again, in December: "A boy (named) received corporal punishment for using filthy language to four girls. The girls had written down the remarks and signed the paper. The boy owned up to the accuracy thereof. This boy has been dismissed from the school." A week later he was "readmitted after severe reprimand."

This charming photograph was probably taken in about 1905.
By kind permission of Archie Earle.

Meantime, schooling continued. "Five girls over 11 years of age attend Cookery classes at Nettlebed School on Tuesdays, 1.45 - 4.00 pm, as arranged with the Education Committee and Mrs R Fleming (of Joyce Grove). The children will be driven in a conveyance when the weather is wet, by kind provision of Mr Fleming." Staff changes were also taking place. "31 January 1913: Miss Gladys M Heath, who has acted as Monitoress in the School since Easter 1909, has succeeded in passing Part I of the Teacher's Preliminary Certificate Examination – she is a former scholar..." She left that February, having been "appointed Assistant Mistress at the new Council School at Sonning Common. Edith Leader appointed in her place, a former scholar who left 2.1/2 years ago, aged 14."

In contrast to Stoke Row School, where little mention was made of the Great War, Mr Baker made quite a number of references to it. "18 September 1914: In view of the great crisis in our country's history, viz the war between Germany and Austria and the Allies – Belgium, France, Britain and Russia; the following features have been introduced into the schoolwork:

Drawing: Flags of the Allied Countries.

Singing: The National Anthem, the Marseillaise, and patriotic songs are being learned. Recitation: Poems of patriotism and valour will be taught.

General Information: Important dispatches and war news are read each day during Reading or Composition lessons.

Geography: Sketch maps from the papers will be cut out and studied with the atlas and the position of the chief towns in the war will be noted. The positions of the great armies will be followed."

124

Mr John H Baker, Head Master and author, enjoying his retirement at his home, Rifleman's Cottage, Woodcote, in about 1960. By kind permission of Miss May Baker.

Young men were being called up fast by October 1914 and so: "Owing to the War... The Education Committee feel there will be insufficient youths to form an Evening Class... and will make no grant."

The timetable was revised in January 1915, in accordance with suggestions made by Mr Hunt, the HMI. "Physical exercises will consist of 20 minutes lessons per week. Additional lesson in recitation, oral and written compositions, substitutes for English grammar lesson for the Lower Group. Drawing lessons once a week for the boys and girls..."

On 30 April 1915: "Edith Leader, Monitoress for the past two years, appointed Supplementary Teacher at Checkendon. Frances Kate Randall, a scholar here in Std Ex VII has applied for the vacancy and is strongly recommended by the Master." Edith Leader was presented with a clock that June.

The Great War, as it was always known until the Second World War broke out, was already affecting the village. On 18 June 1915: "Two boys, H Earle and F Randall, granted permission to be absent... for agricultural labour, owing to the scarcity of labour, due to the War."

And on 12 November: "Mr C B Hunt, the HMI, has taken a commission in His Majesty's Army and will be replaced by Mr H J Dean. The Committee has decided to give Certificates in lieu of books for Attendance and Good Conduct." This, too, was probably on account of the war.

On 31 March 1916: "Jack Randall was successful at the recent Labour Examination and so will be eligible to leave the school. In *Change in the Village*, George Bourne explained: "The Labour Examination entitled children, usually boys, to a 'Labour Certificate' which would allow them to finish school as 'half-timers', and go out and earn a little money."

Later, in February 1917: "Special lessons have been taken this week on the National Food Supplies and the Great War Loan." Special lessons were given on 'Birds, Insects and Crops' and 'Food Economy' in June 1917, and later that month: "An extra 10 poles of ground is being cultivated by the Gardening Class, owing to the urgency of food production. A return of the particulars of the above has been made to the authorities. Potatoes have been planted in 18 of the 30 poles of ground cultivated."

The children were constantly kept informed about the War. On 22 June 1917: "Lieutenant Eric Blore, RFC, kindly gave the children an account of his work at the Front in an 'Observation Balloon', illustrated with B B (blackboard?) sketches." He was also a part-time actor and eventually went to Hollywood where he often played the very formal role of an English butler in films.

In the September of 1917: "The form for school needlework sold has been returned to Oxford with remittance of £1. Papers have been received from the Education Secretary with Government proposals for the collection of:

a) horse-chestnuts for the Munitions Dept. (These were used to make gunpowder!)

b) gathering of blackberries for the Government jam factories to supply the Forces. It is proposed that the authorities grant the schools about two half-day holidays per week until about the middle of October, so that the children may gather the above under the teachers' supervision."

In the autumn of 1917, Mr Baker recorded: "the Vicar, Rev J Hughes, who volunteered under the National Service Scheme, has recently been appointed as Military Chaplain."

By 12 October: "During the past 4 weeks the total quantity of blackberries picked by the children and teachers amounts to 4 cwts."

The school was closed on Wednesday 30 April, "owing to the Children's Concert for the benefit of St Dunstan's Hostel for Blind Soldiers."

Although the Armistice was not far off, no-one knew it in September 1918, and all available manpower was being used. Mr Baker decided to volunteer under a scheme run by the National Services Authority.

"I, Beatrice A Baker, have been appointed by the School Managers and the Oxfordshire Education Authority, to take charge of the school from today, owing to the temporary absence of the Master, who is engaged as a 'War-work Volunteer'. Miss Edith Leader commenced duties today as Supplementary Teacher in charge of the Infants Class." She stayed until November of that year.

Fortunately, about a week later: "The Monitoress, Miss Frances Kate Randall, has been successful in passing the recent Oxford Junior Local Examination and will now be eligible to be recognised as a Pupil Teacher."

In October: "The blackberries this week were sold to the Red Cross Hospital at Henley, being refused at the Railway Station, owing to the Railway Strike."

Thereafter, the school gradually returned to normal. On 2 December 1918 the Headmaster made this entry: "I, John Baker, resumed my duties as Head Teacher today, with Mrs Baker as Assistant. Frances K Randall, the Pupil Teacher, will attend the Maidenhead Girls Secondary School in the new year, after completing 100 attendances at this school."

News of the signing of the Peace Treaty between the Allies and Germany at the end of June 1919, resulted in Mr Baker arranging "a conversation lesson on the end of the War."

In about 1919, the school held a pageant and there was dancing around the maypole. This newspaper photograph was kindly lent to me by Mrs Ada Britnell (nee Wells) who had marked herself with an X.

127

The following praising and constructive Report was received from the Board of Education, following the visit of Mr C B Hunt, who was once again the HMI, on 17 December 1919:

"Mixed & Infants: The Head Master is evidently keen on his school and is endeavouring to conduct the work on enlightened lines. There is no doubt that Reading and History are being handled so as to appeal to the children's imagination, a result due largely to the Master's provision of a good school library and to the general soundness of his viewpoint.

It would be advisable, however, for him to undertake with the top class, a close study of select portions of the literature of the course and to attempt to cultivate in the scholars a more expressive style in the recitation of poetry. The course in Arithmetic seems to need some revision, so that the children may be better trained to use their common sense. New Geography books are desirable in the Middle part of the school.

Probably in the answering some of them are allowed to take the lead too much. They are, however, a friendly set of children who work willingly. The Monitoress gives useful assistance.

The Infants' Mistress is capable and energetic (this was Mrs Beatrice Baker). It would doubtless benefit her to see methods of teaching employed in the best Infants' Schools. The Infants' reading books are very dilapidated. The Mistress teaches Needlework very practically."

Probably as a result of the HMI's suggestions, in early February, 1920: "The Master attended a Conference in Handicraft addressed by Mr Read, the HMI, at Henley Technical School."

Mr MacPherson, Assistant Horticultural Inspector reviewed the School Garden work that March. "The class consists of 14 boys and he was pleased with the interest they took in their work and the satisfactory condition of the garden plots. Out of a maximum 155 marks, 127 were awarded."

That summer "The master attended the Educational Handwork Association's Summer School at Falmouth from 26 July to 21 August – taking a course in Senior Handwork (Woodwork and Metalwork)." This was to prove very useful later, as the Bakers began to produce a series of plays and pageants.

He was certainly very proud when he entered: "10 September 1920: Noel J H Baker (his son), a pupil in Std VI, has been awarded a free place in the Royal Grammar School, Henley, by competitive examination. The scholarship provides free tuition and books for pupils up to the age of 18 years."

In September 1920: "Application to hold Evening School Classes in Mechanical Drawing and Woodwork has been granted. Tools and benches are being forwarded."

The Evening School Class commenced again in October 1920 and "The Master has obtained a Teacher's Woodwork Certificate as a result of attending the Summer School at Falmouth."

In December of that year "Six of the older children left at Christmas, having reached 14 years of age." and "Mr Heath, the Attendance Officer, called for the last time as he is retiring at the end of the month, after 18 years service." Mr G Willoughby, the newly appointed Attendance Officer, came on 7 January 1921.

This photograph, of Mr Baker and his pupils, was taken about 1920. The girls in the back row were: Carrie Page, - ? -, Renee Page, Kate Randall (Monitoress), Annie Franklin, Ada Slade, Edie Green, - ? - . Boys in second row: Tommy Wells, - ? -, Francis Stevens, - ? -, Charlie Wise, Solly Wells, Fred Wise, Bill Slade, ? Potter, Ted Page. Boys next to Mr Baker: Jack Randall and Stanley Wise. The girl at the end of the bench was unknown. On the bench: Elsie Green, Phillis Tudor, Nellie Green, Polly Tudor, Polly Wells and Amy Heath. The name of the last girl at the end of the bench is not known. By kind permission of Mrs Ada Britnell (nee Wells).

During March 1922: "Materials for handicrafts (basketry and bookbinding) have been received." and soon afterwards "Five exhibits in Nature Study have been sent for the Agricultural Show at Thame." These entries show the variety of interesting lessons at the school and probably one reason why unwarranted absenteeism was almost never mentioned after 1900. The HMI's Report in the summer of 1923 was long and detailed, but high in praise, especially on Mr Baker's "eagerness to improve his methods" and how he "made use of team spirit and an effort to induce self-reliance by means of private study in the highest class."

HMI continued: "The Infants' teacher (Mrs Baker) works hard but visits to good modern Infants' schools would be of assistance to her." 1924 continued much as usual, with a big Sports Programme in the summer and a thorough cleansing of the school in September, after which the Evening School commenced again, for "a session of 10 weeks – proposed to take Reading, Writing, Composition and Modern History (Social)." But the Bakers were already looking to make a change in their lives and on 13 October 1924: "The Master and Mrs Baker attended a meeting of the Managers of Alnutt's School, Goring Heath." They took charge of this school the following year.

Before they left, however, there was to be one last performance. 12 December 1924: "During the winter term, especially interesting features of the work of the Upper Classes have been Country Dances and dramatising the story of Dick Whittington, also designing and painting the scenery for the play."

This 1924 photograph shows the finale of the play The Sleeping Beauty, performed by Highmore School. The King was Bill Green and George Earle is just behind him. The girl in the white dress was May Baker and the boy behind her is Fred Edwards. By kind permission of Mrs Lenna Green (nee Archer).

On 19 December 1924, the sad words were recorded in the log book: "We, John H Baker and Beatrice A Baker, finish our duties today as Master and Infants' Mistress, with the kind permission of the Managers." They had been in charge of Highmore School from 1907 to 1924, that is to say, 17 years – it was the end of a golden era! Later, Mr Baker wrote several more books about the local countryside and the ordinary folk that he loved so much, including *The Story of the Chiltern Heathlands* (1931) *The Land of the Gap* (1937) and *Whitchurch* (1956) – alas, they are now all out of print.

Miss E T Varley started as Headmistress on 6 January 1925, and in a clear cursive handwriting, she stated: "I, E T Varley, trained Certified Teacher (University College, Reading) commenced duties as Mistress of this School today. Alice East, Uncertificated Assistant, also commenced in the Infants' Department. Dorothy Brightman, Monitoress since last May, assists in the Mixed Department."

Mrs Florence Green (nee Carey) remembered Miss Varley as being "shy but kind. She wore glasses and had dark hair, which she wore with a fringe. She always wore a dark skirt, a white blouse and often a sleeveless jacket."

The School Report from an Inspection by Mr B M Dunn in November 1925 was congratulatory:

"This school is conducted on stimulating lines and the courses taken, though simple, are attractive and informing. Elementary subjects are very fair and, while the standard of these is being raised, they already furnish quite a useful foundation to much of the work of general interest that is being carried on in the school. One of the strong points in this is the practical and illustrative way in which it is worked out, for the Head Mistress has realised the need of such help for rural schools and History, Geography, Handicraft and Observational work all benefit by this.

It is suggested that if a little more training preparatory to History and Geography were given to the older Infants, more ground could be covered in the Senior Division before the children leave.

Drawing, Physical Exercise and Ear Training are taught with equal zest and the results show decided promise; but, a fuller knowledge of staff notation and a sweeter vocal tone are objects which yet remain to be secured.

The Head Mistress is to be congratulated on her keen and whole-hearted work and her uncertificated assistant on a praiseworthy beginning which could yet be improved by a wider knowledge of suitable methods and teaching devices."

Miss Varley noted very little of interest to modern readers of the log book, just dates, attendances, medical matters, names of assistants, etc. Nevertheless, the Report by the HMI, Mr C B Hunt, in June 1928, painted a very pleasant picture:

"Mixed and Infants: The Headmistress is able to instil into the children some of her own energy and enthusiasm. Thus there is a very pleasant tone in the school and progress is, in general, creditable, despite the inconveniently cramped conditions under which work in the main room is carried on. The assistant teachers, both of whom came less than a year ago, are giving the Headmistress careful and efficient support.

Among good features of the work may be noted the liking for reading, instilled by the teaching and reflected in the freedom and fluency with which a number of the older scholars express themselves in writing. Keen interest is also taken in Nature Study. Some points in the teaching of Arithmetic and Drawing would repay attention

131

and a tendency of some of the older children to answer in a hurry is open to the objection that it impedes consecutive reasoning."

Perhaps the most important clue to Miss Varley's character as a teacher came out in the last sentence: "The Headmistress carefully supervises the general progress of the work and that of each individual child." Miss Varley continued the Evening Classes at Highmore, too. "8 November 1928: I am now half way through the Evening School course, the attendance is very good and all 14 students are keenly interested in their work."

There is little doubt that she was devoted to the school and it was the centre of her whole life. On 4 March 1929, she noted: "I, E Varley, was absent this afternoon. This makes 2.1/2 days in 5.3/4 years." Mrs Biggs (nee Hayward) came in 'on supply' during these times of teachers' absenteeism. Mrs Biggs helped out a great deal in the years that followed and she and Miss Varley became firm friends.

Mr Arthur Denham and his wife showed much interest in the school too, noting in the log book in 1933:

"Very glad to have an opportunity of entering a note in this book. On my visit this day, I found the children very happy, well disciplined and intelligent, as I have invariably found under Miss Varley on previous visits."

The report of the HMI (still Mr C B Hunt) in January 1937 was as praising as ever:

"There are 25 children on the books, taught by the same two teachers as were here in 1934 – Miss Varley and Miss Hall. Excellent training in behaviour is evident and keen effort is the rule. The Headmistress continues her whole-hearted and stimulating work and the response of the children in her class is, on the whole, in accordance with the spirit she inculcates."

Although Assistants came and went throughout the 1920s, one stayed longer than all the rest. On 30 September 1942 Miss Varley noted: "Miss Hall terminated her duties here today, after being Assistant in the Infants' Department for ten years."

However, Miss Varley soldiered on. 3 March 1953: "Miss Varley absent for funeral, her first abstention for seven years."

On 4 June, 1954, the last entry was made in the Highmore School log book: "Closed for the Whitsun holidays." Miss Varley had been Headteacher for almost 30 years, during which time she was hardly ever absent.

Very little is otherwise known of this lady, no one knows what happened to her after this date, she may have retired to live with her father at Tilehurst. Many ex-pupils have spoken very highly of her and remember her with affection.

Another log book does not appear to have been started by Miss Varley's successor, Miss Durrant, who came from Cromer in Norfolk.

Hazel Stevens related the fun the children had in summer, when they were allowed to take their milk breaks on the green in front of the school. "We used to have 1/3rd pint of milk in bottles. My friend, Helen Wrigley, didn't like milk, so I always had hers – we drank the milk out of the bottles through straws, poked in the hole of the cardboard lids. The lids were then used to make pom-poms, with coloured wool. Mrs Baldwin, at the Rising Sun, ran a tuck-shop from the side window of the pub and sold sweeties. We usually had 1d for Rainbow Sherbert – I used to love that – it made your tongue go all colours!"

Group photo taken at Highmoor School in about 1960. Back row: Tim Chapman, William Lunnon, Philippa Spicer, David Lunnon, Annette ?, Anthony Harwood, Adella Grismanauskas, Graham Chapman. Middle row: Allan Wrigley, Susan Giles, Kay Summers, Miss Durrant, Jess Wilder, Beryl Busby, Peter Ginn. Front row: Malcolm Grismanauskas, Mandy Harwood and Kim Chapman. Kindly lent by Joyce Spicer.

Kay Summers recalled dancing around the Maypole on May Day and both she and Adella Harper (nee Grismanauskas) recalled the thrill of watching Princess Margaret's wedding on the television in Miss Durrant's sittingroom in the school house in June 1960. Adella also remembered that when the Queen went to India in 1961, Miss Durrant encouraged the children to bring in newspaper cuttings on the subject and she put a map of India on the wall, so they could follow their sovereign's progress. (See the chapter on the Maharajah's Well). Most pupils remember this mistress as "large and comfortable... she always wore a tweed skirt and flat shoes." Malcolm Grismanauskas was "rather scared of her", but remembered her taking the children for a walk up to Highmoor Farm "to see the animals."

He recalled: "She also put on Christmas plays and once dug a small canal in the garden of the schoolhouse, to show us how a lock works. We had a sand pit and a small pool. We did drawings about special occasions, such as Christmas and these were sometimes put on show against the school wall that faced the Green."

His sister, Adella, remembered that each child had its own garden plot, about a yard square, and that these plots ran alongside the path to the front door of the school. She also brought to mind eating hot dinners, sent from Nettlebed School in metal containers. "One day the Hunt was coming over the hill but only the children who had finished their dinners could go out to watch it. I hadn't eaten my pudding, so I was not allowed to go – Miss Durrant could be very strict."

The Vicar and his wife took an interest in the school plays and pageants. This 1920 photograph was taken in the Vicarage garden. The theme that year was Robin Hood. Noel Baker very kindly lent this photograph but was unsure of the names of the children.

The boys at the back are unknown, but the Vicar is Rev 'Bravvy' Hughes. Middle row: Ted Page, Jack Slade, Bill Green, Frank Willoughby (with bow), May Baker, Tommy Stevens (with bow), Nellie Edwards, Fred Edwards (with bow), the 'monk' is unknown.

Of the three rather worried looking little children, only blond-haired Jack Willoughby, on the left, was recognised. By kind permission of Mrs Faith Bowell (nee Allum).

Religious Education

Like Stoke Row, Highmore School was a Church of England foundation and religious education was of paramount importance. As at Stoke Row, the Diocesan Inspector visited twice a year, awarded certificates and prizes and made his report.

On 5 October 1908: "Augustine Chard took the Scripture lesson and spoke of 'The Growth of the Church amongst the Heathen.' The children's answers and behaviour were delightful."

The Report of the Diocesan Inspector at the end of July 1911 was particularly praising: "This school is doing steady and useful work on good lines. In each class the children showed a competent knowledge of the subjects offered and I was very glad to observe that they had evidently been taught to think for themselves and were able to apply their knowledge to the circumstances of their daily lives. The singing of the hymns was very good indeed and a real pleasure to me to listen to it."

In 1936, Rev R H Lloyd wrote: "This school made a good impression. These children sang a rather difficult hymn nicely and prayers were said with reverence..."

The Vicar called in to the school at least once a week and often took the Scripture lesson. Indeed, in 1946, the only item of any difference in the normal school proceedings was on 18 May: "Rev B ('Frank') Weston, the new Vicar, called today." He was probably just visiting then, for he was not inducted until the following year.

Attendance and Health

When school reopened after the summer holidays in 1902, the average number of pupils was much as it had always been, 60. "Children are restless and inattentive after the long holiday. Rev Harnett awarded prizes 'For Industry during the Holidays', thus:

Boys: Sidney Delafield 2/6d, Frank Baldwin and Henry Earle 6d each
Girls: Beatrice Horwood and Nellie Pooley 2/6d each
Lizzie Baldwin, Rose Heath, Annie Slade 1/- each.

Not only were there the usual health problems but special ones as well. In October one boy was "away all week after eating poisonous berries." and on 26 April 1904, Mr Lucas "Left school for 45 minutes to send for the Doctor as Dick Evans seriously hurt in play-time. It proved to be a broken leg."

A summary of attendance for the Winter Quarter of 1904 showed the following figures: "Boys: 26.8, Girls: 30.2. Out of 60. A bad term!"

The winter of 1906 was very bad and there was much illness. "Several scholars were sent home today... having very bad sore throats, very suspicious as to whether of Diptheric origin... Sickness has lowered the percentage of the school attendance." This type of comment continued throughout January, February and March of 1907.

135

From the beginning of 1909 entries in the log book became briefer and were mainly concerned with attendance, especially when affected by the weather. Some children seemed to be able to attend whatever the weather, though they may have lived near the school.

On 6 August 1909: "At the close of afternoon school, in the presence of the Head Teacher and the boys and girls, a Silver Watch, awarded by the Oxfordshire Education Committee, was presented by the Vicar to Archibald Stallwood for having attended the school for over seven years without being absent or late." Mr Archie Earle, nephew of Archie Stallwood, very kindly donated this watch to my collection of local memorabilia which I hope to place into the Oxfordshire Archives.

The next month the log book stated: "One boy in the Mixed Dept has been absent for a whole week, having no shoes fit to wear." Nevertheless, the number on the books had risen to "65, average attendance: 63.5."

Still there were difficulties, not only with health but also the related problem of hygiene in a village that relied for much of its water on one well, though some people managed to trap winter rainwater from the roof in underground tanks or cisterns. In the summer, however, the water was soon used up.

On 10 June 1910: "Dr Susmann examined children and sent eight home due to lack of cleanliness. They will be allowed to attend after 7 days, if they are fit." That July there was an outbreak of chickenpox which meant poor attendance during the last half of that term.

On the whole, attendance levels were very good during Mr Baker's time. On 30 December 1911, he was able to record: "During the past year 9 children have made perfect attendance. ...Several boys would have made full attendance but for the Choir Excursion to Hastings, which took place in school time."

There was a serious outbreak of Scarlet Fever in the village during the spring of 1912. 15 March: "3 children sent to Smith's Isolation Hospital at Henley." On 29 March: "School closed for three weeks due to Scarlet Fever. 21 children absent out of 53." and on 13 April: "...one week extension of closure."

Even by 1 May 1912: "School reopened with 26 in Mixed and 18 in Infants equals 44 out of 54 on books. 5 children still in Isolation Hospital at Henley. The school rooms have been thoroughly cleaned and disinfected." When the school reopened in September, there were: "31 boys and 25 girls" on the books.

By the time the school reopened on 8 January 1913, there were 53 children on the register. However, in March 1913: "Whooping Cough and Scarlet Fever at Nettlebed, so Cinema Lessons have been temporarily discontinued."

An even more serious event occurred on 7 April 1913, when: "Thomas Tudor, 8 years, a pupil in Stage I, has died in Reading Hospital. He suffered from a disease of the glands and was operated on without success. This sad loss is much felt by all the school children, being the first death in the school during the past 6 years." On 11 April: "The Master and older children attended Thomas Tudor's funeral."

Rewards still helped attendance. On 19 December 1913: "Application has been made to the Committee for a Silver Watch, to be awarded to Albert Edward Green, who has made 6 years perfect attendance 1908 to 1913. Children who have attended best during the past School Year, Sept 1912 to July 1913:

Perfect attendance: 7.	99 per cent: 19
98 per cent: 5.	For Proficiency: 14 awards.

Early in January 1916 there was: "A Tea and Prize Distribution to the three children who had made a perfect attendance: Noel Baker, Elsie Green and Charles Edwards." Mr Baker also remarked: "The closure (for Christmas holidays) seems to have had beneficial results in improving the health of the children."

This was fortunate, for by 24 February: "Owing to a deep fall of snow, 40% of the children are absent this morning. The correspondent (Rev J Hughes) has advised the Master to close the school this afternoon on account of the very inclement weather." This snow continued through much of March and caused great sickness and absenteeism. Similar events occurred in 1917.

There was another death in the village in April 1917: "Dr Coles, the School Medical Officer, visited on Wednesday to investigate a fatal case of spotted fever. Certain children are being excluded. The school will be thoroughly disinfected with burning sulphur."

From 1918 onwards, the entries in the Highmore School log book were usually weekly, rather than daily, but they did show that the numbers on the books were down to 19 in the Infants and 37 older children in the Mixed Department.

As at Stoke Row, perhaps because the Army had found what appalling teeth the agricultural class suffered, the School Dentist began to appear on the scene. On 15 February 1918: "The School Dentist, Mr Carpenter, gave an address to the children on the care of teeth..."

A few weeks later: "Mr Carpenter called on Tuesday morning and made a preliminary examination of the teeth of children over 6 years of age. About 39 of the children were examined. Of these only 50% of the parents have given their consent for their children to be treated. Voluntary sums brought by the children to be treated amounted to 14/- and this was handed with forms returned to the Dentist." 22 March: "Usual lessons on Thursday were not taken, owing to the visit of the School Dentist and Dr Susmann to extract some of the children's teeth."

Although the Armistice was declared on 11 November 1918, no mention was made of it by Mrs Baker, now in charge, perhaps because the school was closed for three weeks at the time, owing to outbreak of various illnesses, scarlet fever and influenza being among them. The school had been redecorated during Christmas holidays, but the early months of 1919 proved to be very difficult. There was a great deal of bad weather, deep snow and illness, resulting in a poor attendance throughout the winter, especially of younger children and those who lived further away.

Although very little of interest was noted in the Highmore School Log Book in the 1930s, quite a number of photographs of the school pageants have survived. This one shows the May Queen, whose baptismal name actually was Queen Elizabeth Stevens, leaving her home, today called 'Longwood', on Witheridge Hill. The remainder of her entourage were dressed as characters from Nursery Rhymes. Kindly lent by Mrs Faith Bowell.

The May Queen is paid homage by Puss-in-Boots in the Fairy Tales Pageant, c 1930. By kind permission of Mrs Faith Bowell (nee Allum).

By 2 May 1918, this had affected the Mistress: "Mrs Baker is absent through illness. Her doctor has certified her as unfit to recommence her duties for one month from 28 April. Managers are making arrangements for a supply teacher." Not only were the children's teeth examined, but their eyesight too. "21 November: "Mrs Pearce (Health Supervisor) visited and inspected several children. Several children's eyesight was found to be defective." One of these was Dolly Franklin, whose story is told in the final chapter of this book.

This is one of the last entries of any length made in the log book. Most of Miss Varley's weekly entries were extremely brief and largely concerned attendance, absences, medical visits etc. When she took over in January 1925, she noted: "57 children on registers, 4 being admitted, 2 have left." However, by June the numbers had increased to 65.

In June 1929, the attendance was only "33.6%, due to a rather severe outbreak of measles." Nevertheless, most children seemed to have recovered in time for an outing to Littlehampton in July.

A little girl in the Infants (Hilda Slade of 'Longwood') died of Diphtheria on 22 December 1929 and was buried on Christmas Eve. What a very tragic thing to have happened at the festive season, how devastated the parents must have been.

By 1934, due to the Senior children having been transferred to Rotherfield Peppard, "The number of children now on the books is 30 and these are taught in two classes." Attendance continued fairly evenly until the outbreak of the Second World War. On 18 September 1939, Miss Varley "admitted 19 evacuees." and "Mrs Cleary, LCC (London County Council) commenced her duties assisting with the Oxfordshire children and the evacuees" on 28 September 1939.

This influx seemed to have affected school life very little and Miss Varley's first entry for 12 January 1940 was only that "Mrs Guy, the Horlicks representative, called." The children were given this nourishing drink in the winter for several years.

On 14 May 1940: "Returned to school today instead of 20 May. [Wireless appeal to open all schools]". Miss Varley "Admitted 15 evacuees" on 17 June, and on 1 July: "School windows wired [Air Raid Precautions]."

On 2 August 1940: "School closed for two weeks for Oxfordshire children. Evacuees, however, attending under the supervision of Mrs Cleary." Perhaps this was to keep them out of mischief! In November, Mrs Cleary transferred to North Leigh, Oxfordshire. Other changes took place too, perhaps because of the risk of showing a light: "2 December 1940: From today until February, morning school starts 9.30 am, afternoon school finishes 3.35 pm."

Very little of interest was detailed in 1941, no doubt this was because of the restrictions placed upon the school by the war, although in October, Dr Susmann, who had been attending the school for many years, immunised the children against Diphtheria.

By 1944 there was very little entered into the log book. The school was small once more, most of the evacuees having returned to London.

In March 1944, "School closed because of whooping cough." Mrs Mappover, Wartime Social Survey for the Board of Education, called on 16 May 1944, but no reason was given.

There was a severe snowstorm on 30 January 1945 and, not surprisingly, "Only 3 children attended." Miss Varley did make a brief note about the end of the Second World War and the Victory in Europe: "Tues 8 May/Wed 9 May: VE Celebrations."

In September 1951, Miss Varley "admitted five Polish children." These were sons and daughters of the soldiers billeted in the camps in the woods and who had been joined, in some instances, by their families. "A severe outbreak of measles and whooping cough" occurred in May 1952. "Only five children arrived this morning."

Neither sickness, bad weather nor anything else of note was mentioned again before the school log book closed in 1954.

Rotherfield Senior School

Rotherfield Central Senior School at Rotherfield Peppard. This is now a private house. By kind permission of Mrs Mary Ramsay (nee Clements).

In 1931 a small Church of England Senior school was built at nearby Peppard and was known as the Rotherfield Central School. Almost immediately, the Senior children at Stoke Row and Highmore School were transferred there.

The first Head Master was a Mr Reason, who loved music. A later Head Master was a Mr F C E Anson, from Churchill, Banbury, Oxon. Among the teachers at various times were: Miss Ball (General Subjects), Miss Flanagan, (Form II Drawing and Geography), Miss Smith, (Form I Needlework), Miss Sumner (Cookery) and Mr Nash (Woodwork and Sports).

Later teachers included Mr Ewart Martin, who eventually became Head Master, a Mr Denslow, Miss Ida Bradshaw and Miss Nancy Jones. The pupils were also taught Gardening (including the grafting of fruit trees) and Current Affairs – a very avant garde subject, then!

When Mrs Joyce Martin (nee Pitt) was 11 she went to this comparatively new Senior School at Rotherfield Greys. Like Mrs Mary Ramsay, (nee Clements) who kindly lent the photographs shown below, she was very happy. "It was an absolute joy to be there – we did needlework and cookery as well as all the usual subjects."

A group photograph taken at Rotherfield Senior School in 1937. The Headmaster, in the centre, was Mr F C E Anson and is flanked by Miss Flanagan, Miss Smith and Miss Sumner. By kind permission of Mrs Mary Ramsay (nee Clements).

The Lighter Side

One of the first entries in the Highmore School log book to note an item of pleasure for the children was in January 1902 when the Vicar, Rev Francis Russell Harnett, MA, of St John's College, Cambridge, who was probably a keen amateur astronomer, took "the Upper Division... to the Vicarage, to view the planet Venus through his telescope."

On 2 June 1902, the Master "spoke to the children about the 'Proclamation of Peace'." This was to mark the end of the Boer War, and on 13 June, there were: "One or two children away, to see the Prince and Princess of Wales at Reading." (An event not mentioned in the Stoke Row School Log Book).

A few weeks later, Mr and Mrs Talfourd Inman "invited children and parents to tea and prize distribution on Thursday." This was probably at Highmore Hall, where the Inmans lived and was to mark "the Coronation of His Majesty Edward VII". In fact the whole school had a week's holiday "on account of the Coronation Celebrations and Festivities."

In July 1902: "The annual treat given by Mr & Mrs Inman (of Highmore Hall) took place in the form of an outing for the Mixed Dept to Henley to see the Olympic Regatta." Mr Talfourd Inman continued to sign the log book and make favourable comments.

In the February of the following year: "Police Constable Timms came into school to warn children of the dangerous habit of carrying matches. This accrued (sic) because of there having been two fires on Common land in Highmore."

The first outing mentioned in the Highmore log book was two years earlier than in Stoke Row, but it was not for the whole school, only the choir, who went to Margate on 17 September 1909.

Mr Baker "gave to the Evening Class a lantern slide lecture on Canada, scenes and industries" in November 1909 and showed the same set to the children just before Christmas.

A School Concert was given on the evening of 11 February 1910, and in the May: "Specimen work by older children in brush drawing and practical arithmetic, sent for competition to the Oxford Agricultural Show. Prizes for arithmetic and scale drawing."

Later an interesting set of lantern slides, "illustrating scenes on the Thames were shown by the Master to pupils of the Day and Evening School by the Master on Wednesday, after school." Mr Baker seems to have enjoyed giving lantern slide shows and in November: "A set of humorous lantern slides were shown to the children, between 2.45 and 3.45 pm, the weather being too wet for outdoor recreation." To children who didn't even know of the cinema, it must have been a great joy!

Another treat was in store that month. "Master read to the children a story, 'The Jackdaw of Rheims', illustrated with twelve coloured lantern slides."

On 25 May 1911: "School to be closed for one week nationally for the Coronation of King George V, according to the King's special request."

Lantern slide shows were not only for pleasure, but also for instruction. In October 1911: "Instead of the usual reading lesson on Friday afternoons, the Master showed a series of Historical lantern slides, illustrating the Early British, Saxon and Norman periods."

Mrs MacIntyre, the new owner of Highmore Hall, came along, bringing the words and music of *Land of Hope and Glory*, askng, "Can it be taught to the children?"

On 8 November 1912: "A Children's Concert was held on Monday and Wednesday evening. Very successful, full attendances, proceeds, including Mr Fleming's subscription, £5, to be spent on providing books for the School Library."

The Lantern slide shows continued, too. On 14 February 1913: A set of Lantern Slides, illustrating the Coronation of King George V were shown during the General Information lesson, supplied by S H Benson of London... gratis."

And the following week: "An interesting set of lantern slides 'Swiss Pastures', were shown to the children instead of the usual Geography lesson. The Master attended Nettlebed Village Hall to see a sample exhibition of Educational Cinema films... Robert Fleming, Esq kindly offered to provide Cinema Educational Exhibitions weekly... Nature Study, Geography, Science, History and Literature."

The crowning of the May Queen, 1928. The part was played by Valerie Braham who lived at 'Fipps Cottage'. Her page was John Goodwin and her unhappy attendant was his sister, Mary. The Jester was played by Robin Denham and the boy with the feather in his cap was Tom Cheshire. By kind permission of Mrs Mary Wilder (nee Goodwin).

At the end of February 1913, "the Vicar, Rev Philip Dalby, visited the school this afternoon, accompanied by Mrs Dalby and Miss Penney. Mrs Dalby presented Miss Gladys Heath, the late Monitoress, with an oak bookcase, subscribed for by the children, teachers and friends."

The Cinema instruction continued at Nettlebed: "...subjects: the Wasp and the Caterpillar. The chief features of the lessons were drawn attention to by the Master, the teachers taking it in turn each week."

However, it seems that the Science lessons at the 'cinema' were not proving entirely successful. "Mr Bartlett, the HMI, considers the Cinema pictures on Science to be too difficult for the children to follow, as scientific subjects cannot be clearly demonstrated, owing to lack of apparatus."

That autumn, it was considered sensible that "Cinema lessons to commence earlier now, owing to the short days. Generally there is a break of 10 minutes between each set of pictures, for the teacher to answer questions and to give relief to the children's eyes."

The School Garden Class joined the School Garden Boys of Stoke Row School on 24 July 1914 to "go to the garden Show at Crowmarsh. A profitable and enjoyable time was spent."

By October 1914, evacuees were beginning to flood in from the continent. "The children have given pence amounting to 10/- towards providing clothing for a little Belgian girl, belonging to a family of refugees, who are being accommodated at 'The Bungalow' on Witheridge Hill and supported by local families." The kindness of the village towards the Belgian refugees was repaid in the spring of 1915. "Older pupils receiving tuition in French, through the kindness of Monsieur Victor Moonens, the Belgian refugee who, with his family, are now residing in the village..."

In February 1921, "the Master took a party of 14 of the children to Reading for an educational visit to the Museum and World's Service Exhibition" and a Minstrel Concert was held that spring. In the April, "the children observed the Eclipse of the Sun through smoked glass."

Empire Day was always a great event and the school was closed on 24 May 1921, to celebrate the fact. "Lessons were taken during the week on the subjects of Britain Overseas and Our Great Empire Builders."

Another treat was in store, too, on 31 May 1921: "The teachers and some of the children attended the Royal Berkshire Hospital Special Matinee at the Palace Theatre, Reading." 1921 was another long hot summer, one of the worst on record in that respect. 22 July: "The long drought and extreme heat has made work in the school trying, so some lessons have been taken out of doors, under the trees, when it could be arranged."

Captain Pearson, MC, who lived at 'Witheridge Hill Farmhouse', visited the school in September "and gave the children a very interesting account of life in India." Probably, after that hot summer the children could relate well to this talk! The school was closed again on 3 March 1922 "on the occasion of Princess Mary's Wedding."

In October 1922, Miss Edith E G May, made her first appearance as a School Manager. This lady had been a Nurse and had retired to Highmore, where she wrote a jolly little book entitled *Chatter from a Council Cottage*. She visited the school and entered in the log book: "I had a very cordial reception from the children who sang songs very nicely. They all seemed very happy."

Miss May visited again early in December and "informed the teachers and children that several children had gained prizes in the recent Essay Competition held by the RSPCA. Colonel May has given a book on bird life for the best essay on 'Our Friends, the Birds'."

Mr Baker's efforts to help the village as a whole not only extended to Evening Classes but now there was to be another innovation: "2 November 1923: The cupboard to be used in connection with the newly formed Village Circulating Library, is to be kept in the school. The Master will act as Librarian." This must have been a wonderful provision, for few people could afford books and the Library at Henley was far away.

Also that November, "Miss May visited and chatted to the children about the origin and history of Guy Fawkes Day. Also about arranging a course of lessons on Mothercraft and Personal Hygiene for the older girls."

On 30 January 1924, there was "a Rehearsal of the School Entertainment in the Village Hall. The preparation has caused great interest in the School and has been a stimulant to effort on the part of the children. The programme consisted of:

I.   Nursery Rhyme Play – Juniors and Infants
II.   Games and Folk Songs
III.   Fairy Play *The Sleeping Beauty*.

Scenery for the five scenes was designed and painted in the school on sheets of canvas and calico, attached to wooden strips. Ideas and designs were drawn first on strips of paper, scale one inch to one foot. The older boys took considerable part in the work; distemper powder colours with size was used. The effort provided much interesting work for the drawing and handiwork lessons."

It also helped financially: "The School Fund for providing games apparatus has benefited to the extent of nearly £5. The total receipts were £13." The performance was repeated a few weeks later: "The School Entertainment is being given this evening at Nettlebed to benefit the Henley War Memorial Hospital."

1926 saw the first recorded 'seaside outing' from the school, when the children went to Bognor on 21 June. Although the Bakers had left, the school continued to put on plays and pageants.

Mr and Mrs Denham bought a small thatched cottage early in the 1920s, they enlarged it and called it 'Little Manor House'. (More of this in the chapter on the Gentrification of Cottages). Mrs Denham was a very artistic lady and an excellent needlewoman and she made all the costumes for a series of productions.

At the end of January 1930, "Commander Lewis, RN, spoke to the children regarding 'The League of Nations'" and in March "the children went to church on Ash Wednesday." On 29 November 1934: "School closed for the Duke of Kent's Wedding." On 6 May 1935, the school closed for King George V's Silver Jubilee and on 4 November 1935, it closed again for "the Royal Wedding" – this was the marriage of the Duke of York (later to become King George VI) and Miss Elizabeth Bowes-Lyon (later Queen Elizabeth, the Queen Mother).

This delightful picture shows a scene from The Sleeping Beauty, with Annie Meheux and May Baker. By kind permission of Mrs Ada Britnell (nee Wells).

It seems there was little of interest to report in such a small school in the later 1930s – not even the school productions were mentioned in the log book. However, they were certainly worth a mention. The tableau, *Madonna, with Lilies* which was put on at Highmore School, largely by Mrs Denham, in about 1936, was obviously the subject of a great deal of talent, combined with hard work.

Several beautiful photographs have survived of these sets and were probably taken by Gilbert Adams, son of the royal photographer, Marcus Adams. Both were friends of Mr and Mrs Denham.

146

This beautiful tableau, photographed by Gilbert Adams, was arranged by Mrs Denham in about 1936. The Madonna was Frances Carey, whose parents managed The Dog and Duck. The cherub above was Margaret Stone and the one standing was Pam Springell. The two on the right were (standing) Kathleen Brakspear and (kneeling) Lily Treadwell. Kindly lent by Mrs Kathleen Kucor (nee Brakspear).

One noteworthy event was on 18 June 1945: "Commenced school dinners." In the September "Mrs Gardiner terminated as Caretaker after 5.1/2 years." and a few weeks later: "Mrs Stone commenced as new Caretaker."

On 20 November 1947: "School closed for the Royal Wedding." (This was the marriage of Princess Elizabeth and the Duke of Edinburgh) and on 12 December: "Police gave the children Road Instruction." This was an indication that motor cars were becoming more prolific on the roads in the area, roads where hitherto children had been able to play with impunity.

On 26 April 1948: "School closed half day for the Silver Wedding of the King and Queen (King George V and Queen Elizabeth, later Queen Elizabeth the Queen Mother).

Lessons were taken outside in the summer of 1949 and in the summer of 1950: "Children attended School Musical Event at Nettlebed from 9.00 am to 11.30 am."

"Avis Gardiner won the Silver Cup for Highmore School in the Area Sports at Woodcote" in June 1951 and that September, Miss Varley "admitted five Polish children."

Another of these exquisite photographs. The Madonna is again Frances Carey, The angels at the back are unknown but at the front the one on the left is Lily Carter and on the right is Florence Carey. The cherubs are Kathleen Brakspear, Pam Springell, Lily Treadwell and Margaret Stone. Kindly lent by Mrs Kathleen Kucor (nee Brakspear).

Mr Denham's name crops up again several times at this point, for instance when he "gave each child a box of paints" on 17 December 1953. Otherwise, little mention is made in the log book of the great generosity of the Denhams to the children, almost from the time they arrived in 1920 to when Mr Denham died in 1960.

Many people still alive today remember with joy the bonfires and fireworks they always provided on November 5th and the gifts they distributed every Christmas. Mr and Mrs Denham were also very kind to the old folk and anyone in trouble.

The Closure of Highmoor School

Tony Hall recalled the furore that occurred when the school was closed: "During the 1950s, and since, the County Education Authority implemented a policy of closing smaller rural schools and offering what was claimed to be better primary education at larger establishments, where one school with several teachers taught children from more than one village.

As its attendance roll fell, Highmoor came under increasing scrutiny, and in 1964 notice of closure was served on the Governors. As soon as the parents of the last 16 to 20 children were informed, they decided to object and fight to keep the school open.

Letters to the Authority, meetings with Councillors, an item on the BBC Radio News and an individual appeal to every member of the Oxfordshire County Council culminated in a visit to Highmoor by Charles Peers, Chairman of the Education Committee, to try and make the parents understand how much better educated their children would be when (as the parents saw it) they were 'taken off in a bus to Peppard each morning', to a bigger school with better facilities. The parents did not believe a word of it and Mr Peers remarked as he left the meeting: 'They are the most recalcitrant lot of parents I have ever had to address!'

In due course Highmoor School closed and Peppard School turned out to be better than had been feared. Highmoor School premises were sold and converted into a private house. Miss Durrant went on to become Headmistress of a school at Banbury.

This was a poignant episode in the long and worthy history of this small rural school, and reflected the way the village was changing, from being based on agriculture, which required large numbers of local workers, to a select dormitory for people employed elsewhere."

The last known photograph of Highmoor schoolchildren, taken in May 1962. Standing: Mandy Harwood, Tim Chapman, Elspeth Railson, Peter Ginn and Kay Summers. Seated: Joyce Benn, Sandra Norris, Sheila Pound, Alison Hartley and Susan Giles. Squatting: Kim Chapman, Valerie Giles, Malcolm Grismanauskas, Hazel Stevens. The last boy on the right is unknown. By kind permission of Allan Wrigley.

9. Downing a Pint

Stoke Row Public Houses

A saying in Stoke Row in the early part of this century was probably a parody of a popular one of the time: "If you want a beer and a jolly good fight, go up to Stoke Row on a Saturday night!"

Visitors to the village had plenty of pubs to choose from. At one time there were five, four of them owned by the Henley brewer, Brakspear. Most of the following information, covering 1753 to 1800, comes from the Victuallers Recognizances, now in the Oxfordshire Archives.

The Crooked Billet

Owned by Brakspear's Brewery of Henley-on-Thames, this is a Grade II Listed building, being "C17 with C18 additions". Unfortunately no written records appear to exist until 1753.

In the years 1753 to 1773 (some years are missing), three publicans were shown for the Parish of Ipsden in the Langtree Hundred, but none of these entries had public house names so it is not possible to identify the pubs, except that Richard Gill appeared to run one from 1753 to 1769 in the parish of Mongewell, once part of Stoke Row. This is very likely to have been The Crooked Billet, since this name appeared in full for that pub after 1774.

In 1770 the name Robert Messenger of Ipsden appears and this point marks a break in the name of Richard Gill – he had held the pub for 16 years. From 1771 to 1774 there were no entries under the Langtree Hundred.

However, 1774 was the start of publicans having to give annual sureties of £10 each to the Justices, as a guarantee of good conduct in their pubs, as these had become such "dens of vice and bad behaviour". From 1785 the entries were made in the September of each year. Tenants often stood surety for one another. From 1774 to 1822 the amount of £10 for surety never changed.

1775 saw Robert Messenger again as landlord of this pub for a year but the following year the name of Richard Gill appeared once more and the next year it was shown as Richard Gill, junior. These records end in 1821, but, even so, it appears that Richard Gill, senior, probably held The Crooked Billet for most of the time from 1753 to 1777 (24 years) and his son Richard Gill, junior, from 1777 to 1822 (42 years), that was quite a record!

Kelly's Directory of 1848 also listed a Richard Gill being landlord. Unless this was the grandson of the first Richard Gill, it could have been Richard Gill, junior, who would therefore have held the pub for 61 years – I suppose it is possible, had he taken it over from his father when he was quite young, say, at 21 years of age.

The Gill family continued to hold The Crooked Billet, though. *Cassey's Directory* of 1868 shows Edwin Gill and in 1883 Kelly's Directory lists Thomas Gill. These men seem to have helped out from time to time in successive years but in the main this house was tenanted by the Saunders family after 1882. Wells Brewery owned The Crooked Billet at this time and from the Register of Licences, now in the County Archives, we find that Samuel Saunders was licensed to sell ale from 1882 to 1891.

In *School on the Ground Floor*, John H Baker describes The Crooked Billet in 1913 as being "the last word in remoteness and peaceful situation. A meadow slopes behind the house. On one side is an orchard and garden and on the other a yard and a large shed where the landlord carries on his trade as a 'bodger' (ie a chair-leg turner)."

The Crooked Billet, before the post-mark date of 1904.
By kind permission of Cecil Lambourne.

It is probable that Samuel Saunders died about 1891, for his widow, Sarah Tracey Saunders, took over from that time and continued until 1936. She was affectionately known as 'Granny Saunders'. In 1936, 'Bill' Saunders became the publican, though until 1961 he also turned chair-legs when not behind the bar. (see Bodging and Trades).

Fitzroy ('Fitz') Ruddle told me that in the 1930s a horse, which probably belonged to Silas ('Bill') Saunders and was kept in the paddock at the rear of the pub, used to poke its head in the stable-door at the front of the pub and quaff beer from a glass if it was proffered to him!

About 1929 the Wallingford Brewery, who had taken The Crooked Billet over from Wells, sold this public house to Ushers of Trowbridge who, in about 1930, sold it to Brakspear of Henley for £770.

From 1966 to 1986 'The Billet' enjoyed great fame under the much-loved licensee, 'Nobby' Harris whose wife, Eileen Saunders, was the daughter of the former landlord. This meant that the Saunders family had tenanted this house for almost a hundred years. Fitz Ruddle recalled: "Nobby Harris used to tell his friends 'pull your own and throw the money up on the mantleshelf!'"

The Crooked Billet in about 1910. Seated is Mrs Sarah Tracey ('Granny') Saunders, with her four sons and grandson. Kindly lent by Mrs Maggie Saunders (nee Stallwood).

Ben Salter took over when 'Nobby' retired, but moves he made to improve the pub were not popular with some of the locals.

Today the licence is held by Paul Clerehugh who has developed a fashionable restaurant there which attracts visitors from London and further afield.

During the late 1980s, filming of parts of several main screen and television films took place at The Crooked Billet, including *Jeeves and Wooster*. The actress Kate Winslet, famous for her role in *Titanic*, and her husband Jim Threapleton, recently held their wedding reception there. Many famous musicians and singers, usually of the jazz and folk type, including Dis Disley, Peter Sarstedt, John Otway, Labi Siffre and 'Wild Willy' Barratt, have appeared at The Crooked Billet in recent years.

The Crooked Billet has a large fireplace, with seats on either side. This photograph with two men sitting in the inglenook is still on the mantleshelf. The man on the left was Charlie Saunders who later met with an unfortunate and fatal accident. He was working at nearby Wyfold Court, when he lifted a sewerage manhole cover and was killed by the ensuing explosion. By kind permission of his sister-in-law, Mrs Maggie Saunders (nee Stallwood).

'Nobby' Harris at the Crooked Billet in 1984. By kind permission of the Henley Standard.

The Cherry Tree

This, too, is a Listed Building, Grade II: "Probably late C17 with early C18 front."

Francis Sheppard, in his book *Brakspear's Brewery 1779 - 1979*, states: "This was probably a cottage converted into a beer-house, sometime after 1830, and called 'The Traveller's Friend'. In 1869 a change in the law brought such pubs under the partial control of the justices. Around Henley they were said to be generally "stuck about in the most uninhabited and wild parts of the country, where constables are almost afraid to risk their persons." Owned by Brakspear's Brewery of Henley-on-Thames, it was bought by William Brakspear in 1896."

The Tithe Map of 1847 shows that there was a "Beerhouse and Orchard" here, under the ownership of J Champion. The photograph below, thought to date back to 1850, may have been taken when the pub was first opened. Unfortunately, it is not possible to decipher the name on the board above the door. Certainly it pre-dates the extension, on the east side of the pub, which has a brick dated 1858.

The topmost of the marked bricks bears the initials JC (James Cox, the local builder?). Initials scratched on other bricks include another JC, FC (Frederick Cox?), JH, BN, MT, EA, AA, WL and BS, which shows how many men were employed on the building of this small extension.

Lascelles Directory of 1853 gives the name of the publican as: "Martha Pembroke, beer retailer, The Cherry Tree."

The Cherry Tree c 1850, before the extension, which is dated 1858.
Kindly lent by Edwin Stallwood.

154

In 1868 *Cassey's Directory* names Charles Whittick as not only being the publican but also a grocer. Perhaps his wife sold goods in the then relatively new extension at the side? The Register of Licences shows that from 31 August 1882 through to 1886: "William Hillier, licensed to sell ale" and *Kelly's Directory* mentions him again in 1887 but this five year stint was quite a record for the early history of The Cherry Tree, for thereafter licensees changed almost annually until 10 February 1916, when Robert West Gregory became the licensee. On 11 May of that year, according to the Quarter Sessions Records, his wife, Mrs Sylvia Gregory, was "licensed to sell ale" and continued to do so until about 1920.

The standard of entries to the Quarter Sessions Records became very poor at the end of the First World War, but on 4 August 1921 until 16 February 1924, we find "Edwin John Stallwood or Mrs H Stallwood licensed to sell ale."

Mrs Margaret ('Maggie') Saunders (nee Stallwood) recalled: "In 1921, when I was about 14, my parents became licensees of the Cherry Tree and I had to help to clean up this pub, which had been allowed to get very dirty and dilapidated, as there had been an elderly widow running it before then." (This was probably Mrs Sylvia Gregory, mentioned above).

Mrs Lily Tayler (nee Johnson) looked back to the 1920s when her cousin, Uda Ada Stallwood, and she used to work for Mrs Stallwood. They "started at 7.00 am to scrape a tin bath full of potatoes when visitors came down from London." Edwin John Stallwood continued to be licensed to sell ale until he died in April 1944 and his wife, Harriet, took over until her son, Percy Stallwood, returned from the

Army in March 1947 and took over from his mother. He ran the pub until he retired, though for over 40 years he also made tent pegs in the barn at the side, as his father had done before him. He was assisted in this by Albert ('Bert') Carter. (See the chapter on Trades).

Four generations of the Stallwood family. Left to right: Edwin Stallwood, his father James, a barefist boxer and rent collector, Percy and his son Edwin. Kindly lent by Edwin Stallwood.

In 1973 Percy retired and his son, Kenneth ('Ken') became the third generation of Stallwoods to have held this house. He told me, "My mother, Irene Edith Stallwood, was a registered breeder of Golden Retrievers, from about 1950 until her death in 1962. At one time she had about 40 of these dogs, which she sent all over the world and showed at Crufts and many other major dog shows. Their pedigree prefix was 'Cherry Tree Golden'."

Very sadly, Ken Stallwood died in October 1994 at the early age of 53. Quoting from his obituary in the *Stoke Row News*: "Ken was a popular landlord, chatty and with his own brand of humour. Like his father before him, he was a very active member of the Stoke Row Cricket Club and was also a great host to motor cycle clubs."

However, his wife Daphne, aided in his spare time by her son Mark and other friends, continues to run the pub. In February 1995 Richard and Sue Boughton wrote in our village magazine:

"A pub like Daphne is running is part of our heritage and a unique advantage of living in Stoke Row. Even villagers from other areas are 'Cherry Tree locals' because of the original atmosphere. It is the centre of the village Sports Association and of course interesting news and gossip. It represents a marvellous meeting place for people wishing to get to know other villagers and their families. Daphne welcomes everyone with a smile and can provide an excellent beer if you so desire."

The Farmer (formerly The Hope)

Miss Catherine Hope, who was 95 when I met her in 1994, and had been a schoolteacher in Checkendon all her life, explained that her great uncle, John Hope, built this public house and named it after himself. In 1870 he sold 'The Grove', the house opposite the Well, so it is likely that he built The Hope with the money from that sale. When he opened it, he was licensed to sell beer.

In 1882, 1883 and up to 18 December 1884, John Godwin was the licensee. One wonders why he surrendered his licence so near to Christmas, always a profitable time.

Again, as in the case of the early history of The Cherry Tree, there followed a long series of publicans, each one only holding the licence for a year or two.

However, on 28 November 1914 George Whitfield took over. The Whitfields stayed until 1931 and several photographs in my collection show his name over the door. Les Franklin looked back to the time when, "at the rear side of The Hope there was a big old black barn and in it George Whitfield had a barrel organ which he would play sometimes to entertain the local children."

Les Franklin also told me that "George Whitfield had a crystal wireless set in the late 1920s, which he kept in his kitchen. George Wilson, the Headmaster of Stoke Row School, supplied three sets of headphones so that the local men and lads could take it in turn for an hour each to listen to the new 'wireless'."

The Hope in about 1914. It is interesting to contrast this with the photograph near the end of this section, which was taken when the house was sold in 1995. By kind permission of Miss Catherine Hope.

Geoff Boyson told me: "The Hope was always referred to as 'the top pub' and The Oak as 'the bottom pub'." Alf Turner, senior, said: "The young 'uns met up at The Hope and the old 'uns used to meet down at The Oak."

In February 1931, George Whitfield died and his widow, Edith Althea Whitfield, was then licensed by the Quarter Sessions to sell beer and continued to do so until May 1938. She also ran a sweet shop at the side of the pub.

In one of the 'Old Timer's Tales', published in the *Stoke Row News* in January 1966, Jacob Bauer recalled: "The sweet shop was at The Hope and if I ran out of pocket money, I would write home for six 1d stamps (which presumably he then sold). It was sometimes the custom for a box of envelopes to be placed on a sweet-shop counter. Inside the flaps of the envelopes different weights were marked, from 1/2 oz upwards. We would pay a halfpenny, chance our luck and pick one out. On one occasion my sister hit the jackpot (16 ozs) and took it all in Bull's Eyes!"

After another temporary landlord, James ('Jim') Thomas Lawrence took on the licence in August 1939 and held it until February 1946. During the Second World War he was a Sergeant in the Home Guard and The Hope was its HQ.

From 1946 William John Rolf and his wife ran The Hope, but very sadly, in March 1951, the following report appeared in the *Henley Standard*: "Mr William John Rolf of The Hope public house at Stoke Row was found dead, presumed drowned, on the river bank on the Marlow side of the Marlow Regatta Course."

The tragic corollary to these newspaper reports of the suicide of Mr Rolf was told to me by Geoff Boyson: "Following the death of her husband and shortly after the inquest, at which the Coroner returned the verdict that he had 'drowned himself, whilst the balance of his mind was disturbed', Mrs Rolf, so distressed by all that had occurred, went out walking in the woods and walked on and on until she dropped dead of a heart attack."

From 1951 until 1962 Harry Douglas Clarke was the publican. Fred Powell recalled: "during his time a surgery was held at The Hope, where one waited to see the doctor in a verandah type place at the back. He held his surgery in the Lounge Bar, but one had to go to Nettlebed for the medicines." (See the chapter on Health).

Outside The Hope in 1916. This photograph shows some of the local men who were home from France on leave. Back row: The boy is unknown, but the man with a moustache is Charlie Franklin. Dickie Earle is third from the left, wearing a hat. Albert Carter is fourth from the left, smoking. Ernest Walter is holding the bike, with his baby, Ruby (later Mrs George). The lady in the overall is Mrs Tucker, Mrs Rose King (nee Lester) wears a hat.

Front row, standing: Soldier on the left is Archie Stallwood, later killed in France by a sniper's bullet. The soldier on the right is George Franklin. The children seated at the back are unknown, but in front, second from the left, is Edie Chapman and third from the left is Queenie Tucker. This photograph is reproduced by kind permission of Peter Franklin.

From 1 September 1962 Arthur Frederick ('Tim') Walker, "a great fisherman and raconteur", managed The Hope which by then was owned by Wethereds of Marlow, but a great change came about in 1978 when ex-farmer James Cox sold his farm, bought this pub from Wethereds and altered it to make what he thought looked more like an old farmhouse. He also renamed it The Farmer, which displeased many of the locals who had known it as The Hope for over a hundred years. In fact James Cox did not stay long and once again there were a succession of owners until Alan and Marylin Mason bought the freehold on 8 March 1988.

At the end of July 1994 the pub was closed down and converted into a private house, now called 'Hope House'. Two houses were also built in the car park.

The Farmer (formerly The Hope) at the time when it was put up for sale in 1995.
By kind permission of Savills of Henley.

The Jockey

This was the name of a very old pub, according to the newspaper report quoted below. However, I could find no reference to it in the Oxfordshire Archives, though there was one for The Plough and Key, which was held by Ann Brown between 1775 and 1796, but nothing thereafter. Maybe it was known locally by the name of The Jockey, or the husband of the tenant was a jockey, or the reporter who covered the attempted murder simply misunderstood the name he was told? Perhaps we shall never know. However, like the nearby Black Horse, it lay on the 'Judge's Ride', along which the Assize judges rode from Oxford to Henley, dispensing justice along the way.

'Berncote', formerly The Jockey. This house was demolished in 1995.
By kind permission of Miss Doris Bowell.

This house later became known as 'Berncote' and Mr Danny Greenaway, son of the former owner, told me that when he was climbing about in the roof he discovered that the existing roof was built over a former structure which had a double pitch, with a leaded valley in between. There were swivelling metal hooks on the walls, which probably retained shutters for the windows and to which horses may have been tethered. Also, under the tarmac of the road outside, there were brown cobblestones. The 'front' entrance was always referred to as 'the back of the house' and the rear, which gave on to the garden, was always called 'the front of the house', which lends credence to the idea that the pub's entrance was on the lower road, ie the Judge's Ride. There were still old ovens there, too and the cross ties on the outside wall of the house had a huge bolt in the centre – this held the ovens in position to the chimney. This chimney, being unsafe and unused, was pulled down in 1985. Over the ovens were large cupboards in which the flour was stored to keep it dry. In *The Land of the Gap*, Mr J H Baker noted that Frank Hilary was a baker and grocer there in 1843.

Mr Greenaway had perused the deeds of 'Berncote' and these revealed that in 1836 Miss Mary Neale sold the property to Edward Reade, the local landowner, who probably rented the cottage to a tenant. In 1868, Edward Reade sold the property to Major General Waddington, who then sold it to Rev Henry Gibbons of Wallingford.

In November 1884 there was an attempted murder at this house. The woman who was attacked had reputedly beaten the stable lad in question. The following report is taken from the *Oxford Chronicle*, 7 November 1884:

ATTEMPTED MURDER AT DOGMORE END

Intense excitement prevailed throughout this neighbourhood on Wednesday, by the rumour that a murder had been committed at Dogmore End, about six or seven miles from this town (Wallingford). The facts of the case – so far as we have been able to gather them in the short time at our command, are as follows: Mr Lawrence is a baker and grocer, carrying on business in a small shop situated about mid-way between Ipsden, Dogmore-end and Checkendon.

The house was formerly licensed to sell beer, and was known as 'The Jockey'. It subsequently went by the name of Berncote Cottage; and it has been occupied by Mr Lawrence for about two years. What the circumstances were that led up to the shocking murder attempt we are unable to say.

It has been gathered from the injured woman that about half-past eleven on Wednesday morning, she was sitting in her kitchen, peeling potatoes, when turning her head, she saw a man advancing towards her, wearing a mask. It being the Fifth of November, she was not so very much frightened, until she saw the man raise a pistol.

Before she could speak, a shot was fired, which entered her right side. She called out, 'You have shot me.' and the masked man replied 'Yes, you b...... and I will shoot you again.' Instead of doing so, or making any further attempt, he ran out of the house as fast as he could. The poor woman staggered to the front door and fell.

She must have been there some time; for it was more than half-an-hour afterwards when a groom in the service of Mr Morris, of Basset Manor, found her lying in an unconscious state. An alarm was given, Dr Horne of Wallingford was sent for, and information given to the police. Some of the people living near said they had seen a young man (answering to the description given by Mrs Lawrence) making his way to Goring.

Dr Horne, on arriving, found that the bullet had traversed the poor woman's ribs from the right side round by the blade bone; but he was unable to find the bullet, and decided to send for an experienced surgeon from Reading Hospital, to assist him at the examination the following day.

Meanwhile, the police, with Mr Morris and Mr Hope, were on the alert, and after searching Ipsden Heath, they got scent of a man on the highway at Woodcote. They followed on the same track and at Moulsford they found a young man sitting in the inn, eating some food.

Mr Hope went in and sat down by him, noticing that he kept his hand in his right hand pocket. As soon as the man saw the opportunity, he bolted, but was captured by the policeman outside. In his right pocket was found a small pistol, loaded, and he also had five cartridges. He offered a desperate resistance, but was eventually captured.

161

The unfortunate fellow, who is charged with having committed the strange act, appears to be the son of Mr Buckner, a shoemaker of Aston, a most respectable man. He is barely nineteen years of age, and what his motives were are not clear. It is said, on one hand, that he worked for Mr Lawrence, and was badly treated. On the other hand, it is stated that a cash-box was taken, containing over three pounds and the money was found upon him." Whether the woman died or not is unknown.

Jack Greenaway, father of Danny, first came to this house as a tenant in 1905. On 18 September 1911 Rev H Gibbons sold it to T W Breach, Esquire, who then sold it to Cecil Hatt. From here on it gets more complicated. Cecil Hatt appears to have sold it to T W Breach again and then it reverted to Rev H Gibbons. However, he died in 1917 and left it to his widow, Mrs Christine Gibbons, who sold it in 1919 to Roland Page, the property owner of Stoke Row.

In 1923 Roland Page sold it to Mr T H G Higgs, who then sold it to Mr T E Collier in 1937. When Mr Collier's daughter, Miss Cherrie Collier, died in 1947 the house and land were then sold to a man who was thought to have lived in High Wycombe, a Mr E T C Britnell. In 1954 Mr Britnell sold it to John ('Jack') Greenaway who was gamekeeper and woodman for Mr Vanderstegen of Cane End and had rented the cottage throughout all these changes of ownership since 1905. His family continued to live in it until the death of the surviving unmarried daughter in 1994. Thereafter the house was demolished and a beautiful new one built in its place by Alwyn Dyer.

The Oak

This house, which stands at the top of Stoke Row Hill was built as a pair of cottages and in 1823 it was extended to the rear, when it became an ale-house. It is a Grade II listed House: C17 with C19 extension to the rear."

John Wheeler, landlord of The Oak between 1882 and 1892. By kind permission of Mrs Kathy Gedling.

Richard Green was probably a publican of The Oak in 1827, as a copy of the certificate of his marriage that year to Sarah Allum, spinster, of Reading was found with the deeds. Also the baptism certificate of their son, dated 3 February 1828: "George, son of Richard and Sarah Green of Stoke Row, was baptised by Joseph Fenn, Officiating Minister."

Richard Green is also stated to have had an interest in the 1863 Stoke Row Enclosure. In 1882 James Clinch was the landlord and on 21 December 1882 (just in time for the Christmas trade!) John Wheeler took over until 1892. The pub was, by then, owned by Simonds Brewery of Reading, whose logo was a hop leaf. A metal sign was found in the old barn by Douglas Burnett, the owner of the house at that time. Simonds is now a part of Courage, the Reading brewery.

Again, there was a succession of publicans, and, as we have seen in the case of The Cherry Tree and The Crooked Billet, some of them carried on other trades in their spare time. "The old barn at the front of The Oak was, at one time, used as a wheelwright's shop", Alf Turner told me.

Henry Chapman became landlord on 13 February 1904 and was licensed by the Quarter Sessions to sell beer, ale and cider until December 1929. Then William Barefield took over The Oak on 7 December 1929 and he held the licence until February 1939. His wife was Maude (nee Pitt).

The Landlady, Mrs Charlie Edwards, with relatives outside The Oak, c 1948.
Left to right: John, Fred and Winifred Edwards, Mrs Nina Evans (nee Edwards)
Charlie Edwards?, Fred Green and Mrs Phyllis Edwards. Seated: Doris and Joy Edwards,
Mrs Nellie Green (later Mrs Elliott), Stanley and Maureen Green.
By kind permission of Mrs Nellie Elliott (nee Edwards).

From February 1939 until May 1950 Philip Jacob Bauer was the publican. He had originally come down from London and his spare time occupation was mending watches and clocks. Mrs Phyllis Edwards also lived there and was his housekeeper. On 5 November 1951 the pub closed down.

In 1953 the property was sold and converted into two semi-detached cottages. In fact it was bought and used as one house by a Douglas Burnett who was a homeopath and held his practice in the barn at the side of the house.

Since then there have been several owners who have modernised and improved the property. Mr and Mrs Deacon now live at The Oak and have restored the old barn, which formerly housed the wheelwright's shop.

The Black Horse

Although this pub is now technically in Checkendon, since changes were made to the parish boundaries, it has always been considered as being a part of Stoke Row.

The Victualler's Recognizances (Oxon Archives: QSD/V/3) covering the period 1753 to 1774 name a number of landlords in the Parish of Ipsden, but no names were given for their public houses.

The first mention of The Black Horse is in 1779, when Robert Messenger was named as licensee and he continued to be so for eleven years. Thereafter his wife seems to have taken over until, in 1789, William Messenger took on this house. It is probable that he was the son of Robert and he remained landlord for a further 32 years until 1821, when again a woman, Elizabeth Messenger, possibly his widow, became licensee.

There is no record after this date until the *Post Office Directory* started to list the publicans in 1852, beginning with Thomas Munton, farmer.

From then on, keeping the pub for only a few years at a time, were Thomas Christmas, Henry Ring, Thomas Holloway and James Bunce. Walter White then took on the licence and stayed longer, from 1891 to 1903, at which time the house was listed as being in Checkendon.

Albert Saunders, who married Sarah Gill of The Crooked Billet, took over the pub from Walter White in 1905, at which time it belonged to the Wallingford Brewery.

In the 1920s, Higgs Brewery bought The Black Horse and made considerable improvements to it, including the bricking up of the large old inglenook fireplaces. (There is reputed to be a bread oven at the side of one of them.) Higgs also extended the property, so the family, who had previously lived in the main room of the pub, were able to have their own accommodation at the rear.

Sarah Saunders was licensee until 1952, at which time Mrs Margaret ('Maggie') Saunders (nee Stallwood) took over and four years later bought the entire property from Wethereds of Marlow who had acquired it by then.

After the death of the renowned 'Maggie' in 1993, Margaret Morgan (nee Saunders) and her husband Martin, inherited the pub and the adjacent 35 acre farm.

Margaret thinks that "in view of the many outbuildings, the amount of land and the fact that this was on the 'Judge's Ride' from Oxford to Henley, it is fairly certain that this was a staging post for horses en route to London." Today Margaret and Martin run The Black Horse as a free house, selling Brakspear's and other beers. It is one of the few surviving pubs in this area that still have a truly rural feel to them.

Above: the exterior of The Black Horse in the 1930s and below: 'Maggie' in the bar room in about 1960. Both photographs kindly lent by Mrs Margaret Morgan (nee Saunders).

Highmoor Public Houses

Many Brakspear's public houses had land with them, on which the landlords often grew hops (and supplied the Brewery?) whilst their wives kept chickens and grew vegetables. One such, which actually had several acres of farmland with it, was:

The Dog and Duck

This pub was formerly known as The Old Dog and Duck. In 1992, Carole Rosier, Deputy County Archaeologist, of the Sites and Monuments Record Office at Oxford, stated in her report, after visiting this house: "parts of it are of wattle and daub construction and the beams are certainly 17th and 18th century."

In *Brakspear's Brewery* we read: "In the early part of the eighteenth century, Robert Brakspear provided surety for the licensee of the Dog and Duck at Highmoor (paying £10 per year to guarantee orderly conduct) but in 1786 Robert Appleton of New Street, Henley displaced Robert Brakspear, only to have the tables turned on him in 1789, when the firm of Hayward-Brakspear-Moorhouse secured this pub by means of a ninety-nine year lease from the owner, Thomas Stonor, esquire. Even by 1812 The Dog and Duck was still a rented pub. ...In 1872 William Brakspear bought the Dog and Duck at Highmoor."

Once more, much of the following information, covering 1753 to 1800, comes from the Victuallers Recognizances in the Oxfordshire Archives: In the years 1753 to 1773 (some years are missing) between eight and ten publicans were shown for the Parish of Rotherfield Greys in the Binfield Hundred, but none of these entries had public house names and so it is not possible to identify the pubs.

The first entry where a publican is named, along with his house, is in 1775 when, until 1777, Richard Cheney's name was given as publican. The first entry clearly calls the pub 'The Dog and Buck', so perhaps the clerk had had one too many himself!

From 1782 to 1785 William Buckeridge was the landlord and for the following three years it was Simon Reeves, but then many years are missing from the records. James Hill then stayed for five years and in 1799 Michael Lemmon (sometimes written as Lunnon, ie 'from London') held The Dog and Duck until 1811 and perhaps longer, as records are again missing from 1812 to 1817. Edward Eburn is the next mentioned licensee and then, in 1871, we come to some more tangible information.

James Saunders was stated in the 1871 Census to be "aged 35, born at Nettlebed, Victualler and Grocer." Here again, we find that a small shop was attached to the pub. No doubt this was run by the publican's wife and probably just sold the basic needs of life, such as flour, tea, sugar and candles.

The 1881 Census named "Thomas Page. Aged 40, Chair turner and publican, born Beaconsfield, Bucks. Caroline Page, aged 41, his wife, born in Great Kingshill. Children: Mary Jane (16), Elizabeth (12), Ada (8), Henry George (7), Frederick (5), Francis William (3) and Albert (1)."

He was again mentioned in the 1891 Census as "Thomas Page, aged 50. Chair turner and publican." Now we note that they appear to have given up the shop and he has taken to turning parts for chairs. The same children were named and there was another, Edith, 8 years of age. The Quarter Sessions continues to name Thomas Page as landlord of The Dog and Duck right up to 1904 by which time he had held the licence for 23 years.

John H Baker related an interesting story in *School on the Ground Floor*, about an occurrence at the Dog and Duck in 1910. "On my way to choir practice one summer evening, I saw a dapper figure approaching from the upper part of the village. He was dressed as though he was on a walking tour. He carried a walking stick, and from a strap over his shoulder was suspended a small leather pouch for holding binoculars.

I instantly recognised the small, neatly dressed man as resembling the portrait of 'Dr Crippen', at that time widely publicised in the press as being 'wanted' by the police on a charge of murder. Being due at the church for choir practice, I had only time to take a good look at the man as he passed on down the lane in the direction of Witheridge Hill.

On my return home, the maid, Annie, told me that a strange visitor had called. She had answered the knock on the front door with the baby boy in her arms. From the girl's description the visitor was evidently the strange man I had seen in the village. He had asked if he could see the schoolmaster as he wished to ask him if he could accommodate him with a night's lodging. Annie told him she expected the master to return from church any minute, but she assured him there was no room in the house for a visitor, as the only two bedrooms were occupied by the family. On hearing this the man wished her 'good evening' and went away.

I lost no time in sending messages to the Police Constables at Nettlebed and Stoke Row, warning them of a suspicious stranger seen in the locality. About the same time, Dr Crippen's companion, Ethel le Neve, dressed as a youth, was reported as having been seen walking on Nettlebed Common. A day or two after, it was reported that the 'wanted' pair had made their way to the South coast and had embarked on a ship for America. It was on this vessel that the run-away couple, as a result of the first use made of wireless communication, were arrested by the detectives from Scotland Yard.

While in the village of Highmoor, Crippen stayed at the Dog and Duck inn. When served tea, he particularly asked for jam with no pips in it, as they were an annoyance to one who had artificial teeth. In the course of conversation with the landlady he expressed an interest in music and played a tune on her violin.

The Crippen affair caused some sensation at the time. He and his wife, a former variety actress, had led a 'cat and dog' life for some years. In the meantime, he had become attached to his lady assistant in his dentistry business, Ethel le Neve, and he wanted to free himself from the encumbrance of his wife. Instead of adopting the simple expedient of disappearing with his chosen companion, he committed a crude and heartless murder by administering poison in his wife's morning cup of coffee. He followed this up by burying her body in a hole dug under the cellar floor.

Crippen's subsequent trial made a great sensation. Some sympathy was aroused for the misguided criminal, as he stood a lonely, diminutive figure in the dock, making a recital of the purgatory of his ill-assorted marriage, but the inevitable verdict condemned him to expiate his crime on the scaffold." The whole affair obviously left a great impression on Mr Baker.

On 8 October 1914 Edward William Hall Taylor and his wife took on this house and they stayed until 1927. Alistair MacIntyre, who grew up at Highmoor Hall, recalled that Mr Taylor also ran a taxi service. He died in September 1927, aged only 47, and his widow continued to run this pub until she, too, died in May 1930, aged 49.

The Dog and Duck, when the South Oxfordshire Draghounds met in November 1934. The sign reads 'Tea – Beach's Jams'. Kindly lent by Mrs Ada Britnell (nee Wells).

Within living memory, in August 1932, Charles Francis Carey was "licensed to sell ale" and this he continued to do right through the Second World War until 1945. Peter White of Nettlebed told me: "Mr Carey used to re-cover billiard tables with baize, when not behind the bar." Yet another publican's sideline!

The Dog and Duck, along with other local pubs, must have been very prosperous while the Americans were stationed in the local camps in 1944. Later, when the Poles and Lithuanians took their place, no doubt the chatter in the bar was quite incomprehensible to most of the 'locals'! (See the chapter on Wars).

Harry and Flo Venn ran the Dog and Duck from 1953 until 1980. Before his retirement, Mr Venn had worked for the Southern Electricity Board, being responsible for the Wayleave arrangements in the area. The Venns used to organise coach outings to the seaside every year – these started specifically for the Darts Club and later became days out enjoyed by all the villagers. (See the chapter on Recreation).

In 1980 the Clares, Peter and Patsy and their daughters, came and stayed for over ten years. The Clares entertained many keen owners of Classic cars during their tenancy, a custom that continues to this day. This photograph shows two such motor cars. Kindly lent by Patsy Clare.

Patsy Clare showed me the Victorian window panes in the front door. On one side is a dog, probably a bull mastiff and on the other side is a duck. A local sport on the pond at the rear of the property in Victorian times was to tether the ducks by one leg and then to see how long the dog would take to catch them, hence the pub's name!

Carole Rosier, the archaeologist, was particularly interested in the barn at the side of the pub, where there is a very unusual floor, created of upright sections of tree trunk 3" - 8" in diameter, driven into the ground, some of which are quarters.

She mentioned Loudon's *Encyclopaedia of Cottage, Farm and Villa Architecture* (1833), and wrote: "He refers to the method of the construction of these floors and notes the employment of this technique in buildings of the common kind. That Loudon should include them may be an indication that they were not uncommon at the time that he was writing, although the one at the Dog and Duck would seem to be a relatively rare survival. None of my Oxfordshire contacts were aware of another in the county and therefore it is of some interest."

No doubt this barn served the successive publicans well as a shop, a 'bodger's workshop', a garage for the taxi, a billiard table re-lining workshop and goodness knows what other sidelines!

On 19 April 1994, David and Debbie Taylor took over this pub, and continue to run the restaurant set up by the Clares. They have also made quite a number of innovations in order to attract custom – these include a Vintage Vehicle Run, Hog Roasts, Barbecues, etc.

The Green Man, Highmoor

In 1776 Catherine Harris was named as landlady of this pub which, at that time was called The Blue Man, probably stemming from the age when Ancient Britons smeared themselves in woad. John Lovegrove continued under this name for three years, but in 1785 Francis Basdon took over and the name was altered to The Green Man, which was a popular fertility symbol, made from grass at sowing time.

In 1806, under the tenancy of William Treadwell, the name reverted to The Blue Man, but in 1818 John Curtis renamed the pub The Green Man, and it appears to have stayed thus from that time onwards.

Messrs Holmes and Harper of the Greys Brewery, Henley, appear to have owned this pub. Robert Frewin held the licence here from 1882 to 1893. Thereafter there were a series of landlords, including our old friend from The Oak at Stoke Row, John Wheeler, in 1904, perhaps up to 1915. After 1919 there was no mention of The Green Man in the Quarter Sessions records. Perhaps the Dog and Duck proved too great a competitor? Certainly by 1936 it was a private house.

The Green Man in 1996. By kind permission of Mr Giles Robinson.

The Lamb at Satwell

The Lamb at Satwell, pre-1915. 'The Fish Man' (Fred Frewin from Stoke Row) and a carrier from Nettlebed are both waiting outside. The lady is unknown, but in the garden is 'Grandpa Yeatman'. By kind permission of his granddaughter, Mrs Kate Benn (nee Taplin).

This pub was formed from a pair of cottages, said to have been built in 1520 but, unfortunately there is no written evidence for it before 1804, when William Treadwell is quoted as Licensee and gave a surety of £10 for himself; the other was given by John Tanner. Thereafter all records are missing and it is not until August 1882 that the owners are stated as being Greys Brewery Ltd, Edward Aldridge was licensed to sell beer.

Florence Yeatman and her mother with a Brakspear's drayman, c 1910. The name of the little boy is not known. By kind permission of Mrs Kate Benn (nee Taplin)

George Webb stayed from 1883 to 1889 and Oliver Nash from 1891 to 1896, at which time the freehold was bought from Greys Brewery by Brakspear. The pub at that time included a shop, no doubt it was very useful for the people who lived down that end of the village, far from the centre of Highmoor.

At the beginning of the 20th century, James Yeatman and his wife, Elizabeth, took on The Lamb. Mrs Kate Benn explained: "'Grandpa Yeatman' died on Christmas Day 1915 and is buried in Highmoor Churchyard. 'Granny' Yeatman continued to run The Lamb until 1919."

In 1919, George Whitfield, who had for many years been the publican of The Hope at Stoke Row, was licensed to sell beer and did so until 1924. Arthur Baldwin came in 1927 and stayed for ten years. When he left, a gentleman with the grand sounding name of Samuel Walter de Voil became licensee until 1946 when Phyllis Grace de Voil (probably his widow) was licensed to sell beer.

During the tenancy of Mr H J Illing (1974 - 1987), the bricks with which the inglenook fireplace had been blocked up were removed and this revealed a series of four fireplaces, each built in front of the other. At the base of the fourth one, Mr Illing found a pair of duelling pistols, which he gave to someone to value, but they were never returned. However, a ghostly visitor came instead. Mrs Beryl Illing wrote to me in 1996 telling what happened:

"We took over The Lamb in February 1974. Between then and July my husband ('Larry') was totally convinced there was an inglenook fireplace behind the blocked up wall. The oak beam was still in place. Until then there was only a small stove, which stood against the blank wall. Larry decided to excavate and found that there were four fireplaces in situ, all reducing in size until we found the ultimate inglenook. Larry also found some bones (either a cat or a rabbit) buried within the rubble. Consequently we had a magnificent log fire and it was well received. It wasn't long afterwards that a few ghostly incidents started to happen.

1) I opened the door of the stairs and went up two of the steps to put on the light, and on so doing, saw a figure facing me. He had a well proportioned paunch and an old cardigan with buttons down the front.

2) During one night I awoke about 3.00 am and 'something' rose from the end of the bed and disappeared. It didn't scare me.

3) Early one evening, after we had opened the pub, there were half a dozen customers in the bar and all of a sudden there was a noise above, in our bedroom, as if furniture was being dragged over a wooden floor (we had fitted carpet). All the customers heard this and all offered to investigate with Larry. There was nothing disturbed.

4) My husband was in bed, nursing a bad attack of 'flu' one Saturday afternoon. My son and I were downstairs watching TV. We didn't disturb Larry until I took him a cup of tea about 5.30 pm. I asked him if he'd had a good sleep and he said "I would have done if someone hadn't come along the landing and disturbed me!" I assured him that it wasn't us.

We can only conclude that, by dismantling the fireplaces, we had obviously disturbed our friend, whom we named 'George'."

Several publicans have held the licence here since that time, including Alan Stephens and Linda Myatt, Sue and Terry Kearney, Terry Smith and Brian Choat, but none have reported 'the ghost'. At present Finn and Bodil Kruse, who are Danish, are the licensees and, together with their chef Lawrence Stafrace, run an excellent restaurant with Danish gourmet dishes and a welcoming ambience.

The Rising Sun, Witheridge Hill

1804 is the first date given for this pub under the Victualler's Recognizances. In this and several subsequent entries, it is referred to as 'The Old Sun'. John Irving was publican then and continued to be so until 1810 or perhaps even longer, as the records are again, frustratingly, missing until 1817. In 1882 the owners were stated to be Brakspear although for a time they leased it from H H Gardiner, and then in 1901 from Robert Fleming.

Brakspear had a series of licensees until July 1886 when Shadrach Blackhall came – he kept the pub until 1892. From 1893 to 1904 James Delafield was licensed to sell ale. He was followed by a series of short-staying tenants but in July 1916 George Turner took over. By February 1918 Annie Turner was widowed and she continued to run it until 1931.

Alfred Botting, who lived on Witheridge Hill from the time he was born in 1917 until 1927, remembered that the children often bought sweets from the window at the side of the Rising Sun and continued to do so until the school closed. Albert ('Bert') Baldwin, who was one of the sons of the local postmistress, was a very long-standing tenant, 1931 - 1965.

Margaret and Dick Hall managed The Rising Sun from 1965 until 1981. They ran an excellent and far-famed restaurant. 'Maggie' was very strict, though and would not serve any customer who came late for a pre-booked table. It is reputed that Princess Margaret came to dine and one of her friends was told, later in the evening, "Please don't sit on the table, you wouldn't do it in your house I don't suppose, so don't do it in mine!"

It was during the tenancy of Chrissie and John Ashton (1985 - 1989) that The Rising Sun Players were formed. These young people performed Shakespearean plays in the garden, under the direction of Youth Leader Danny Hall, until 1997.

Louise Wickes was licensee from 1989 until February 1994 when, very sadly, she was killed as her car crashed in a snowstorm, while she was visiting her mother in the north-west of England.

In April 1994 Barry Armstrong and Christine Thompson took over this pub and made many improvements, including altering the bar so as to make more space in the restaurant. Their aim was to "bring back the 'locals'" – they certainly have succeeded!

The earliest known photograph of The Rising Sun on Witheridge Hill, taken about 1900. The little girls, very neat in their 'pinnies', have come from Highmoor School, close by. By kind permission of Mr Archie Earle.

The Rising Sun in about 1980. Photograph by kind permission of John and Chrissie Ashton.

The Woodman, Highmoor

This, too, is a Listed Building, Grade II, "probably late C18." Originally owned by Wells of Wallingford, there is a date stone, 1872, on an extension at the rear of the property. No other records can be found until 1882, when the name given was John Leader, who was enabled to sell both beer and ale. According to *Kelly's Directory* of 1882, he also kept a shop, probably quite a small one. This he continued to do until 1887 but in 1889 his wife, Emma Leader, took over the running of this pub which she continued to do until 1896.

What happened between then and 1919 is uncertain, but in that year Albert Leader (probably the son of the former licensee) took on the licence and this he held until 1935.

By then it was owned by Brakspear's Brewery of Henley- on-Thames, having been purchased by them from the Wallingford Brewery in 1930 for £1075. At that time according to the sale particulars, it was "licensed to Albert Leader, who has been in occupation for 30 years on a quarterly tenancy of £18 per annum."

The Woodman in 1937. By kind permission of Brakspear's Brewery.

In October 1937 Edith Mary Stallwood became the publican. This lady was known as 'Edie' Stallwood and her husband was Fred, always known as 'Bremmer'. It seems that, although she ran the pub until 1954, he probably had some other occupation, perhaps connected with the nearby woods. (See also the chapter on Wars).

175

From 1954 to 1958 Albert Henry Potter was licensed to sell ale. He was said to have been "the youngest publican in Oxfordshire at the time." However, when he married, his wife did not care for the public house life so he went into computing and now lives in America.

In May 1958 Herbert Ernest Sparks took over The Woodman. He had been a printer. It was during his tenancy that the very large pond in the garden suddenly vanished. It seems his wife was hanging out the washing one day, heard a great gurgling sound and found that the pond water had disappeared into a sand pocket. It took many lorry-loads of rubble and earth to fill the enormous hole.

In April 1950, a Seafire aeroplane crashed in the adjacent field. (see the chapter on Wars). Wood from the cherry tree, knocked down by the plane, was used to make tables for The Woodman – they were there until it was sold.

Andy Bryan, who was publican at The Woodman from 1968 until it closed in 1984.
By kind permission of the Henley Standard.

In 1968 Andrew Robert ('Andy') Bryan took on the tenancy. He was a great supporter of local sports and village events and also kept chickens in the field at the rear. His 'old Dad' sold their eggs from the barn at the side of the pub.

The Woodman was closed and sold as a private house in 1984 to Mr and Mrs Bryan who, in turn, sold it to Alec Thomas. In digging out a vegetable patch, which had obviously been used as a rubbish-dump in later years, Mr Thomas found many curiosities, including a crate of bottles from Ive's Brewery of Henley, a horse harness and a 19th century Persian sword-blade. This latter object was recognised with delight by Ron Taylor when I took him there in 1995. It had been given to him by an elderly gentleman when Ron was evacuated from London to Highmoor in 1942.

There is also a pane of glass in the window of what was the Public Bar, now the owners' winter living-room, which has the name 'F Voile' scratched on it. Alec Thomas made considerable alterations and improvements to the house which was again sold in 1996, this time to Guy and Tessa Ferguson, who have rebuilt the barn.

Outside The Woodman in about 1950. The two gentlemen with the horse are unknown. By kind permission of Sam Gardiner.

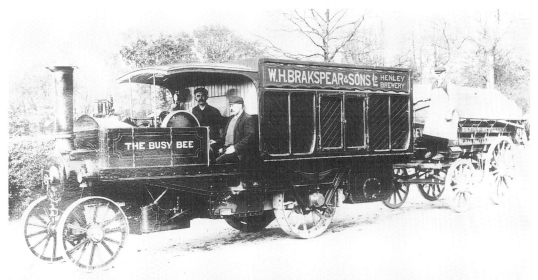

Many of the local public houses are, or were at one time, owned by Brakspears of Henley. This is one of their vehicles, the famous 'Busy Bee', delivering beer to local pubs such as those in Stoke Row and Highmoor, in about 1920. By kind permission of Brakspear's Brewery.

10. The Stoke Row Sawmill and Star Brush Factory

The old sawmill at the far western end of Stoke Row is, at the present time, owned by 'Two Heads Global Design Exhibitions', but it started its life in 1921, when it was built by Smallbone, the builders, of Streatley, for 'The Star Brush Company'. Harold Wynn told me: "Being a new factory it was a very modern one for its time, occupying a total of five acres and incorporated all the shafting underground, so there were no overhead belts or shafting cluttering up the place." It had become the principal local employer by the time Hamiltons took it over in 1957.

In the autumn of 1982 I planned to write an article about the Brush Factory, or the 'Star Brush' as it was usually known locally, for the *Stoke Row News*. I was shocked when I telephoned the Manager Frank Langham for an appointment, only to be told: "You'd better hurry up, we close down on 15 October!"

I recall quite clearly the atmosphere of that day and wrote in the November issue of the village magazine: "It was a cold misty, September morning when I arrived at the mill and the ambience was increased by the fact that I had unwittingly arrived at the time when the thirteen remaining men were having their coffee break. Therefore I found myself wandering around the silent, empty plant, feeling the chill of pending doom all around me. The signs of recent change were already there, just a few bikes in the shed that had been built for several dozen many years before. There was a bare space out by the road where I had often noticed huge piles of logs waiting to be taken into the sawmill. A general air of foreboding seemed to pervade the whole place."

The Star Brush Factory at Stoke Row, 1982. Photograph by the author.

Hamiltons had been known for their brushes for over 150 years but in latter days concentrated mainly on those used for decorating. They had representatives all over the world. An old catalogue revealed that their range of products was very large and the intriguing names conjured up all sorts of pictures in my mind. Among them were *butchers' block brushes* and *scrubbers* of every kind, including those which had 'wings' of bristle affixed to the front so as to enable the user to get into every corner.

Their 'Victory' range of household brooms and brushes included a brush which was ideal for the old stair banisters which had turned upright rods often very ornate. There was even a picture of the old wooden round lavatory brush which could so often be seen hung out of the window of what was euphemistically known as 'the littlest room'!

Hamiltons made shaving brushes too and artists' brushes of every size and type from both sable and bristle but it was their decorators' brushes for which they were most famous. Some of them had very curious names: *stipplers, limers, mottlers, dabbers,* the list was endless.

Even in today's market of plastic and nylon brushes, the bristle brush has never been surpassed. When Hamiltons owned the sawmill, the bristles used came from China. Frank Langham explained to me: "The stiffest ones come from Chunking and the medium ones from Hankow, two regions which specialised in rearing the pigs which provide these wonderful natural fibres. The bristle tapers upwards to a fine point and has along its length fine hairs which retain the paint in a way that no nylon fibre will ever do."

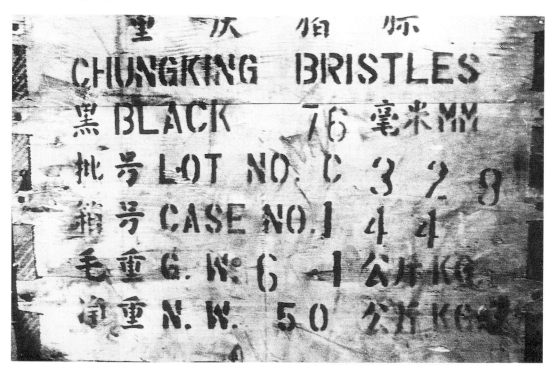

All around the factory site were wooden boxes in which bristles had come from China. Photograph by the author.

Since the brush backs were made at Stoke Row and the bristles inserted in the Harrow factory, these boxes had come down from Middlesex with other items in them. Even so, the sight of the Chinese lettering which probably only meant 'gross weight' or something similar, excited my thoughts. I found myself imagining where they had come from and thought of the peasants who raised the pigs so far away.

Slicing the timber c 1950. The man on the left and those on the right are using 'peevies', tools with a long handle and an iron hook on the end for keeping the timber in position. Left to right: Ted Evans, Ivor Osman, unknown, Bert Thatcher (the foreman) is in the far distance, by the door. Bob Packer is on the right (nearer) and Fred Earle (further). Photograph kindly lent by Mrs Lenna Green (nee Archer).

The Hamilton trademark *Semper Idem* (Always the Same) was one of the first to be registered. The Star Brush logo was a brown star with a white star in the centre of that. I have a small nail brush in my collection of local ephemera. It not only has the company's emblem in the centre but also the words: "STAR BRUSH, BRITISH MAKE" and was probably manufactured in about 1965. This was an important claim at a time when brushes with colourful plastic handles and backs inserted with nylon fibres were fast coming on to the market and attracting the housewife away from the old wooden type. Even the wooden ones still being sold, cheaply imported from Romania, via Italy and Holland, were beginning to damage the industry. The Chinese, who once only sold bristles, were also beginning to export brushes.

Frank Langham showed me around the mill. The beech wood was delivered in the form of mature tree trunks, about a hundred at a time. These trunks were a minimum of ten inches in diameter and were usually over seventy years old. The mill used about a thousand cubic feet of good wood every week. The trunks were fed into an automated band-saw, the only new machine in the place. Before the advent of this novelty the Osman brothers had operated the original, hand-fed band-saw for many, many years, going back to the time when the logs were brought in on horse-drawn trailers. By 1982, the new machine was only seven years old, built by a company in Auxerre, France, where the five smaller band-saws had been made in the 1920s.

The automatic machine cut the logs into planks which were then put into wire 'cages' and fed into the drying kiln for up to twenty-one days, until they were down to ten per cent of their original moisture content. The kiln was built at the outset of the firm and was fired by the 120 sacks of sawdust and five tons of off-cuts that were produced every week. This kiln was said to be the biggest in southern England. It held 48 cages, each eight foot cubed. They ran on a 'railway', which was eight feet wide.

The furnace provided the plant with central heating – all very economical. At the time of my visit, Norman Kearn of Woodcote was filling sacks with sawdust. He had worked there for twenty-seven years and had eight years to go before he would retire officially.

After the planks were dried they were put through a ribbon-saw (sometimes known as a multi-ripsaw), which reduced them to strips before they were cut into small blocks by the men who operated the bandsaws. At one time, it was a very skilled job to cut these blocks to the correct angle, until Bill Johnson thought of the idea of cutting the whole block at an angle, so that two heads could be cut off from each block, thus saving a good deal of waste and therefore money. Other blocks were also produced and cut in different ways to make several widths of handle.

All of these bandsaws were still referred to by the names of the men who had operated them, all of whom had retired by then, or even died. Such names as Albert Main, Laurie Wells, Tom White and Bill Green were used right up to the end with affection, to denote each machine, so long had those men operated them.

Loyalty to the Star Brush appears to have been the hallmark of the firm. After 40 years of service each man received £20 from the Board of Directors and (believe it or not!) a book on brush-making. Harold Wynn was one of the longest serving employees with 52 years of unbroken service to his credit. Bill Green worked there for 50 years, many of them as Foreman, and was Acting Manager for two years before he retired in 1974. George Johnson gave a total of 42 years, although his long spell was broken by military service during the Second World War.

Bill Johnson worked in the mill from 1936, starting at 14/7d a week, at a time when such money was considered to be very good. Bill George, George Walter and Alf Turner were among others who notched up many years at the factory. Bert Thatcher had been with the company for 40 years and was Manager when he was interviewed for the *Reading Mercury* in 1962.

181

Tom White, cutting blocks for the brushes c 1950. By kind permission of Mrs Lenna Green.

Some of the staff at the Stoke Row Sawmill just after the Second World War.
'Art' Britnell is on the extreme left and Bill Green is third along, both in the middle row.
Jack Ruddle is also on the left in the front row. The names of the others are unknown.

Days were very long at the mill, especially in the early times. Len Summerfield wrote to the *Henley Standard* in 1982, "We used to start work at 6.00 am and those men who came from Russell's Water had to get up at 4.30 am in order to cycle to work. Our lunch was cold tea and sandwiches which had to be prepared the night before."

But it was not all work. There seemed to have been a happy atmosphere there – a bit more than happy sometimes, for practical jokes appeared to be the order of the day, perhaps to relieve the tedium of the machine-minding. One that stood out in Bill Johnson's memory was when "George Walter's wellington boots were put up on one of the cages – it took him all day to find them!"

Not everyone appreciated the jokes however, nor liked life at the mill. In about 1940, Eric Summers started working there. He related: "Freddie Cox told me about this job and I was attracted to it, partly because it paid well. As I might have known, the work was very arduous. I had to stand outside, cutting up brush-backs from silver birch wood, on a saw driven by an old Sunbeam engine. Another of my jobs was to make chaff from loads of hay by feeding it through a very noisy machine. This chaff was to feed the horses which pulled the timber, before Star Brush bought mechanised transport. This work gave me headaches which, together with the many unkind tricks that the workmen perpetrated on each other, made me look elsewhere."

George Johnson said, "Mothers used to warn their sons: 'Don't you go and work there, you'll lose your fingers.' Several men did, but it was largely due to carelessness and 'larking about'. There were guards on the machines but they used to take them off so as to be able to work faster on piece-work. When the Inspectors came (which was well known beforehand) the guards would be put back."

Ted Evans who worked there until 1942 recalled: "There used to be a man there called Dan Murphy who stirred his tea with his pipe, and he wasn't the only one! One day, a concert party came to Stoke Row and among their number was a baritone who was also a steeplejack. He stayed on in Stoke Row for a few days in order to mend the chimney at the sawmill, which he did by lashing several ladders together, having pulled up one after another from the bottom. He tied himself to the chimney too and mended it before descending by the same method!"

During the Second World War 'fire-watching' became an important job at the sawmill where an incendiary bomb could have caused havoc. Bill George was 36 years old and waiting for his call-up papers when he started work in February 1940. He remembered that the ground was frozen hard and the dust blew everywhere.

"I found the fire-watching quite exciting. After I had only been there a month a German plane dropped a *Molotov Bread-basket* over Nettlebed and the blaze from there could be seen for miles around. The *basket* itself was carried on the wind and landed in a field opposite the Sawmill." He laughed as he thought back to the reaction of Mr Bartlett the Manager when Bill picked up this container. "He thought I'd 'had it', but it turned out to be just a bit of sheet metal shaped like an umbrella. In fact it lay about the place for about a fortnight until someone reported it."

One Sunday night though Bill did get a fright when a plane, "it might have been of ours", dropped a flare over the factory. Bill 'joined up' in 1941 and Dickie Day took over the fire-watching.

Ted Evans also did stints at this work: "I was also a fire-watcher at the sawmill at weekends when I relieved Dickie Day who did it every night of the week."

Some of the wood was felled locally around Checkendon. However, Fred Powell recalled: "Beech came to the Star Brush from as far afield as Spencer's Wood, near Reading. When I was a boy, coming from Kingwood Common on my bike I used to hang on to the tail of the sawmill lorry!" Harold Wynn told me: "Hamiltons owned Lambridge Wood, about 204 acres near Henley, and also Withy Copse.

Later they brought a great deal of beech from the Meon Valley in Hampshire. Only beech could be used because a softer wood would break during the high-speed turning.

One of the fellers was Jack Foster, who carved his sign on every tree stump quick as lightning as soon as they had felled it. It comprised three fishes, intertwined. You could walk through a forest and see at once which trees he had felled!"

Timber cutters at work in 1929. Left to right: Ted Evans, Ivor Osman, Bert Thatcher (later Foreman and then Manager until his death in 1972) and Jack Somerfield. By kind permission of Ted Evans.

When Bill Johnson left the services in 1947 he returned to the sawmill where he had worked since 1936, when he had stacked dry boards at 1/4d a gross. This time he went out timber cutting, often with his brother George. "We reckoned to be in the woods by 7 o'clock in the morning. We biked everywhere carrying all our equipment with us. We often had as many as three cross-cut saws ranging from three foot to seven foot long. Then there were the beetles and the wedges, huge axes and water in a billy-can, so we could boil up and make tea." Their work was supervised too. "In the beginning the forester would come along to see what you were doing and if you knew your job. You weren't allowed to cut down small trees or to skim other trees by dropping yours carelessly."

Bill explained: "Half the time you couldn't let the tree fall where it leaned. You had to beetle it out by coupling with wedges. You made one cut, inserted a wedge, by tapping it with a beetle and then you would have to make a back saw in front and put in another wedge – this was known as coupling up. After you had done this you chopped the back of the tree to let it go over the wedges. You never heard of a sledge-hammer then, only a beetle, which was made of wood banded with iron rings. Thus the wedges never got burred over which, if you'd used a sledge-hammer, would have resulted in rough edges and you wouldn't have been able to couple up then.

When the motor saws came in anyone could do it and often made a mess of it. There was no pride in the work after that; the men often didn't care about the trees."

The mill employed a firm who had machines specially made for pulling out the tree stumps. In order to stop them becoming bogged down these machines had flanges on the sides which made them look, as Bill said: "For all the world like Boadicea's chariot!"

When the wood had been felled it had to be brought back to the factory. Bill told me: "For local work six Shire horses were used and kept in the stables at the back of the factory." (This is now a private house).

Tools used by a bodger and some by a tree feller, including beetles, wedges and axes.

185

The men and boys who worked at the Sawmill in the 1920s.
Photograph kindly lent by Patrick Anstee.

Beattie Evans was often frightened by the horses. "Sam King's horses were very frisky and often reared up. Sam managed them very well but I was afraid of them!" This photograph by Eric Guy shows Sam King, hauling logs up Stoke Row Hill in about 1940, with horses owned by the Stoke Row Sawmill. By kind permission of Mrs June Black (nee King).

For more long-distance work, the firm had a number of lorries, made by Scammel and specially designed for hauling the long logs. Ted Evans also told me George Newman was the first man at the sawmill to drive the big Scammel lorry in the 1920s.

"He had to go to Scammel's factory, up north, for a week, to learn how to drive one of these huge monsters, and specially how to kick start it because it was too heavy to 'wind' by hand. There were six ratchets on that lorry. They were adjustable retaining bars to keep the trunks on the lorry securely. There were three on each side, you could let the four at each corner down how you liked, but you had to be very careful when you were unloading and let the middle one down or the logs would roll on to you!" After the Second World War, Foden lorries superseded the horses.

One of the horses in front of its competitor, the old Scammel lorry.
By kind permission of Mrs Lenna Green (nee Archer).

Harold Wynn was born in 1901 in Reading and started at the sawmill as soon as it was built in 1921. He went along for an interview with Mr Bartlett who was to be the new Foreman. "You can start Monday." he was told. "I did and stayed there for 52 years!" he stated proudly. He eventually became the Foreman of the Machine Shop.

Harold didn't remember how much he earned when he started at the mill, but "after a while I was getting £3. 7. 8. 1/2d a week, when my father was getting only 27/6d, though he did have a rent-free cottage." He continued, "We had to start early, seven o'clock, but luckily I was able to bike in from Checkendon just down the road.

We stopped for breakfast at 9 o'clock. You brought your own bacon and eggs, but the company employed Charlie Boocher, an old soldier known as 'Darkie', to do the cooking. He had been out in India with the army and was full of Indian phrases that he'd learned out there, such as *Char* (tea) and *Pani* (water) He cooked the food over a wood fire and brewed the tea in a *Dixie*." I asked him what a *Dixie* was. "Oh, that was a big black cast-iron pot, oval in shape. Each man had his own enamelled plate and mug. You got your tea by dipping it into the Dixie. You put condensed milk into it then – lovely it was. At lunchtime the men brought out their sandwiches and again 'Darkie' brewed up the tea.

It was this man's task to sweep up and do other odd jobs about the place. He had to operate the semi-rotary pump to raise the water up to the foreman's house, the one by the road. The mill office was also in this house. Water was piped down from Woodcote by gravity in the early days and the mill was sufficiently below the head of water for this to be successful, but the house was on higher ground you see. So they built a reservoir by the mill and the water had to be hand-pumped up to a tank in the roof. There was an overflow pipe sticking out of the roof and when that started to flow old Darkie knew the tank was full!" Later, of course, all the water was pumped automatically to the site.

It was Harold's job to "mend what other men broke!" He had several men working with him, chiefly Alf Turner and Jock McCarra. One of the jobs they had to do, about every fifteen years was to remake the kiln pipes. "They were about 1.1/4 inches in diameter and over the years they became burned out by the fierce heat. There were five bends in each pipe and sixteen coils to the set. That meant eighty bends, each about three inches radius. It was quite a job but I made a jig which did it much quicker." Another typical task was to replace a cylinder liner. "To do this we used an age-old trick with two kettles and a piece of ice usually begged from the travelling fishmonger. You put the insert in a hole made in the ice and this shrunk it a fraction. At the same time you poured the boiling water over the cylinder head which expanded it and then you were able to tap it into place very gently."

There was a very big engine to drive all the equipment and machinery. It was made by Garrett and called a CCS V. Harold explained, "The letters stood for Compound Condensing Superheated and the V was the Roman version of Five."

The engine at the Star Brush factory c 1960. "It was always kept in superb condition by Tom Absalom". By kind permission of Alf Turner.

Jack Day, hauling timber with a tractor c 1940. By kind permission of John Day.

*Timber unloading with tripod block and tackle for the Star Brush factory, c 1920.
By kind permission of John Day.*

A Dennis lorry hauling timber at the Sawmill, c 1930. Kindly lent by Pat Preece.

Alan and Pamela Thatcher in the Star Brush cart with Arthur Povey, c 1938 .

A large number of photographs were taken in 1950 commissioned by the Star Brush senior management. Some of them were used in a booklet published in 1951 when their new showroom was opened at Eden Grove, Holloway, London. This one of the entire staff at Stoke Row was kindly lent by Lenna Green.

Harold Wynn (showing his cheque) when he retired, in about 1970.
By kind permission of Mrs Lenna Green.

This well-composed photograph was commissioned by the Hamilton Star Brush Company in about 1970. The man with the cheque was Bill Johnson who had been awarded £100 for thinking of an idea whereby twice as many brush backs could be cut from the same piece of wood. In this way a great deal of waste was eliminated – no wonder the firm were pleased with him!

The gentlemen in suits and ties were directors from the London office. Mrs Ethel Ireson was on the left and Mrs Langham wife of the Foreman was on the right. The man in the beret was 'Ches' Black from Poland, who later owned the London House Stores.

11. Earthenware, Bodging and Other Trades

Pottery and Brickmaking

One of the earliest references to Stoke Row is to Dagmer, now Dogmore, meaning 'the place of the diggers'. What they were digging for, especially in the Romano-British period, was clay. As many gardeners in the village have come to find out, Stoke Row is built on a hill largely composed of this material. To be more accurate, it is mostly clay with flints but the western end of Stoke Row also has an area of Reading Beds clay. Unfortunately, it has rather too much silica in it and that is why the bricks 'spall' (spoil/break up) quickly. Nevertheless, 'shards' (pieces) of Romano-British pots have survived intact near Swan Wood, Highmoor, where there was obviously a Romano-British pottery – not far from the one that thrived later at Nettlebed.

In Oxfordshire Museum Service Publication No. 13, *Oxfordshire Potters*, there is a list of the names of potters of Stoke Row, taken from the *Reade manuscript, the Parish Registers and various Directories. It also lists their birth date, if known, and the dates they were believed to be working:

Name	Occupation	Dates	Sources
Swain family	Potters, Brickmakers and Limeburners	(?)1612 - late 18th	Reade MS; Parish Registers
James Smith	Potter	(d 1791)	Parish Reg. 1791
Peter Smith	Potter and Brickmaker	c 1800-28	Reade MS.
William Smith	Potter	(d 1834)	Parish Reg. 1834
Wm Wichellow	Potter	(b 1792) (d 1851) 1839	Reade MS; Parish Marriage Register, 1839
Martha Wichello	Earthenware manufacturer	1839-54	Reade MS; Parish Register, 1839, *Gardner's/ PO Directory*, 1854

Name	Occupation	Dates	Sources
George Hope	Potter	(b 1817) (d 1890) (?) 1854	Census, 1871; Parish Register; OS Map 1881-1890
Samuel Harding	Potter	(b 1853)	Census 1871
Robert Munday	Potter	(d 1853)	Parish Reg. 1853
Geo Readings	Potter	(b 1804) 1861-1871	Census 1861, 1871
Jos. Wm Slade	Potter	1865	Parish Reg. 1865
Ebenezer Harding	Potter's apprentice	(b 1856) 1871	Census 1871
Chas Wm Robbins	Potter	1891- 1897	Parish Baptism Register, 1896; *Kelly's Directory*, 1891 and 1897.
Wm Timson	Potter	1896-1901	Parish Register 1896, 1901

*This refers to a history of the area, handwritten in a book by Mr Edward Anderdon Reade, who was instrumental in providing the Maharajah's Well to Stoke Row. In 1983 I typed out this rather cumbersome and wordy document, placed copies in the church vestry and with various interested parties in the village and, with the blessing of Rev David Salt, placed the original in the Bodleian Library.

The Oxfordshire Potters concludes from the list above that "the Swain family came to Stoke Row from Checkendon, attracted by the lime and brick kilns already in the vicinity. The family figures in the parish registers from 1612, although they do not give occupations until the 18th century. No documentary sources, such as wills with inventories, survive to link the family with the pottery industry. Even assuming a brick-making trade operating in the 17th century, as was likely, one cannot tell at what point the pottery began to be made there... By the 18th century, the Smith family owned the brick kilns and the industry began to expand, and to include pottery. James Smith was known as 'Potter Smith' (d 1791) and his son, William, was also a potter (d 1834). William Wichellow occurs in the Parish Registers as a potter from 1839 until 1851 when, upon his death, his widow, Martha, ran the pottery."

"...after this George Hope, born in Checkendon in about 1817, expanded the business considerably. In 1863 he is described as a farmer and potter, and a year later as farmer, brick and tile maker and potter. He was a man of some standing in the community, Parish Overseer, Poor Law Guardian, surveyor and waywarden until 1889, but little more can be found about the pottery business itself." George Hope also built The Hope (later The Farmer) public house, presumably with his own bricks, and named it after himself! (See the chapter on Pubs).

The researchers of this interesting little book continue: "The 1871 census tells us that 29 men and 7 boys were employed at the works, but of course, some of these will also have been working on the farm. George Hope died in 1890 and Charles William Robbins, who took over the works, was listed in the directories as a brick and tile maker and threshing machine operator and as a potter in the parish register in 1896.

Only one other potter occurs in the sources, William Timson, in 1898 and 1901. Pottery production probably ceased between 1897 and 1899, when the works changed hands again. However, the Stoke Row Brick and Tile Company continued in the directories until 1939."

Josh Main remembered the brickworks very well. In his 'Old Timer's Tales', published in the *Stoke Row News* in September 1966, and in his 'Memories', which appeared in the same publication in June 1992, he told of his early working life there.

"I worked at the Vanderstegen Brickyard in Busgrove Lane from the time that it started, soon after the first War, to the time when it was sold to the Tilehurst Brick and Tile Co, about 1935. My grandfather, who lived in one of the cottages that today forms part of 'Clayhill', the house on Stoke Row Hill, worked there, too. He was responsible for the kilns at night, whilst the baking was in progress and he rested during the day." Ted Evans told me that the whole village smelled of sulphur when old Mr Main was firing the bricks!

Charles Main and his wife, Elizabeth, the grandparents of Josh Main. Photographed by Fred Viner of 198 Kings Road, Reading in about 1900. By kind permission of Mrs Elsie Wickham (nee Main).

195

From working in the gravel pits he moved on to the brick yard, which was situated down Busgrove Lane, where the Vanalloys Business Park is now. It was there that they dug the clay for the bricks and sand and gravel for the mortar for the building of the Star Brush factory in 1920. Josh worked in the brickyard, with his grandfather, for about twelve years. "You had to be sober then, for the holes dug out for the clay were about 16-18 feet deep and often full of water. You had to push your barrow across a 10" wide plank, and if you didn't keep the wheel of your 'navvy' barrow true, then you fell in!" he laughed.

"In fact, you pushed the barrow forward and it was when you were pulling it back behind you that these amusing incidents occasionally occurred. You got to know the barrows, and if you thought it was going, you let it go, quick!" he explained.

"The brick clay was blue, green, red or yellow and was mixed with a little sand and fed into a 'pug mill', driven by a portable engine. This worked up the clay after the fashion of a concrete mixer and forced it through an opening the size of a brick, or tile, on to our workbenches, where we cut off four bricks at a time with wires stretched across a frame. Or else it came down in a ribbon on to a table and into four boards, from which they were cut with wires, six or eight at a time, and so were always known as 'wire cuts'. They then had to be carried on a barrow, the wheel of which ran on a metal track, to keep it in position."

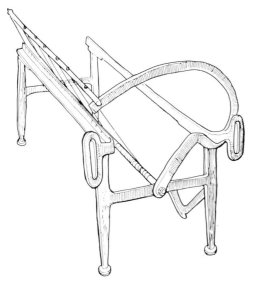

Cutting frame for making bricks. Reproduced by kind permission of John Rhodes of the Oxfordshire Museums Service.

Handmade bricks were fashioned in a similar manner but were rubbed in sand and thrown on to a board which had a piece of wood the shape of the 'frog', which is a recess in the brick to take the mortar. They were then trimmed off separately to width. The green bricks were picked up between two pieces of wood, two at a time, and stacked on four pallets on a special long barrow with the wheel in the middle of the platform." Alf Turner, junior, informed me: "half a brick sideways was called a 'brickbat' and a quarter of a brick was called a 'quarter' but half a brick longways was called a 'Queen Closure' when they were laid in brickwork."

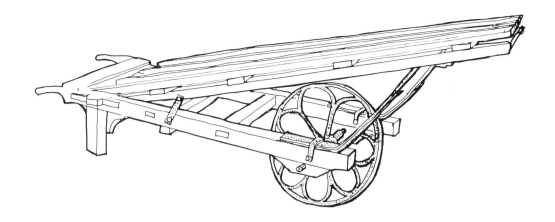

An off-loading barrow. By kind permission of John Rhodes.

Josh continued: "We then had to run the barrow along 6" wide steel strips to air dry the bricks out in the yard, where the boys had to cover them with green boughs and thatch. In due course they were moved into the kilns for firing.

The kiln, which was one of the 'Scotch' type, was built by Harry Godwin. The walls were of two leaves of 9" brick, spaced about 2'6" apart, jointed in sandy loam and the middle filled with rubble and it had tunnels in the sides for the fires. The raw bricks were then stacked on to a device made of clay pipes so they could drain off. They were protected in bad weather by 'faggots' of leafy wood 'tops'. From there they were barrowed again into the kiln and there stacked neatly in the 'tunnel'. We were paid 12/6d per thousand for making and stacking."

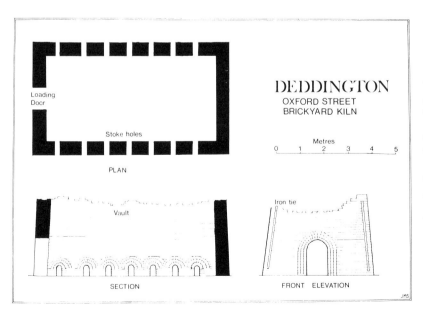

DEDDINGTON
OXFORD STREET
BRICKYARD KILN

Loading Door

Stoke holes

PLAN

Metres
0   1   2   3   4   5

Vault

SECTION

Iron tie

FRONT ELEVATION

A plan of the Scotch kiln at Deddington. The Stoke Row kilns were of a similar type. Taken from 'Oxfordshire Brickmakers', by kind permission of John Rhodes.

197

Josh went on: "Each kiln held 40,000 bricks and was itself made of bricks. It was about 10 ft high. Each of the two walls which made up the tunnel was a yard wide and they were built in ascending manner internally, so as to create a 'tunnel' which was narrower at the top than it was at the bottom. Into each, at the base of the exterior, were built ten oven holes, each one foot wide, and these went right through to the centre. The coal for them came in by traction engine from Goring Railway Station. The top of the kiln was made from bricks and covered over with loam. The back was similarly blocked up when the fires were started and so was the front of the 'hatchway'. The bricks were baked for three or four days in these very hot ovens."

Josh Main later worked for the builders 'Smallbones' of Streatley – who probably used some of the bricks that were made by the Stoke Row Brick and Tile Works!

Bodging

Of all the crafts and trades practised in Stoke Row and Highmoor over the years, 'bodging' must have the most intriguing name. As most people in these villages know, the term has nothing to do with a 'bodged' job, for the work called for great skill and experience.

In January 1968, Geoff Boyson wrote a very clear description of the craft in the *Stoke Row News*:

"The beechwood legs and spars for chairs, which were finished in High Wycombe, were fashioned by pole lathe and treadle lathe turners who usually set up their crude shacks of corrugated iron and sacking with calico windows in the woods where they bought their timber.

They produced a large variety of turned parts for chairs known as *Wheelback, Giant Arm, Kitchen, Windsor, Church* etc, examples of which can still be seen in some homes in the village.

The work was extremely hard and poorly paid. For example, piece work rates 'between the wars' were as follows:- One gross (144) of 'forefeet' (front legs) and 9 dozen stretchers = 6/-. A gross of common forefeet and 6 doz. stretchers = 6/6d. A gross of best forefeet and 6 doz stretchers at 9/- included an extra hand process known as 'toeing in' and it took two men a full twelve hour day to produce them.

They bought their timber at £1 per cartload of 25 cubic feet, cross cut it according to what sort of leg was required, and then split it with a beetle and wedge. Roughing out was done first with a hatchet, usually blacksmith-made, and then with a draw shave on a shaving horse which was a combined seat/bench/clamp."

75 year old Silas ('Bill') Saunders, checking chair legs he had made in his shed
by The Crooked Billet. This shed burned down recently and has now been rebuilt.
This professional photograph was taken by Walton Adams of Reading in about 1930.
By kind permission of Mrs Maggie Saunders (nee Stallwood).

Geoff Boyson's description of the craft continued: "On the lathe the billets were shaped with a gouge and the pattern marked out with a V-shaped tool called a 'buzz' before finishing with a flat chisel. The legs and spars were then stacked between rails for seasoning.

The late Bill Saunders of the Crooked Billet was a well-known local bodger. He started work at the age of 10, joining his father in the wood trade. His uncle laid the foundations of his bodging career and originally provided the timber, but after the First World War, when he started on his own, timber became scarce and he obtained it mostly from the Wyfold Estate and Checkendon.

In 1913, when Bill's brother was taken ill, he often took the 'pimps' (bundles of kindling) into Wallingford before he started turning. He produced for only three firms, Mealings, Allens and Holts and at first took the legs to Wycombe himself by horse and cart. Later he hired a lorry and eventually the firms collected them. Bill's stools and rolling pins were also in great demand. He was 78 when he finished working as a bodger."

In 1994 Mrs Lily Tayler (nee Johnson) told me she still had a rolling pin, a chopping board and a cricket set, made from local wood by Bill Saunders of The Crooked Billet.

Sometimes the old bodgers were subject to unkind pranks. Les Franklin recalled one of them: "For instance, 'Preacher' Smallbones, who lived at the foot of Newnham Hill, always preferred to work in the afternoons and in the evenings at his tent-pegging and chair-leg making, trades which he carried out in a shed on Alma Green in the corner of George Lester's yard. The naughty boys of Stoke Row would sometimes cut the string of his treadle lathe and, when he was working by candle-light, would throw bricks at his shed to rock the candle!"

Albert Carter, always known as 'Bert', always had a pipe between his teeth and worked in a barn at the side of The Cherry Tree. Here he is seen turning chair legs on a pole lathe, sawdust and shavings all around him. By kind permission of John Holroyd.

Being the landlord of a pub, where most of the work was done in the evenings, and running another business during the day, often went together. Percy Stallwood explained how the family business of tent-peg making was started and carried on at the rear of The Cherry Tree.

"Although my grandfather, Edwin Stallwood, ran the business it was his wife who kept the books. She wrote beautifully and even wrote out an agreement once for him to purchase a horse from a Gipsy horse pedlar from Woodcote. This agreement was signed with only an X by my grandfather, who was unable to read or write, but it was agreed to be legally binding.

He also drew a sum of money from the Post Office by signing with a cross, even though this was the proceeds of the Village Sports Day, he was so well known and well liked that no-one would have doubted his word, anyway."

Frank Page, who owned 'Beechwood' (now 'Red Cow House') on the corner of the Village Green and the Reading Road, had a timber yard at the side of his house (ie facing the Village Green) and he also employed 30 or 40 men on tent-pegging.

Tent Peg Making

Although chair parts were also made in villages nearer to High Wycombe, Stoke Row and Highmoor were the principal villages in the Chilterns for the making of tent-pegs. The main reason for this was its proximity to the Royal Army Ordnance Depot at Didcot, since most of the pegs that were made, particularly in the First World War, were for the army.

Even during the Second World War, the army bought over 10 million of these wooden pegs – one day in 1942 the Stallwood family received one order for two million and even as late as 1945 another order was for 500,000.

Bert Carter again, in his younger days, second from the left, in this early and rather posed photograph, demonstrating the arts of 'bodging' parts for chairs and making tent-pegs. Date and site unknown. By kind permission of Mrs Pat Preece.

Most of the tent-peg makers worked in 'shelters', (also known as 'shops' or 'shacks') made of four upright poles, topped with sheets of galvanised, corrugated iron, set up so as to have a fall to the back, to encourage the rain to run off. Around this structure were sacks, which had been cut open to make them into 'sheets', which were then hung like curtains to keep out the draught. Banks of sawdust and shavings piled high on the outside of the sacks ensured that the shelters were quite cosy in winter, "unless the north wind blew hard!"

In the winters, lighting was minimal, usually by means of a candle in a 2 lb jam jar. This form of illumination cast no shadows and gave a circular light. A piece of wire gripped the neck of the jar and was extended to make a loop so that it could be suspended from the roof and held over the 'collar' of the 'tent peg horse' for the worker to see what he was doing. If he moved away from the 'horse' he had to take the candle jar with him.

The methods used for making the pegs were always the same. First of all, the trees were felled. In the days before the mechanised cutting of tree trunks, they were sawn by two men with a cross-cut saw. The wood was then cut into lengths and split into halves, with a 'beetle' (a type of hammer) and a 'wedge'.

The half logs were then split into sections using a 'molly' (a round wooden hammer) and a 'flammer' (an L-shaped axe). Once the wood for the tent pegs had been split and the 'pairs' of pieces were made ready, then it still needed 24 movements to make a peg, including the notch and the edges. All this work was done on a specially-made 'tent-pegger's horse'.

Frank Page and George Ruddle, making tent-pegs in their 'shelter' in about 1930. Kindly lent by Mrs Pauline Mann (nee Ruddle).

The 'peggers' as they were usually known, worked from 7.30 am to 6.00 pm and each man could make 600 pegs a day, about 3000 a week (of the 9" type). Once the pegs were made, they had to be stacked correctly. In season this was often done by their wives and children.

Peggers' piece work rates 'between the wars' were:

9" - 1/4d per 100;   13" - 1/6d per 100;   18" - 3/6d per 100;
24" - 7/6d per 100;   36" - 12/6d per 100; 42" - 18/- per 100.

Government inspectors went sent around the tent peg makers on a regular basis. Josh Main told me: "It was the job of these inspectors to pass or reject the pegs and they would come down from London when an order was near completion. Not knowing anything at all about tent peg making, but probably feeling it was up to them to make some sort of demonstration of knowledge, they would pass almost every pile and then choose one which they would demolish with a kick of their foot and mark a few with a black arrow denoting rejection. The peggers would gather these up, take them back to their shelters and shave off the offending mark ready for the next batch which, needless to say, passed the test!"

He also told me "When young men started to learn the craft, they always got blisters on their soft hands. The answer to this was to take a needle and thread and pass it through the blister to draw out the water. The blister then soon dried out and eventually the hands became calloused enough to withstand any amount of wear." Although the trade today is virtually extinct, several people, such as Don Williams of Bix, have started to take up the old craft again and give demonstrations at local events.

Six Stages in making a tent peg: 1. George Ruddle and his 'mate', cutting a log to size. All these photographs were kindly lent by Mrs Pauline Mann (nee Ruddle).

Top left: 2. Splitting a log, with 'Molly' and 'Flammer'.

Top right: 3. Sectioning a split log.

Left: 4. Sawing tent peg lengths on a saw horse.

Above: 5. One of the 24 movements required to shape a tent peg.

Left: 6. George Ruddle proudly holding a range of various sized tent pegs: 6", 9", 12", 13", 18", 24", 30" and 36" long.

205

George Ruddle's shelter, with piles of tent-pegs stacked outside, in about 1948.
By kind permission of Mrs Pauline Mann (nee Ruddle).

In the *Stoke Row News*, 1979 - 80, Rev Cyril Isherwood remembered: "The woods, which were more extensive than they are now, since so much has been cut down, were a means of much activity and work.

There were a number of places where deep trenches, oblong, like a pie dish and deep enough for a man to be able to crouch beneath a tree trunk which was laid across it and to pull down a two-handled saw, whilst another man on top pulled it up. Slowly but surely, they sawed the long planks of wood ready for the builder. It took a long time, but in those days there was no rush and hurry and care and time were put into the work which was made to last. No tree was cut down until the leaves had fallen and the sap gone down.

If there was a young sapling in the way of the tree where it would fall, it was carefully hooked aside until the tree was down and then allowed to grow to take the place of the one that had been felled and so the woods were gradually replenished.

There is still the remains of one of these trenches in the wood where the footpath goes from Uxmore to the Black Horse, although much overgrown since those years when country life was so different from what it is today. In the days before any thought of electricity, wood was largely used for both cooking as well as heating. 'Wooding' was quite an important event, when women would go into the woods, sometimes with an old pram, and pick up bundles of dead wood that had fallen on the ground.

In the old houses, where the chimney was large and wide enough, hams were wrapped and hung up to be cured by the smoke of the wood fire, and so would have tasted very different from so much that we have today.

Mr Cox, the builder, employed a man solely to cut up wood for their fire, which was a large, wide, open grate with an oven underneath. I can remember seeing the hams high up in the chimney, gradually being smoked, though I never tasted one.

Not only were the woods useful for 'wooding' but also for 'chucking', which meant a number of people going round with axes and breaking up stumps of old trees that had been cut down. This provided large chunks of wood which made good fires and so saved coal.

People would go with old prams or any kind of wheeled conveyance and load it up with sacks full of 'chucks' and so were ready for winter to keep the home fires burning."

Making rifle-butts in the woods around Highmoor during the First World War.
Left to right: 'Barber' Saunders,- ? -, Arthur Springell, Sid Saunders,
- ? -, ? Butler, ? Powell, Harry ('Brusher') Slade, Jimmy Stallwood
and Steve (?) Saunders, who had only one eye.
The identity of the man in the bowler hat is unknown.
By kind permission of Bill Kimber.

207

Blacksmithing

George Seymour was a farrier rather than just a blacksmith. He preferred to term himself 'a shoeing and general smith'. There was no doubt about the fact that he loved horses. He had been in the Royal Veterinary Corps during the First World War, but was invalided home from Gallipoli, having been kicked by a mule and suffered a wound to the head.

He later took over the licence of the King's Arms at Skirmett from his father, but when he died, George felt the need to be closer to his mother and other members of his family and so he moved to Stoke Row. His brother, Tom Seymour, who was also a blacksmith, lived at Shiplake.

Around 1924 George took over the forge beside the house, then owned by the Delafield family, which is now known as 'Cherry Tree Cottage' in Newlands Lane. For a while, the Seymours lived in School Lane but in about 1928 the cottage to which the forge was attached became vacant, so George moved his family in. He then only had to pop through the door and he was in his workplace!

The forge was fired with special coal which kept very hot. Mr Seymour's main work was shoeing horses, (especially for the Star Brush factory) and making parts for farm machinery, though he sometimes did ornamental ironwork. Another of his jobs was to put iron 'tyres' on wooden cart wheels. For this work he used a circular iron platform, that held the wheel, while he put on the heated tyre which was quickly doused with water so it shrank to fit.

George Seymour, outside 'The Forge' on the Reading Road.
By kind permission of Reg Seymour.

208

Cherry Picking

When they were in blossom, the cherry trees at Highmoor and Stoke Row were a great attraction to trippers from Reading. The chapter on the Maharajah's Well demonstrates the value of the cherry orchards, the one beside the Well providing an income for the Well Keeper. In the earlier years of this century, the local women and children picked the cherries and sold them in the markets of Reading and Oxford.

The season lasted about eight weeks, from early June to the end of August and by the 1920s often as much as two tons of cherries left the village daily on carts, the bulk of which went to Oxford Market. By this time the men were doing the work as well. Wally Biggs, of Stag Farm, Stoke Row, preferred to cart his cherries into Reading three times a week, where they fetched 2/6d a sieve. The cart licence cost 15/-, so a fare paying passenger was welcome on the return journey.

Mr Biggs recalled: "The main varieties of cherry were: *May Dukes, Ambers (Whiteheart), Coxeters, Napoleons, Beef Hearts, Governor Woods, Purples, Watlington Blacks* and *Shiners.*" How many people could identify even a few of those, even though some may be still growing around here today?

Cherry Orchard, Stoke Row.　　　　　　　　W. J. Taylor, Post Office, Stoke Row

Cherry trees in bloom at Stoke Row, circa 1905. Kindly lent by Cecil Lambourne.

The fruit had real value to the local women and children, who depended on the extra income for clothing, especially shoes. Many of the 'townies' did not always appreciate this, as is shown by an extract from the *Henley Standard* of 29 July 1892:

"In accordance with an ancient custom, Highmoor was visited by great numbers of people on Sunday last. The majority of the visitors were conveyed in brakes from Reading. The place of rendezvous was the Commons at Lower Highmoor (the area between the Dog and Duck and Highmoor Hall) which is well covered with cherry trees. On their arrival the most nimble of the visitors immediately made an ascent of the trees, throwing the cherries down to their friends.

The inhabitants have great cause for complaint in the wilful destruction of the trees and the inroads people make upon the private property of persons who live on plots of land surrounding the Commons.

An old widow, whose maintenance for the greater part of the year depends on the sale of her fruit in the cherry season, had one tree entirely spoilt by the visitors.

There can be no doubt that if the persons who committed this damage were aware of the circumstances of the old lady, they would have at once desisted when they were requested. Probably more will be heard of this in the Police Court.

It is hoped that these visitors, who will probably pay us another visit next Sunday, will not attempt to strip or damage the trees in close proximity to the cottages, as there is a distinct agreement between the Lord of the Manor and the tenants as to the trees so situated.

There are certain trees accessible to all, but those mentioned in the agreement are reserved for the special use of the neighbouring cottagers. It is well that this should be made known and that the 'cherry pickers' should distinctly understand that a recurrence of last Sunday's conduct may lead to serious consequences."

Arthur Smallbone remembered a time when he earned himself the nickname of 'Electricity', which was something of a novelty at the time. "A new power cable had recently been erected through the upper branches of the tree and, not realising that it was live, I took a hold of it and was thrown off the ladder with my clothes on fire. Fortunately I landed on the hedge and suffered no permanent injury, other than a burnt out watch and waistcoat.

One time I picked 500 lbs of Whitehearts from a single tree at The Hope at the rate of a sieve an hour."

Setting the long 'fruiting' ladders was a considerable feat of strength and balance and required judgement born of long experience. Later on, people from the towns came out on a 'pick your own' basis and the extension to the Crooked Billet was built with these visitors in mind.

Many a charabanc came out to Stoke Row to view the cherry blossom in the spring. They came again in the summer, this time loaded with those who came to pick the fruit. It was hot and thirsty work and all the local public houses benefited from visitors.

As recently as the 1960s, Stoke Row and Highmoor were spectacular at cherry blossom time, but sadly, today, the trees are not pruned and cared for as they were and many have deteriorated.

A sketch of the old Stoke Row Windmill. Kindly lent to the Stoke Row News by Mrs Absalom.

Flour Milling

Few people realise that there used to be a windmill in Stoke Row. It stood in the south-east corner of the Village Green, on the site of a pair of cottages which are today known as 'Coggins Cottage' and 'Millstone Cottage'. The former, named after Constable (later Sergeant) Coggins, the village policeman who lived at this house, which was once owned by the police. It has a millstone at its front gate and 'Millstone Cottage' has one as its doorstep. The foundations of both these houses are thought to have been partly those of the windmill.

In his memoirs, published in the *Stoke Row News* in January 1966, Jacob Bauer wrote: "Often, with local children, I would climb up inside the windmill among the wooden wheels, and have played on the steps of a cellar which connected the mill with 'Windmill Cottage'." This cottage still stands today, in the corner of the Village Green. There is reputed to have been an underground passage between the mill and 'Windmill Cottage', the miller's home."

Miss Cecily Turner, the well-keeper and school teacher wrote in the same magazine in July 1966: "The mill was a substantial structure, built of brick and flint stones. The miller was known as 'Miller Munday'. People used to go gleaning in the fields years ago, then took the corn to be ground at the mill. There was always a roadway to the mill across the Common (now more often called the Village Green). My earliest recollection of the mill was with one broken sail, children used to play in and around it. Some years before the cottages were built it had fallen into decay. I do not think it was used since 1840."

Other Crafts and Trades

Many other rural crafts, such as charcoal making, hedge-laying and besom broom making, were carried out in Stoke Row and Highmoor. John Cotterell was the most famous of the besom broom makers and followed the craft his father taught him. John's sister, Edna Lambourne, recalled: "In the summer, on Sunday evenings after tea, the whole family would go for long walks, though it was usually partly so my father could look at the underwood for peasticks and beanpoles for the following year, or at birches for besom broom making." Happily, John's son, Mark Cotterell, has taken up the craft again and is often to be seen at Steam Rallies and Craft Fairs, demonstrating his handiwork.

John Cotterell, with one of his finished brooms. Kindly lent by Mrs Edna Lambourne (nee Cotterell)

Employment in the Village Today

In more recent years these old village crafts have been replaced by other forms of employment at the two small factory sites, one of which is the recently rebuilt Vanalloys Business Park. In her book *In for a Penny*, Betty Searby tells the story of the business that her husband, John, and she ran successfully for many years, converting vans into mobile shops, using metal alloys (hence the name Vanalloys). It is a most interesting book, in which Betty records many of her amusing poems and stories.

In one of the 'Getting to Know your Neighbour' series that I wrote for the *Stoke Row News* in 1982, John and Betty also told me how they started in 1948, fitting out standard trailers to suit the customer, eg fish and chips, cakes and bread or ice-Cream. "J Lyons and Co commissioned several for marketing their product 'Bev' coffee, Mecca ordered some as refreshment stands for the Royal Parks and many more were used as offices when so many buildings had been demolished.

Later the trailers were redesigned with aluminium extrusions, with or without wheels and often with colourful awnings. Then John got the idea of making mobile fruit displays which shopkeepers could wheel out to the fronts of their shops. This gradually brought Vanalloys into shopfitting and in the end they were doing work for shops up to 50 miles away. Altogether they fitted out almost 1000 grocery and greengrocery shops – they also made windows and entrances for garages, ladies' and gentlemen's outfitters, and even bookmakers!

They also produced some 50 shops and kiosks for Marshall Shops Ltd for the sale of cigarettes and confectionery. They also put in office fronts for British Airways all over the northern hemisphere, from Norway to Khartoum. Qantas also have a Vanalloy shopfront in their Piccadilly office and so we see this little Stoke Row firm has connections all over the world, from Scandinavia to Australia."

In the early 1990s the old buildings were replaced with smart brick built units, where people work in industries from photography to clock repairing and light engineering to refrigeration.

There are also several little firms on the smaller Crest Estate, between the church and Uxmore and the old sawmill is now used by a company specialising in exhibitions.

The Vanalloys Business Park, drawn in 1995 for the Stoke Row Appraisal by Avril Bryant.

12.   The Villages at Play

At a time when people in towns paid for their entertainment in theatres, music halls and later in cinemas, country folk amused themselves. Before the popularity of the motor car, recreation in these two villages usually took the form of Sports Days, Concerts and Outings. Above all, it was local sports that occupied the minds of most of the men and provided the main topic of conversation in the local pubs.

It was not only sport that provided entertainment. The Church and Chapel also occasionally gave the local adults and children 'somewhere to go'. Ted Evans recounted: "Every two or three years during the early 1920s, an Evangelist came to Stoke Row at the invitation of William Brazil, a strong supporter of the Chapel. Mr Moon, for that was his name, parked his black caravan on Alma Green and put up a marquee. Part of the fence was taken down around the site, which was more or less a small field with Alma Green Cottage in the middle, and people came in droves every evening. There was no charge, but a collection was taken during the service.

When I was about 11 or 12 years old, the Vicar of Highmoor, Rev John Hughes, gave a series of lantern slide shows on weekday evenings in Highmoor Church. The programme started with a few hymns and then followed the slides, usually of the Holy Lands. Part of the show was a great novelty as it consisted of jerky, moving pictures; probably this was an epidiascope. Again there was no charge, just a collection."

Few people know that Stoke Row had a Ladies' Cricket Team in 1909.
This photograph was taken in August of that year and kindly lent by James Bennett.

Stoke Row Football Club c 1920. Fred Carter kneeling front right,
the others are unknown. Kindly lent by David Carter of Maidstone.

Unknown young cricketers at Stoke Row, c 1910. Kindly lent by John Holroyd.

This photograph shows a Bank Holiday Sports, including a Marathon Race. It was taken in 1911. Kindly lent by Mrs Kathleen Dyer (nee Howells).

Highmoor Athletic Club Cricket team, c 1940. Standing: Bill Archer (later killed in the RAF), George Meheux (captain), George Stevens, Cecil Welsford, Robin Denham, Laurie Wells, Harold Summers and William Brakspear (umpire). Seated: George Jackson, Reg Green, Agnes Treadwell (scorer), Charlie Edwards and Harry Wise.

This 1900 photograph shows that a small band had been brought in for the occasion, and there were boat swings and other family amusements. Kindly lent by Hilary Fisher.

"In the early 1920s," Josh Main related, "Wokingham London Road team came to play cricket at Stoke Row and brought a pigeon with them. They beat Stoke Row and this meant they had won the League. The Pigeon was then sent home with the good news!" He then added: "Quite often the season ended with a 'Social'."

In 1950, the Stoke Row Cricket Club celebrated with a 'Swop the Sexes Fancy Dress'.

Back row: 'Boodle' Slade, Jim Carter, Alan Rosser, Mrs Hilda Tilby, Mrs King, Mrs 'Tutty' Edwards, Mrs George Ruddle, Phyllis Edwards and Mrs Aggie Brown.

Second row: Ernie Stallwood, Sonna Powell, Fred Carter, - ? - , Sheila Brown, 'Mick' Franklin, Nina Johnson, Bernie Heath, Percy Collis, Reg Fullbrook, Bill Slade, Alf Turner, Bert Bonner and Ivy Collis.

Third row: Mrs Rosser, Mrs Dora Carter, Floss Brown, Mrs Bert Carter, Margaret Stallwood (golliwog), Mrs Lil Carter, - ? -, Mrs Millie Cordery, Mrs Ivy King

Seated on ground: George Ruddle (fairy), Eddie Rosser, Johnnie Brown, Isobel Gillett, Beatrice Johnson, Maggie Butler, Colin Collis, Bill Butler and Bill Brakspear (umpire).

This photograph is reproduced with the kind permission of Peter and Julia Franklin.

Stoke Rovians often put chairs from The Cherry Tree into a metal tyred lorry belonging to Albert ('Bert') Carter (seen here smoking his pipe) to go to 'away' cricket matches. By kind permission of John Holroyd.

A lovely picture of Clifford and Johnny Brown fishing at Henley, in about 1926. By kind permission of Mrs Ruby Chapman (nee Brown).

Charabanc outing from Highmoor, c 1925. Note the legend on the side of the vehicle that shows it was owned by J White of Castle Street, Reading. His logo, J W, in an oval ribbon, tied with a bow, was painted on the side. The speed limit was 12 miles per hour!

Ted Evans remembered the games children used to play in school break times – among these was "flicking cigarette cards to see who could get them the furthest. The winner got the lot then!" The aim was to collect a set of these little cards, which were about 3" long x 1.1/2" wide. A card came with each packet of cigarettes. Woodbines were 5 for 2d, 10 for 4d and Players, which were better quality, cost 11.1/2d for 20. Subjects included Kings and Queens of England, Actors and Actresses, Flags, Footballers, Signalling, etc.

Boys also made whistles from tree boughs. They sometimes used elder, "but young ash was the best. You cut it down with a knife, put it into your mouth to wet it and then you twisted it and the bark came loose After that you cut a V in the top and you blew through the end, pushing the bark up and down to vary the notes."

'Tipcat' was another favourite pastime. "You got bits of stick, about 4.1/2" long and about 3/4" thick and shaved the ends off to a point. Then you laid the stick down flat and hit the pointed end with another stick. As you did so, it spun up into the air and then you hit it as far as you could. The winner was the one who hit his stick the furthest!"

Another much-played game was 'Ducks and Drakes', which involved skimming stones across one of the many old water-filled clay pits in the locality. One hot summer's day when they had decided to have a bathe and had taken all their clothes off, they were splashing about and having a great time when Miss Turner, the maiden lady schoolteacher, came past and they had to stay under the water until she had gone. "It would never have done for us to be seen in the altogether!" he confessed.

On dark nights the village lads would play a dangerous game known as 'Dicky, Dicky Dyke'. This was done with a lamp, a battery operated bicycle lamp was safest, but often they could only get hold of carbide or oil lamps. "You hid the lamp under your clothes and then showed it for a few moments before covering it up with your coat again, while the others shouted: 'Dicky, Dicky Dyke, show us your light!' When the 'flasher' was located he was 'out' (of the game). The modern meaning of 'flasher' was unknown then!" Ted laughed.

One year a Concert Party came to Stoke Row and took over the Village Hall. They gave a show every night and charged 6d. Ted thinks they "came from the North" and one of the group was a girl, known as 'Micky Kelso'; she dressed as a man and was a stand-up comic. There was also a "wonderful baritone". When the audience declined, towards the end of the week, this singer would do decorating jobs about the village, especially where heights were involved. He fearlessly climbed on to the Church roof to repair it and also painted black the metal chimney of the Star Brush factory.

This Concert Party probably rented the Village Hall for a small sum, about 5/- a week and, though some of them lodged with people in the village, others slept the night in the Hall. One night they played at Checkendon and another at Highmoor. Ted and his pals went to see them there as well, even though they had already seen the show in Stoke Row – and they had to walk there and back!

When they were older, Ted and his friends used to go up to Nettlebed to "the pictures" in the Working Men's Club. When they were still at school they were allowed in for 3d but when they went out to work they were charged 6d. They went most Saturday nights while the film shows lasted and had great amusement from the antics of Harold Lloyd, Charlie Chaplin, Snub Pollard and Tom Mix.

There were also exciting serials, like The Phantom Foe, which encouraged the local young folk to return week after week, to see what happened to the hero or heroine. Again, they walked to and from Stoke Row, usually in the dark, but it was quite safe to do so then, for there were so few cars about.

Another story Ted told me was about a wind-up gramophone that the local lads had. Ted was very friendly with Roland Page and Cyril Walter. They all owned this old American cylinder phonograph. The machine had lost its spring, so they jacked up an old cart, and harnessed the flywheel of the phonograph to the band of the hub of the cartwheel with string and made it play records that way. He recalled: "We had great fun altering the speeds of the records – one was *The Laughing Policeman!*"

Mrs Daisy ('D') Newman (nee Wells) related: "Among the 'recreations' that the children enjoyed most was, believe it or not, to watch Mr Absalom of School Lane kill a pig by slitting its throat. Older pigs, known as 'bacon' pigs then had their hair burnt off, but if the animal was under three years old it was known as a 'porker' and its hairs would come off when the carcass was put into boiling water.

It was then hung up and Mr Absalom would make a slit down the middle and take out the 'chitterlings' or entrails which were then sold at 3d - 6d, dependent on the size of the pig. The women who bought the chitterlings would wash them, over and over again in salt water and eventually they were fried – very tasty indeed!" Daisy remembered, her mouth watering! "The local boys would be given the pig's bladder which, again when washed in salt water, was blown up to make a football."

Albert Powell of Wellside Villas started up a boxing club for the young lads of Stoke Row – they used to meet in the Village Hall. Mr Powell had been in the Army – in the Sudan in 1901, spending the summers in the cooler area of the Troodos Mountains of Cyprus. He was also in the First World War and was one of 'The Old Contemptibles' at the Battle of Mons in France. Of course, the boys looked up to him.

A Darts Club outing, from the Dog and Duck, Highmoor, in the summer of 1953. The day was spent at the Arnold House Hotel, Brighton. Kindly lent by Pat Sparrowhawk.

Back row: Ken Bradford, Kim Wells, Stan Harwood, Bill Lunnon, John Britnell, Alf Stevens, Dick Wells and George ('Preacher') Smallbones.
Second row: Gladys Bradford, Val Lunnon, Mrs Jim Wells, Ruth Howlett, Sid Saunders, Roger Bradford, - ? - and Arthur Webb.
Third row: Skib Webb, - ? -, Ann Britnell, Mrs Webb, Harry Venn, Louise Stevens, Annie Britnell, Louisa Wells, Ada Britnell and her husband Art.
Children also went: Derek Venn, Chris Bradford, Patsy Lunnon, Johnny Stevens, Linda Britnell, David Lunnon, Pat Bradford and William Lunnon.

The childhood memories of these country people nearly always seem to have been happy ones. Mrs Joan King (nee Cox) who now lives in Sonning Common, and her brother Bob, grew up in Highmoor. They lived in the further of the pair of Church cottages, opposite the church. When the family left Highmoor, Joan was aged fourteen and her brother was eight.

In later years she wrote this for the Sonning Common Women's Institute: "My childhood was spent in Highmoor in the 1920s and 1930s. The beechwoods surrounding the village were our playground; we spent many happy hours playing 'houses' or hide and seek, or just wandering in the leafy glades.

Every Christmas all the village children were invited to a party in the Memorial Hall, given by Mr Arthur Denham, a village benefactor. We had a lovely tea and played the usual games, my favourite being 'Nuts in May'. The schoolchildren gave a display of country dancing, which we practised for weeks. To round off the celebration, each child was given a present from the tree, and an orange and sweets.

The same benefactor arranged a super bonfire on Guy Fawkes night on the school common; we children had to collect as much brushwood as we could in the preceding weeks, to help to make the bonfire. On the night, each child was given a packet of fireworks – Sparklers, Golden Rain, etc. There was a handsome Guy and colourful rockets, and we all had a grand time.

In spring, we searched for primroses and violets and then bluebells. Our summers were spent in the woods, or playing cricket on the common. Later, we went mushrooming and blackberrying, and collected acorns. We sold the acorns to a lady who kept pigs. (This was Mrs Stallwood (nee Leader) of the Woodman public house). She gave us one penny for a gallon – a gallon of acorns was an awful lot! The money we made [which wasn't much] we used to spend at Nettlebed Fair in October, which was one of the highlights of the year. In winter we went wooding, collecting all the old dry wood for fuel at home.

There was no television; we had to make our own entertainment. Every week in Highmoor Memorial Hall, we had a Family Social Club, which cost 3d. On arrival we would draw for a partner, the children separately from the adults. The first half of the evening we played games like darts, rings, shove-ha'penny and whist, one pair against another, recording our scores on a card; the highest score of the evening gained a prize. We had refreshments, tea and cakes, then the second half of the evening was dancing and games, Musical Chairs, etc. We all enjoyed our evening out! Some other forms of entertainment were Concerts – sketches, songs, recitations, performed by local people, and also travelling concert parties, which were always well attended.

Henley was our nearest town, and we would often cycle there. There was also a bus, run by a man from Stoke Row; I think his name was Jackman. After a Saturday evening at the cinema, the bus would be crowded coming home – but Mr Jackman would always say 'There's plenty of room at the back!' although we were packed like sardines! Consequently, when we came to Greys Hill, we had to get out and walk to the top.

Another time on the bus, in a very thick fog, Mr Jackman asked, "Does anyone know where we are?" to which some village wag replied, "You be in the b..... ditch!" (This was Jenny Russell, who lived in Holly Close, her parents looked after the Well, opposite). We eventually arrived home safely. These are just a few of my memories of a happy childhood spent in a close-knit village community."

Three young Stoke Row 'Flappers', 1925. Ivy Lester, Hilda Chapman and Lily Johnson on an outing to Bognor. Kindly lent by Mrs Ruby Chapman (nee Brown).

The Stoke Row Drama Group

The Stoke Row Drama Group has been entertaining villagers for over 20 years. One of its first productions was *Farewell, Farewell, Eugene* in April 1977. That year they also amused the village with a Christmas Revue which was billed to be 'Full of Eastern Promise'.

Since then the Drama Group have usually put on a play every winter and productions have included Sam Cree's *Don't tell the Wife*, Alan Ayckbourn's *Ten Times Table* and Derek Benfield's *Post Horn Gallop*.

They have usually concentrated on comedy – Bill Dunn's role as Dame Daffodil in the 1990 pantomime *Sing a Song of Sixpence* and Gordon Sinkinson's interpretation of Dr David Mortimer in the 1999 farce *It Runs in the Family*, are some that will never be forgotten!

Several lady members of the Drama Group are also members of the SRWI and perform plays each year for its members, and for a few years there was a Youth branch of the Drama Group.

224

STOKE ROW DRAMA GROUP PRESENTS

A COMIC NIGHT
OF DRAMATIC *The Farndale Avenue Housing*
DISASTER WITH *Estate Townswomen's Guild*
Dramatic Society's

Production of

Macbeth

Grrrrrr

A comedy by David M'Gillivray and Walter Zerlin Jnr
This is NOT Shakespeare...at least not as we know it, Jim

STOKE ROW VILLAGE HALL
Thursday 28th, Friday 29th and Saturday 30th March 1996

The front cover of the programme for the 1996 production of the Stoke Row Drama Group.

'Farewell, Farewell, Eugene', presented in April 1977. Left to right: Mrs Gregory, Joyce Skinner, Joyce ?, Laureen Williamson, Gordon Sinkinson, Esme Turner, Sarah Dunn and Stephen Rivers. Reproduced by kind permission of the Henley Standard.

225

1st Stoke Row Scout Group

The 1st Stoke Row Scout Group was formed in 1973 with a Cub Scout Pack: the Scout Troop opened the following year and the Beaver Scout Colony in 1986.

The Group is still one of the most thriving organisations in the village with more than a hundred children and leaders meeting in Stoke Row Village Hall each Wednesday evening. Liz Gibbins told me:

"The boys and girls enjoy a wide range of activities, eg adventure camps, fun days, gliding, hiking expeditions, caving and rock climbing. Also many forms of sport: football, cricket, swimming, cycling and athletics as well as cultural pursuits such as chess, mastermind contests, concerts, drama, cooking, arts and crafts.

The aim of scouting is to promote the development of young people to achieve their full potential in mind, body and spirit as responsible citizens. The method used is an enjoyable and attractive scheme of progressive training. An important part of Scouting is to provide service to the community which in Stoke Row includes helping with the village Litter Blitz, Sue Ryder Home, local hospitals, steam rallies, churches and various charities."

Mrs Wendy Thatcher, Queen's Guide Teresa Kozakiewicz, Mrs Barbara Cox, Leader and Mrs Daphne Stallwood with the boys of the 1st Stoke Row Cub Scout Pack in October 1973. By kind permission of the Berkshire Mercury.

Colin Allum of Stoke Row and Dan Seymour of Peppard (both later became District Commissioners) with Tim Brazil (15) and Neil Simpson (16), both of whom had just won the Chief Scout's Award in July 1980. By kind permission of the Henley Standard.

75 years of Scouting was celebrated in March 1983 by the Stoke Row Group with a 'Gang Show' which traced the history of Scouting. Photo by kind permission of the Henley Standard.

Johnny Morris, the famous zoologist and television personality, presenting World Conservation badges to twelve Stoke Row Cub Scouts in July 1980, namely Richard Weller, Tim Griggs, James Kendal, Robert Sinkinson, Oliver Nowell, Gavin Bartlett, Stephen Collis, Simon Panting, Dominic Wicks, Robin Payne, Christopher Fulton and Malcolm Scanlon. The gentleman with him is Brigadier Dixon of Henley.

Kate Fotherby, leader of the very active Beaver section of 1st Stoke Row Scouts, with their prize pumpkin in 1996. Photograph by kind permission of the Henley Standard.

Film and television actor, George Cole, who lives in Stoke Row, with a group of Cubs in about 1975. Chris Sayer, Colin Maycock, Michael Hartley, Alistair Arnott, Jeremy Brazil, Edwin Trout and Laurence Homer. By kind permission of the Henley Standard.

Watched by Trevor Gibbins, Mrs Jane Brazil cuts the cake on the occasion of her retirement, after 24 years with the 1st Stoke Row Scout Group. For 19 years she had been Chairman of the Executive Committee. By kind permission of Mrs Jane Brazil.

The Stoke Row Steam Rally

The Stoke Row Steam Engine Rally, now a thriving annual event, started as quite a small affair in 1980 and was called by the attractive name of 'Puff 'n' Stuff'. Its founders, among whom were the Greenaway family and Alan Cox, set it up in order to raise money for the restoration of the Maharajah's Well.

At first it was held in a field behind the bungalows that are opposite the church, but for many years it has taken place at Nuffield and includes steam engines, rollers, tractors, vintage cars and commercial vehicles, motor cycles, organs, stationary engines, etc.

In 1998 it attracted more than 250 vintage exhibits, as well as a host of sideshows, which often include demonstrations of traditional woodland industries and country crafts, such as the making of tent pegs, besom brooms, wattle fences, etc.

Between 1994 and 1998 it raised more than £20,000 for local churches and schools, including those at Ipsden, Goring and Woodcote, as well as Stoke Row.

According to the weather, anything between 4000 and 10,000 people attend each year, participants and visitors coming from all over the country to this popular event.

The weather in May 1981 was very wet and resulted in near disaster for the Steam Rally. Even a steam engine had to be pulled out with Richard Jackson's tractor! By kind permission of the Henley Standard.

A Fowler Road Roller beside Stoke Row Village Green, making its way to the 1991 Steam Rally. The owner, Mr Ralph Fear, is at the rear, with Lucy Hemphill. Richard Hemphill was driving the roller. Photograph by Rev John Harrington.

The Women's Institute

The Women's Institute movement was started by a Mrs Adelaide Hoodless in Stoney Creek, Ontario, in 1897, after she lost a baby through the feeding of contaminated milk. This wonderful organisation has now spread throughout the world and for many years in the first half of the 20th century it worked to educate women in hygiene and home crafts. In the latter decades it has widened its role to include influencing government, as well as educating and entertaining its members, and is the largest women's organisation in Britain.

Highmoor had a branch of the WI which was started in 1956, under the Presidency of Mrs Joyce Spicer. She recalled that, among the founder members was Pam Crosland, the Treasurer and Barbara Martin, the Secretary. "Barbara was a very good organiser and arranged many enjoyable outings to London, to Brighton and to theatres, etc. We had excellent speakers and classes in all sorts of crafts. We were very proud of our Christmas Fairs, which helped to raise money for the WI. Also, we had wonderful Harvest Suppers and Christmas dinners." Joyce added with relish.

"At the time of the International WI's 75th Anniversary in 1972, Barbara Martin went to a Garden Party at Buckingham Palace. When she returned, she told us all about it and how fearful she was lest the Queen should speak to her and ask what Highmoor WI were doing to celebrate the occasion. At that time we had done nothing, but we later planted a tree in the grounds of Highmoor Memorial Hall. Sadly, today it is overshadowed by the horse chestnut trees which have now grown so large.

Also, we had a wonderful party at our house, 'Upway'. It was an excellent group, very friendly too, as we only numbered about 25 and everyone worked happily together," she remembered, smiling.

"In the end, several ladies moved away and our numbers became too few to make it viable to have speakers and classes. We closed down in 1986, when Janet Leaver was President. It was very sad. Some members went to Rotherfield Greys and some to Peppard, while others joined the Nettlebed Institute. They were thirty highly successful and happy years for the Highmoor WI."

This photograph was taken at the 25th Anniversary Party of the Stoke Row WI in 1981.
By kind permission of the Henley Standard.

The Stoke Row branch of the Women's Institute was also started in 1956, with a membership of 55, under the Presidency of Mrs Biggs. Lady Brunner, OBE JP, of Rotherfield Greys, who was Chairman of the National Federation of Women's Institutes from 1951 to 1956, and one of the founder members of the WI's Denman College, attended the first meeting. It was recorded in the Minute Book that the Tortoise Stove in the Village Hall was lit early, so as to warm the room. A Mr Mercer gave a talk on 'Magic and Mirth'.

The following year the Institute formed its own Drama Group, which started with a play called *One Wedding, Two Brides!* Since then, at least once a year, and sometimes more often, the SRWI Drama Group has performed plays and sketches to entertain SRWI members and people in other villages.

In recent years the membership has declined slightly. Most women go out to work and have cars of their own which can take them to other localities for their education and entertainment.

Nevertheless, Stoke Row WI still offers fun, education and friendship to about 35 members who meet each month in the Village Hall. They enjoy speakers and demonstrations on all sorts of subjects, and outings to various parts of Britain and Europe as well as helping with village events – including providing the teas at the Steam Rallies. One of its most successful ventures is the SRWI Darts Team.

In May 1996, the Stoke Row WI belatedly celebrated its 40th Anniversary. Among those present for the Anniversary Supper were founder members Sybil Brown, Muriel Asquith, Pat Achurch, Mrs Gregory, Rose Textor, Joyce Skinner and the President Esme Turner. By kind permission of the Henley Standard.

The Village Halls

After the First World War, each village developed what were known as Recreation Grounds – we usually say the words quickly, but in fact we mean a place where people can 're-create' their tired bodies and spirits and generally 'let their hair down'.

Before the Stoke Row Village Hall was constructed, the only place for recreation of any kind was the 'Iron Room'. This very grim, unattractive name was given to a small meeting hall which was erected on the Glebe land between the Church and the Vicarage in 1905 by Rev Herbert Harben Appleford, Vicar of St John's Church at Stoke Row. It was probably constructed of corrugated iron.

By 1909, its ownership seems to have been in some doubt, as testified by copies of letters and a statement which were found in the Vestry in recent years. In spite of the Vicar's efforts, the Hall was always known as the Iron Room. When it was no longer used as a meeting hall, probably when the present Village Hall was erected in the 1920s, it was let as a dwelling until it was pulled down a few years afterwards. A bus garage was later put up on the site.

The Stoke Row Village Hall today is much in demand. Gerry Ackerman informed me that "it is used by various local groups for a variety of activities. Regular users include Beaver/Cub/Scout groups, Aerobics classes five times a week, the WI and Parish Council once a month. Throughout the year the Hall is used for social functions – parties, wedding receptions and dances as well as for fund-raising events such as Jumble Sales, Darts Tournaments and the Church Christmas Bazaar.

The SODC use it for Local and General Elections as well as for Planning Applications and Hearings. Once a year the Stoke Row Village Hall Committee hosts a Senior Citizens' New Year Dinner and the Drama Group puts on a play in spring.

The Committee consists of volunteers and co-opted members from the regular user organisations." Indeed, it seems to be so much used that it may be necessary to replace it in the not-too-far-distant future with a more permanent building.

The Physical Training Recreation Ground Act, 1937, enabled Stoke Row to receive a grant of £600 in 1949 for improvement of its Recreation Ground, which is still in active use and now has a tennis court and car park. The pavilion is soon to be replaced with a much better structure.

There is also an excellent children's playground in the Well Orchard, which is regularly inspected by the Parish Council.

Highmoor has a Recreation Ground, too. Both Parish Councils, among their many responsibilities, keep an eye on these valuable pieces of land. Each village has a thriving Sports Club and Quiz team.

The Memorial Hall at Highmoor has recently been completely restored and it is hoped to rebuild it entirely one day. It is used by the Parish Council and the Quiz team as well as being booked for private functions. However, the chief user is the Highmoor Nursery School, which is run every morning during term time.

Stoke Row Village Hall. Drawn by Avril Bryant for the
Stoke Row Village Appraisal in 1995.

Highmoor Memorial Hall. Drawn by Avril Bryant in 1996.

235

The Stoke Row News

Partly because it is much larger, Stoke Row is more lively than Highmoor, which lost its 'heart' when the school and shop closed. Stoke Row has a Youth Club, Drama Group, Neighbourhood Watch, Babysitting Circle, Conservation Group, Scouts, Women's Institute, Aerobics Class, Sewing Bee and Garden Club.

With a circulation of 350 copies, *The Stoke Row News* plays a valuable part in keeping both villages informed of events to come, Chapel and Church services and news of all the organisations and happenings in both Stoke Row and Highmoor.

It was started in October 1965, as an outcome of the Village Association and has gone from strength to strength ever since. Recent improvements in computer technology have made the production easier, the layout of the 20 or so pages more attractive, and also enabled advertisements to be printed in the village by the team.

The front cover of the Stoke Row News.

However, the cover, with its intriguing diagrammatic map of Stoke Row, designed by Gundrada Sheridan in 1966, is always professionally printed, on the same cheerful yellow background.

The little red helicopter, in the top left-hand corner, continues to be coloured red by local children, in order to commemorate the visit by the Duke of Edinburgh, who landed on the village green in his red helicopter, in 1968, when he came to mark the centenary of the sinking of the Maharajah's Well.

The magazine is produced by voluntary labour, two ladies having notched up about 20 years each doing the printing and collating. This, together with the Highmoor subscriptions and the faithfulness of the advertisers, some of whom have been with the magazine for many years, keeps the price very low.

The author of this book has been Editor of *The Stoke Row News* since 1991 and enjoys all the contact it brings her with people of both villages and outside.

13. The Butcher, the Baker and... the Postman!

Until the Second World War and certainly before the First World War, the villagers were almost self-sufficient. When the motor-car became more common, people began to rely more on shops in Reading, Henley and Wallingford.

Up until 1903 a Shoe Maker was one of the classifications entered in the trade directories, which were issued by Kelly and/or the Post Office annually. Dolly Franklin told me that she and her mother used to go down to Wallingford twice a year to buy clothes, materials and other goods that were not stocked by the local shop. One of the most popular stores there was Field, Hawkins and Ponking.

Other folk have told me that Heelas would send clothes up from Reading 'on approval' to known good customers. People mended their own clothes, including boots and shoes and often sold or traded goods they made, such as honey or home-made fruit wines.

Stoke Row's earliest shop and post office, The London House Stores. The name implied quality. The recruitment poster dates this photograph to about 1913. Roland Page, the owner, is standing in the doorway, the children's names are unknown. Kindly lent by David Howells.

There were thrift clubs for those who wanted to save up for Christmas purchases. For reasons of economy almost everything was used and reused until it wore out completely. For example, dresses were hand-made and when they were past repair they were turned into aprons and eventually into rags for household cleaning purposes. Most people had a goat and a few hens; many kept a pig. Those who needed to transport goods such as logs, had a donkey and these animals nibbled the verges neat. All the cottages had open fires and the children were sent out to gather kindling wood and logs as soon as they came home from school. This wood had to be kept dry for months before it could be used so a good stock was always maintained.

Not all the food consumed in Stoke Row and Highmoor was purchased in the village shops. Fred Frewin delivered fresh fish and fruit daily.

Fred Frewin, fresh fish and fruit salesman, with his pony and trap. His wife is holding the reins. This photograph was taken in about 1910. Kindly lent by Mrs Rina Eaton (nee Hayes).

Stoke Row also had a butcher. Mr Heath had an abattoir at the rear of 'The Haven', in the main street. He delivered meat all around the area for many years.

Cottagers grew all their own vegetables, bottled fruit, made bread, cakes, jams and soups. They bought their milk and butter from local farmers who delivered to the door and sometimes bread or cakes from the local baker too.

Items like tobacco, sweets, rope, buckets, tools etc had to be bought from the shops, but a few local people still have rolling pins, bowls and other wooden goods that were turned locally. The front cover of this book shows people carrying wooden buckets that were probably made in the woods hereabouts and banded with iron by the local wheelwright.

In about 1948 Roland Page, who had had houses constructed next to the garage at Stoke Row, developed two of them into a shop. A year or so later the London House Store closed and the Post Office was transferred up the road into the new shop, called Stoke Row Village Store. Author's photograph of the exterior of the shop/Post Office with its new windows in 1999.

Today the Stoke Row Village Store is owned and run by Peter and Pat Armstrong, who sell a wide range of goods and provide a number of other services, such as dry-cleaning, shoe-repairing and tasty items baked in the shop. Photograph taken by the author in 1999.

Baking

There were two bakers in Stoke Row. One was Mr Keep, who came from Aldermaston and worked at The London House Stores, employed by Mr and Mrs Gillett. Mrs Lily Tayler (nee Johnson) remembered that his 'lardy cake' (ie made with lard) was a rectangular one, as opposed to the round type baked by Mr Lambourne, and was just a little bit better. Lily used to deliver the bread for Mr Gillett and can remember taking it round on foot, in a washing basket, when the snow was too deep to take the cart out.

However, there seems little doubt that the best one was Mr Arthur Lambourne, who was known as the 'Midnight Baker' as he often delivered fresh bread late in the evening if it was required. Mr Lambourne came to Stoke Row in about 1900 and took over an oven which had been built into the rear of Stag Farm (see also Stag Farm) by Wally Biggs' uncle, but it had never been used. About 1905 Mr Lambourne moved into a house built by 'T M' in 1822 on the edge of the Village Green. It had been occupied by a bootmaker, named Mr Rogers. Mr Lambourne rebuilt his workshop extension and converted it into a bakery. The little building beside the house served as a stable for his horse and cart. In 1948 his sons turned this into a bigger bakery.

Right up until electricity came to Stoke Row in about 1934, when women started to buy electric cookers, Mr Lambourne baked many Sunday dinners and especially turkey dinners at Christmas. He was also Churchwarden at St John's for over 40 years.

The Lambourne family, c 1930. Basil, Ivor, Cecil, and Gordon, with their parents.
By kind permission of Cecil Lambourne.

Eric Butler of Sonning Common told me that his mother, Mrs Margaret Butler, used to deliver bread for Lambourne's bakery and did so for 33 years in an old green Ford van, which had a spare wheel on the passenger door. She went out to Kingwood, Peppard and Sonning Common on Monday, Wednesday and Friday and to Uxmore, Checkendon and Woodcote on Tuesday, Thursday and Saturday.

Mrs Lily Tayler (nee Johnson) recalled that her mother bought a quartern of dough (ie enough for a four pound loaf) made by Mr Lambourne and brought it back to Dogmore Cottage in order to put sultanas in it and put it in a tin. It was then returned to Mr Lambourne for baking and brought home again hot, wrapped in a cloth. He also cooked dinners for the poorer folk in the village for 2d a time, especially in the summer when they hadn't got a fire going or if they had no 'cooking range'.

He had a small shop from which he sold dried goods, usually those associated with baking, such as flour, mustard, baking powder, a few sweets etc. John Holroyd remembered that his mother, Mrs Emily Carter, who lived at 'The Grubbins' (their garden was alongside Lambourne's house) used to shout across to Ivor Lambourne if she needed something and he would sell it to her 'over the garden fence'.

June Greenaway wrote in the *Stoke Row News* in November 1969:

"We are all saddened by the closing of the bakehouse, not only because no other bread is quite the same, but because of its close involvement in the history of the village. Mr Lambourne's career started at the age of 15 when he started work in an underground bakehouse in Oxford.

He originally baked at Taylor's shop (The London House Shop) and then at Stag Farm. The oven was put in the present bakehouse and business started there in 1905. After having worked in several other bakeries in Stoke Row he set up his own bakehouse with twin ovens which burned beech wood as well as coal.

Water for bread making was brought from the well in those days by means of a hand-pulled cistern on wheels, or with yokes and buckets. There was a stable at the bakehouse and delivery was by horse and cart.

For many years flour came from the Abbey Water Mills in Reading, which closed down in 1954. It then came from another water mill at Sonning. The latest supplier, Cox's Lock Mill, was originally a water mill but is not now water driven, although the wheat still comes up by barges from Weybridge, Surrey.

Cecil and Ivor Lambourne took over from their father in 1947 when they came out of the Army. In the last years of this family business the output was 600 loaves a day, as well as bread rolls, fruit cakes and buns – doughnuts and 'lardy cakes' were a speciality.

Arthur Lambourne died in 1962, aged 90. Many of his songs, particularly 'My Grandfather's Clock' enlivened the old 'Socials' in the Village Hall.

Cecil is the only remaining member of this large family who is still living at The Old Bakery, which is in the north-west corner of the Village Green – the bread ovens are still there in the adjacent bakehouse"

This picture shows Lambourne's Bakery on the Village Green at Stoke Row, taken in about 1920 by Collier of Reading. By kind permission of the Rural History Centre.

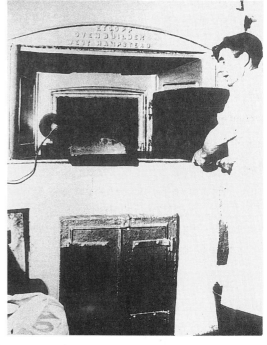

Ivor Lambourne making loaves ready for baking and his younger brother, Cecil, takes loaves from the oven. Photographs by Les Todd and kindly lent by Cecil Lambourne.

Postal Services

The first recorded postal delivery to Stoke Row was in *Gardener's Directory* for 1852: "Letters are received through the Wallingford Post Office." However, by August 1853, it would appear that some arrangements were made to send and receive letters to and from Stoke Row. A letter in the Post Office Archives to the Postmaster General, states: "Under this further report from the Surveyor, I submit that the Treasury may be applied to, to nominate another person to the office at Stoke Row." In 1854 the *Post Office Directory* nominated: "Miss Sarah Needle, National School-mistress and Postmistress. Letters arrive 9 am, dispatched 5 pm." In 1863 the Sub Offices at Stoke Row, was replaced with a pillar box but even by 1877 the post was still in charge of the schoolmistress, Mrs Kate Francis. (See also Stoke Row School).

This photograph, which was taken later than the previous one, probably in about 1920, and shows Rodney Page proudly posing outside his shop-cum-Post Office in his 1904 Argyll motor-car. The lady with the bicycle and dog is his daughter, Maud Howells (nee Page) and the men driving the carts are probably just off to deliver bread. Kindly lent by David Howells.

Rev Cyril Isherwood, in his 'Memories of Stoke Row', recalled: "When we first came to Stoke Row in 1891 there was no means of communication with the outer world, except by letter, as no telephone had been connected – the postman walked from Henley (6 miles). So my mother, who had always lived in the City of London, very soon had the telephone brought to the Post Office, which was also a shop and a bakery and sent the first telegram. (It is now a private home, 'Old London House').

The postage then was a halfpenny for a postcard and a penny for each letter. The charge for telegrams had to include the address of the person to whom the message was sent, so they were only used on special occasions."

William J Taylor was named in *Kelly's Directory* of 1895 as being the Sub-Postmaster at Stoke Row. He dealt with post, money orders, telegraph orders, express delivery, insurance and annuities.

Mrs Agnes Brown, who was the postwoman at Stoke Row in the early 1920s. This photo was taken outside The Oak. She lived at 'Firtree', then just a semi-detached cottage in Newlands Lane. She had four children: Dolly, Johnny, Ruby and Clifford. Photograph by kind permission of Mrs Ruby Chapman (nee Brown).

In 1899 the postman was 'mounted' and there was an allowance given for the keeping of a horse. The post office continued to be run by Mr Taylor until at least 1903. It is recorded in the Post Office Archives that in 1913 the Henley-on-Thames to Nettlebed and Stoke Row mounted posts were converted into a Mail Cart Service to Kingwood. There was a Contract payment and deliveries were revised. Cycles were supplied and an established appointment created.

In the *Henley Standard* on 4 November 1998, recalling entries '100 Years Ago', the following report appeared: "Stoke Row: The funeral of the postman took place on Sunday last. A E Compton, the rural postman for Stoke Row was only 36 years of age and he was taken ill on October 23rd and died a few days later from acute rheumatism.

The funeral was attended by 15 postmen, all in uniform and the deceased was carried by his postal colleagues. The church was crowded as the deceased was much respected on his walk. He leaves a widow and five children."

Ted Evans, born 1909, recalled that there were two postmen when he was a boy. The main one was Fred Jarvis and he operated from a hut on Alma Green. The other one was ex-Navy and he also cut the hair of the village men for just a few pence. The postman who delivered to Stoke Row between 1924 and 1930 was always affectionately known as 'Postie' Preston. Mrs Gillett was Postmistress from 1928 to 1949.

In 1993, John D Rogers, an independent postal historian, wrote an article for the *Stoke Row News* about the Post Office at Stoke Row and Highmoor:

"The Post Office, these days, is only the administrative and regulatory body which draws together three independent parts, The Royal Mail, Post Office Counters Ltd and Parcelforce.

Let us give chief consideration to the Royal Mail and firstly the red letter boxes, of which there are three types, pillar, wall and lamp, according to their mounting. Increasingly installed since the 1850s, their distribution and age give a good indication of the spread of population.

The existence of the two boxes on Witheridge Hill which, though not the first installed there, still mark out the original route used by the letter carrier. Increased literacy gave rise to more letter boxes in well-to-do areas or by large manor houses, examples of which can be seen widely around the vicinity of Henley. Of course, the age of a box is not always safe as an indicator, as larger boxes are sometimes installed later. Lorries demolish boxes which are (usually) replaced with more modern examples.

The modern box by the Stoke Row post office clearly marks the move in the early years of the present Queen's reign to remove and upgrade the smaller boxes in the post office wall or window, which usually had a door in the back to enable the postmaster to remove letters for hand cancellation – now a great rarity. This small type of letter box dates back to early times, when it was the duty of the local Postmaster to provide his own box – often made by the local blacksmith – resulting in an interesting range and diversity, prior to letter box standardisation.

Originally, mail was hand-cancelled at Stoke Row, then all was machine cancelled at Henley as labour costs spiralled and technology advanced. When the Reading MLO (Mechanised Letter Office) opened and full postcoding began, all addresses in the Henley parish were given a postcode starting with RG9. At present, a set of blue dots on the envelope indicate the delivery postcode, but soon this format will change, most addresses will be read by machine and a more sophisticated sorting to house numbers will begin. Here is the link to the volume of mail increase, spiralling labour costs versus increased competition from faxes and electronic mail. This is all a long way from the 1800s when, although it was true that a letter posted in Henley in the morning would reach London by the early afternoon, the volume of mail was a tiny fraction of that handled today, and the numbers of pairs of hands needed to forward each item meant an enormous unit cost – even when wages were very low.

Parcelforce has its automated centre at Winnersh Triangle, processing all local parcels and is one of the most modern in the country.

Recent years have seen a huge number of rural sub-post-offices close in the Henley area. Apart from Highmoor Cross, offices have been lost at Bix, Stonor and Nuffield to name but a few. Village residents must remember that the local sub-postmaster is only paid according to the amount of his transactions and if people do not use their local post-office it can easily become vulnerable to closure."

'Electronic Mail?' Cartoon drawn by Avril Bryant for the Stoke Row Appraisal in 1995.

The Telephone

The Checkendon Telephone Exchange opened in 1908, occupying a room at Checkendon Post Office, where the equipment was operated by the Postmistress, Mrs Pullen. An automatic exchange was built at Nuthatch in 1950 and a relief exchange at Woodcote was opened in 1966. In 1972 there were 930 subscribers on the Checkendon exchange and in 1974 the exchange enabled subscribers to use the new STD (Subscriber Trunk Dialling) system. No date is known for the inauguration of the Nettlebed Exchange, which serves Highmoor, although it is known to have been in existence by August 1915.

It would certainly amaze Mrs Isherwood, who had the first telephone brought to Stoke Row Post Office in the early 1890s so she could send messages to the outside world more quickly than by post, if she could come back today and see that we not only have a telephone in almost every home, but often several. Many are now used for 'email' and to access the Internet, whilst mobile phones are in use the world over.

Shops and Post Offices at Highmoor

Mrs Ada Britnell remembered that, when she was a child, "the woman who lived in the cottage, which later became 'The Little Manor House' on Witheridge Hill, sold sweeties to the children when they came out of school."

There was also a shop, run by George Page, at what later became 'Fipps Cottage' on Witheridge Hill. This old photograph shows that the left hand side of this pair of cottages was a shop. On the wall there is a sign which reads: G Page, Grocer, Draper.

The first record of postal services to Highmoor is contained in a letter dated 26 November 1857 to the Postmaster General: "I submit that, as proposed by the Surveyor, the post between Henley-on-Thames and Nettlebed be extended to Highmoor Hall and Highmoor and that, to accelerate the arrival of the Messenger at the end of his walk, the delivery at Nettlebed be transferred from him to the sub-Postmaster, an allowance of £5 a year being granted to the latter for the duty. Also that the Sub-Postmaster's salary be raised from £4 to £5 a year, according to the scale."

A report from Mr Good, dated 27 August 1858 begged: "I submit that James Bailey, late Messenger from Henley-on-Thames to Twyford, may be appointed to the situation of Messenger from Henley-on-Thames to Highmoor, which is now vacant."

The first Post Office at Highmoor was kept by Mrs Treadwell in the end of a row of terraced cottages known as Post Office Cottages. Thieves were about at Highmoor, even in Victorian times. In 1891, a report to the Postmaster General stated: "Mrs E Treadwell, Highmoor, Henley-on-Thames – Deposit of 2/- stolen."

Perhaps the worry of this theft made Mrs Treadwell give up the job of Postmistress. Frank Baldwin, in his 'Memoirs', related how his mother then took over:

"In 1889 Charles Baldwin and his wife bought the three terraced cottages, built 1860, which faced Highmoor Green, but they had to wait to occupy them, as Mrs Treadwell, the then Postmistress, was a sitting tenant.

Charles and Fanny Baldwin were married in 1881, when he was 28 and she was 20 and they continued living with her mother until they had five children, by which time they had saved up enough money for a home of their own.

...Later, in 1891, Mrs Baldwin took on the job of Postmistress at Highmoor, opening the front parlour of her tiny house, on the end of the row known as Post Office Cottages at Highmoor Cross, as a sub-post office. She delivered post every day, walking both morning and evening the two-mile circuit from Highmoor Hall, down to Lower Highmoor and then often to Bromsden Farm and back to the village. The post was collected from the box at her house and also from the postbox at the foot of Witheridge Hill (by the crossroads, where it still stands today) by the postman from Henley, twice a day.

Fanny Baldwin was one of the few people in Highmoor who had received an education, for which her mother had sacrificed 3d a week... It was through her mother's long-sightedness that Fanny's education stood her in good stead, not only enabling her to take on the job of Postmistress, which was simple enough to begin with, but also fitting her to carry on the work after the death of her husband; thus providing her with a small income to help her raise her family alone."

In later years the work became much more complicated, with pensions, forms etc. but, after her death in 1943, Frank found all her books to be in perfect order and "not a penny out."

Dolly Franklin told me: "In the 1920s the post came in a big red box, brought by a man with a cart. He sat up very high, from where he could see all around. After coming down from the top of Witheridge Hill to the bottom, he then went up the track to Greyhone and Peppard. He came down each morning at 7.00 am and our family used his approach as an alarm clock!" (See the Gentrification of Cottages). Ada Britnell remembered that "the postman was Freddie Green in the 1920s. He wore a cap with a peak at the back and at the front. He had a hut on the lower side of Witheridge Hill, where he made himself tea in between cycling round to deliver the letters. The children teased him dreadfully, knocking on his door and running away!"

Ada continued: "Jim Pickett was the Highmoor postman in the 1930s. He brought post up from Henley on his bicycle and based his day in a little tin hut on the grass verge at the foot of Witheridge Hill. He went out delivering post twice a day on his bicycle and had a *cat's whisker* radio in his hut."

Joan Tait informed me: "Mrs Kitty Baldwin (nee Smallbone) ran the Post Office from No. 1 Council Cottages, Highmoor Cross, from 1943 to 4 September, 1964. Thereafter the Post Office was run from another part of the village and then it was transferred to Shepherd's Green." This was closed down a few years later.

Post Office Cottages, Highmoor, 1982. This photograph was taken before the cottages were modernised. The original Post Office was in the furthest on the right. Later on, Mr and Mrs Baldwin moved to 'Ivydene', just out of sight, on the right. Photograph by the author.

The second Post Office at Highmore Cross, as it was spelled then. The letter box is in the wall at the side of the porch. This house was called 'Ivydene' and has since been enlarged. It is known today as 'Highmoor Cottage'. Kindly lent by Mrs Sibel Betts (nee Delafield).

Heath's Stores, on the 'New Road' at Highmoor, faced the road up to Witheridge Hill and was originally built by George Page in 1856 for his daughter to run. It probably changed hands several times. The Highmore Parish Magazine for January 1936 contained this advertisement.

Established 1856
W S Heath

THE STORES
Witheridge Hill
Near Henley-on-Thames

High-class Groceries and Provisions
Families waited upon Daily
Agent for the Royal Insurance Company

In this picture, taken in about 1930, are Knowlton Sweet, his daughter Gladis (who later married Sam Gardiner) and his son Leslie, with a little girl who was known as 'Ruby', who used to get her 'sweeties' at Mr Sweet's! Photograph by kind permission of Sam Gardiner.

In 1938, *Kelly's Directory* listed Thomas Griffin as shopkeeper but in 1939 his wife took it over. Perhaps her husband had to go into the army. In 1940 Mr D Rattley became the shopkeeper and for many years it was known as Rattley's Stores.

By the early 1960s, the shop was in the hands of a Mr and Mrs Gore, who finally closed it down and turned it into a private house. John and Jean Bridgman bought it in 1970, with some of the shop fittings still visible, especially in the kitchen. They named it, very aptly, 'Old Postings'.

14.   The Villages in Two World Wars

There is little doubt that Stoke Row and Highmoor, in common with every village in the country, suffered a great loss of men in both the First and Second World Wars. Brass memorial tablets on interior walls of both St John's church and the Chapel in Stoke Row read:

In Memory of those from this Parish
who lost their lives
in the Service of their Country
in the Great War, 1914 - 1918.

A J Absalom	F H Green	A Wells
W Brakspeare	G Green	F Wells
E Evans	H Green	G Wells
R Evans	J Green	H Wells
F Evans	G Horwood	J Wells
G Grace	A Stallwood	T Wells
		W Woods

Another brass plaque in the Church makes touching reading:

Henry Edmund Green
A Leading Seaman in HMS Monarch
who passed away 9th October, 1918.
His goodness and cheeriness
were an inspiration to us all.

It should be remembered that although many men bore the same name, this does not necessarily mean that they all belonged to the same family.

However the story of Edward Evans, as related by his son, Ted, is very poignant: "My father had been in the Navy for 12 years and when he came home he worked as a forester on the Nettlebed estate. When the First World War broke out in 1914 our family were at a Fete in Stoke Row. It was August Bank Holiday Monday and a telegram was delivered to my father's hand to order him to report back to the Royal Fleet Reserve at Portsmouth for training.

When Dad arrived at Portsmouth there was as yet no ship for him to join, so we all stayed in lodgings for a while. From time to time throughout the war my mother, Alice Evans, took us children down to Portsmouth when Dad's ship was in. These visits continued until my father died on 4 May 1918 aboard *HMS Terrible*, not long before the end of the First World War.

When my mother realised that Dad was not going to live (he died of double pneumonia, caused by exposure) she sent me with my friend to the cinema. Part way through the film the usherette came down to us and told my friend that they had to go home at once. When I got back I learned that my father had died." Telling me this story almost 80 years later, his eyes were moist.

Mrs Jennie Norris (nee Wixen) recalls seeing the coffin of L/S Edward Evans, draped with a Union Jack, being carried through the village. His seaman's cap was on top of the coffin and was buried with him.

On the wall of the Village Hall there is a Scroll of Honour, which lists all the men who fought for their country in the 1914-18 War. Even those not killed probably came back with many physical and mental wounds which lasted the rest of their lives.

Leading Stoker Edward Percy Evans and his wife, Alice (nee Green) on their wedding day, 4 August 1908. By kind permission of Mrs Irene Webb (nee Alder).

Home on leave. This photograph was taken behind The Hope (later renamed The Farmer), Stoke Row, in about 1915. It appears the men are drinking Wethereds Oatmeal Stout. Left to right: standing: Frank Wells, next to him is Pte Joe Wells of 1st Royal Berkshire Regiment who was later killed in France. On the right is Harry Green who was also killed in France. Seated: Albert ('Bert') Treadwell, Arthur Britnell, Frank Wells and Bill Evans. By kind permission of Mrs Lily Bishop (nee Treadwell).

Left: Sidney Pitt in 'convalescent blues', c 1916. The other soldiers are unknown. By kind permission of Mrs Joyce Martin (nee Pitt).

George Green, seen here aged 19.1/2 years, c 1915. He died in the sinking of HMS Derbyshire, in 1916, as did Lord Kitchener. By kind permission of Mrs Lenna Green (nee Archer).

His brother, Albert ('Jack') Green, here aged 18. This lad died of pneumonia two months after going into the army in 1918. The Armistice was declared shortly after his death. Both these photographs kindly lent by Mrs Lenna Green (nee Archer).

Returning to the village, even during the First World War there were evacuees in Stoke Row. Ted Evans remembers Maude Grindle and May Dabbs who came here to get away from the bombs dropped by the Zeppelins on the East End of London. When they arrived they were louse-ridden and had to be bathed and their clothes fumigated. Ted also recalled seeing a Zeppelin going to bomb London when his mother took him to King's Cross to see his aunt Florrie.

Mrs Daisy ('D') Newman (nee Wells), cousin to Ted Evans, recalled an incident in Stoke Row: "Near to the end of the First World War, when the children heard that an aerial balloon had come down in one of Mr Delafield's fields (off Cox's Lane) they ran off to see it without permission, so Mr Wilson, the headteacher at Stoke Row School, lined all the children up and caned the lot of them! This was an Army balloon, made of khaki material. On another occasion, not long afterwards, they heard that an aeroplane had also come down in a nearby field; at that time Mr Wilson took all the children to see it."

Highmoor

Although Highmoor was a smaller village, almost as many, seventeen, men lost their lives in the First World War. Their names are engraved on a commemorative plaque on the interior wall of Highmoor Church:

Fred Baldwin	George Grace	Reg Baldwin
George Green	George Earle	Albert Green
Wm Edwards	Albert Heath	Fred Edwards
Frank Heath	Francis Godley	George Horwood
Archie Stallwood	James Turner	George Wells

Three of these men are buried in Highmoor churchyard:

George Green, aged 20. Lost on HMS Hampshire 5.6.1916.

TR8/27535 Pte A Green, 36 Trg Reserve Btn. Killed 22.10.1918, aged 18.

45964 Pte R Baldwin, Wiltshire Regiment, killed 12.8.1919. (no age given).

Two other gravestones are dedicated to men not named on the church plaque:

George Ernest Arthur Leake, Capt, DSO, died Rouen, 2.6.1917, aged 29.

Frederick Charles, beloved son of Frederick and Rose Bailey, on active service in France, 30.4.1917, aged 19.

Women also enlisted in the First World War. Mrs Sarah ('Sally') Stone (nee Slade) in her WACS uniform (right), with a friend in 1916. By kind permission of Mrs Beryl Grismanauskas (nee Stone).

Gilbert Stone of Highmoor, who married 'Sally' Slade), when he was with the Royal Warwickshire Regiment during the First World War. Photograph kindly lent by Mrs Beryl Grismanauskas.

256

Officers of the Royal Berkshire Yeomanry, 1914 - 1918. Brigadier Crosland of 'Satwell Spinneys' is second from the left in the middle row. By kind permission of Maggie Cotterell.

Gilbert Stone (left, marked with an X) with his comrades, 'somewhere in France', during the First World War. By kind permission of Mrs Beryl Grismanauskas (nee Stone).

The Second World War

Many men, seeing the possibility of another war looming ahead of them, volunteered for the Territorial Army as early as 1938.

This very patriotic photograph of Tom Wells of Highmoor, in the Territorial Army on Salisbury Plain, shows him in the cookhouse. There was no preparation for a 'photocall' then, as can be seen by the state of his 'whites'! Kindly lent by Peter Wells.

Right: Gordon Lambourne of Stoke Row, home on leave from the Territorial Army, outside his home which was also the bakery. By kind permission of Cecil Lambourne.

Both these men returned from the war, but others were not so fortunate. Another brass plate was mounted on the wall of St John's Church at Stoke Row and also of the Chapel. They read:

To the memory of those who gave their lives 1939 - 1945

J H Bird, L/Cpl. Royal Marines, Killed 6th June 1944, aged 19

P L Clayton, Pilot Officer, RAF, Killed 6th June 1942, aged 20

G L F Hopkinson, Flying Officer, RAF VR, Killed 8th July 1943, aged 21

B Lambourne, Stoker, Royal Navy, H M S Gloucester.
    Killed 22nd May, 1941, aged 24

Jim Bird attended Stoke Row Primary School and, like his two brothers and his sister, went on to Rotherfield Greys Secondary School. The family lived in School Lane. He was a tall lad, weighed 16 stone, but carried no excess fat, for he was fond of boxing and kept very fit. His father was a builder's foreman, so it was natural that Jim should start as an apprentice with Waltons of Henley. He was under age when he volunteered in 1939, but his Uncle had been in the Navy for 30 years and his eldest brother, Brian, was already in the Senior Service, so he decided to join them. As he was only 17.1/2 they would not take him, so he went to the Royal Marines instead and told them he was 18, so he was accepted.

After a while Jim was promoted to Lance-Corporal and was sent on training courses in various parts of the country. While he was in Ipswich he met a girl of whom he grew very fond but, before their relationship could mature he was sent out to France on D-Day, 6 June 1944, aboard *HMS Copra*. It was while he was on this ship that he was killed when he was only 19 years of age. Son of Charles and Edith Bird, the name of Lance-Corporal James Harry Bird appears on the Roll of Honour at the Chatham Naval Memorial, Panel 84. His brother told me that their mother never recovered from the shock of losing her youngest son, so near to peace being declared.

Little is known about Pilot Officer Peter Levinge Clayton, except that his family lived in the house now known as 'Hilltop' opposite the church. He was a member of the Royal Air Force Volunteer Reserve and was killed on 6 June, 1940, whilst serving with the 149 Squadron. He was 20 years old. His parents, Charles Levinge and Esta Edith Clayton, moved to Bishops Stortford soon after the tragic death of their son.

Pilot Officer Clayton is buried in Adegem Canadian War Cemetery (the reason for his being buried in a Canadian cemetery is not known). This is about 20 miles from Bruges, not far from the Dutch border – perhaps his plane came down near there. A separate plaque is on the internal wall of St John's – probably his parents attended this church.

Flying Officer Geoffrey Frederick Laing Hopkinson was yet another young man who joined the RAF Volunteer Reserve. He served in 206 Squadron and was killed on 8 July 1943, aged 21. Mrs Lucy Parslow, who worked for Mrs Hopkinson during the war, told me that Geoffrey lived in London for much of the time, but he used to come home at weekends. She said: "He was a very handsome boy, tall and dark-haired." It seems that Mrs Hopkinson lived alone at 'The Quarries' (now known as 'Chiltern House', on the Reading Road) and, although she had a younger son, David, "she was devastated when she learned of Geoffrey's death." Geoffrey Hopkinson is buried at Enfidaville War Cemetery, about 100 km south of Tunis and the register containing details of his grave is kept at the local Police Station there.

Basil Lambourne's family were bakers – their bakery was beside their house on the Village Green. (See the chapter on Shops). His brother Cecil showed me photographs of Basil, a tall strong good-looking young man, who had a love of open-air life. When he left Stoke Row School he worked for his uncle at Kirklington, but came back later and took employment with the builder, Arthur Butler of Peppard. He liked dancing, too and courted a girl called Winnie Lamb from Goring.

Basil was called up, became a Stoker 1st Class, and saw service in the Mediterranean. During the Battle for Crete, he was aboard *HMS Gloucester* when it went down with only 84 survivors. A telegram brought the news that he was posted 'Missing', but his death was not confirmed until after the war. His parents, George and Annie Lambourne, always hoped and prayed that their youngest son would return safely after all, as had his four brothers, but it was not to be. The untold, appalling story of the *Gloucester* was the subject of a recent television programme and is related in Ken Otter's new book *HMS Gloucester*.

Stoker Basil Lambourne was 23 when he was killed on 22 May 1941. His name appears on the Plymouth Naval Memorial. By kind permission of Cecil Lambourne.

260

John Meheux of Nottwood Lane Cottage, Newnham Hill, was also killed during the Second World War, though not on active service. His brother George told how it happened: "John was at Market Harborough, training despatch riders. Usually there was a column of 15 trainee riders, with an instructor at the back and another at the front. On this particular day the front instructor was not at work, so John came from the rear to go up to the front, but was killed on a bend by an approaching lorry."

Women also served in the forces. This picture is of Sybil Tripe when she was in the ATS Auxiliary Territorial Service, aged 18 in 1939. Kindly lent by Mrs Florence Green (nee Carey).

Stanley Alan ('Mick') Franklin, wearing a beret, squatting in the centre of the front row of a group of his comrades in North Africa in 1942. By kind permission of Peter Franklin.

Ted Evans of Stoke Row, home on leave in July 1940, with three of his children: Flora, Pearl and Alan. Photograph by kind permission of Ted Evans.

Ron Tripe of Highmoor in the Royal Marines, about 1944. Ron is seated on the ground, at the front, on the right. By kind permission of Mrs Kathleen Kucor (nee Brakspear).

Raymond Townsend in 1941, with his father William, who owned the The Grove Nurseries, opposite the Maharajah's Well at Stoke Row. Photograph by kind permission of John Townsend.

William ('Bill') Archer of Highmoor, in the RAF, 1940. He is seated fourth from the left. Bill Archer was killed over Arnhem. By kind permission of Mrs Lenna Green (nee Archer).

At least nine Highmoor men were killed during the Second World War. A plaque on the interior wall of St Paul's, Highmoor, commemorates seven of them:

1935-46 War		
Wm Archer	John Denham	Paul Enfield
Alfred Evans	John Hanutt	Geoff Nares
	Cyril Symonds	

William Archer was in the RAF and was killed over Arnhem in Holland – where he is now buried. Both he and his sister Lenna (now Mrs Green) spent much of their youth at 'The Barn', Lower Highmoor and in Satwell Close, Satwell, Highmoor.

John Denham was the eldest son of Arthur Denham of 'The Little Manor House', Witheridge Hill. When he grew up he went into accountancy and law. He volunteered during the early part of the Second World War and went into the Pioneer Corps as an accountant. Then he was commissioned and took part in the invasion of France in 1944. It was a sad irony that he was killed when a car in which he was travelling and which was being driven by a Frenchman, collided with an Allied tank. He was a very charming and able young man and many people loved him.

Paul Enfield was first reported missing and then presumed dead. He and his wife, Rose, lived in a little house set back from the road, which is now known as 'Appletree Cottage', opposite the Dog and Duck.

Alfred Evans was the father of Mrs Audrey Hutton (nee Evans). He was in the Royal Naval Reserve, was 'called up' at the beginning of WW2 and was killed when the mine-sweeper *HMS Dunedin*, on which he was serving, was sunk.

Unfortunately nothing is known about John Hanutt, but Geoff Nares was the son of Owen Nares, famous actor and 'matinee idol'. Mr and Mrs Nares lived at Lower Highmoor, in a little cottage in the beech woods.

Cyril Symonds was in the RAF. He lived in one of the Henley Trust cottages, next to the Church at Rotherfield Greys. His gravestone, in Highmoor Churchyard extension reads:

Sgt Cyril Symonds, Gunner, RAF. No. 2235152.
Killed 18.12.1944. He gave his life for his country.

Although his name was not mentioned on the brass plaque, the son of the Hamiltons of Satwell Barton is also buried in Highmoor Churchyard. He was always known as 'Jack' and was in the RAF. His stone bears the legend:

John Jackson Hamilton, BA, AMICE.
Killed on Active Service 10.12.1941. Aged 28 years.

Dennis Clark, who served in the jungles of Burma during the Second World War and was awarded the Military Medal. By kind permission of Mrs Eva Holloway (nee Carter).

Frank Bromhead (left) and Tom Meheux of Highmoor (right); both served in the Royal Berkshire Regiment in India and Burma throughout the Second World War. By kind permission of the Henley Standard.

Those who returned from the war rarely spoke of their experiences. A very moving letter from Dennis Clark's daughter appeared in the *Stoke Row News* in August 1995, at the time of the 50th anniversary of V J Day (Victory in Japan).

Dear Editor

Whilst bitterness and controversy surround 'the Forgotten Army', the majority stay silent in the knowledge they did their duty, willingly, for King and Country. There was no thought of gratification or reward, as is so abundant in today's society, thank goodness!

I wonder if the villagers of Stoke Row realise that one such 'hero' lives within their midst.

Born in Stoke Row, one of five brothers who all joined the forces, and two sisters, he joined the Royal Sussex Regiment at the tender age of 19. He spent the next four years fighting in the jungles of Burma. Although he did receive a small wage, most of it was sent home to his widowed mother.

After the war he volunteered to go back into the jungle and recover the bodies of those who had fallen. When this young soldier finally returned home, void of his youth, physically and mentally drained by the horror and trauma, there was no help for him or his fellow soldiers, just a young bride, belief and hope for the future.

He has never forgotten, his memories are vivid, but he has never been bitter and has long since forgiven. He has the usual medals of war, but the one that takes pride of place is his Military Medal (for outstanding bravery in the field), with a letter from the late King, from whom he would have personally received the medal, had he not been ill at the time.

He, and those like him, are the real heroes, who put the past into the history books, look forward and not back, live their lives decently and honestly, without bitterness or hatred.

I am proud that Dennis Clark is my father.

Carol Clark

In the *Henley Standard*, the war in the Far East was commemorated on 15 August 1995, with an article and a photograph of three of the men who survived the horrors of those campaigns.

It included Bill Roberts of Highmoor, secretary of the Maidenhead and Henley branch of the Burma Star Association, who told the story of a Japanese flag and how it has helped veterans ever since. "This flag was captured in Belgium, probably from an embassy. We used to bring it out for social occasions, and people who donated money for branch funds wrote their names on it.

The money raised goes towards the cost of nursing homes and hospitals for men of the 'Forgotten Army', who had been 14,000 miles away from Britain, with literally no supplies and no contact from home. War widows are also provided for."

Tom Meheux, who was wounded at Kohima, is quoted in the same article as saying: "We don't bear the Japanese any bitterness after this number of years. But it is a great sorrow that they have not apologised for the treatment of prisoners."

The Home Guard

Men from Stoke Row came under the Checkendon Platoon of the Home Guard. The following excerpt was taken, by kind permission of the Checkendon WI, from their 1955 Scrap-book:

"On 4 May 1940, Mr Anthony Eden, Secretary of State for War, asked for 'large numbers' of men to come forward and offer their services. It was hoped to raise a force of 150,000 men. Within a fortnight 400,000 men were enrolled. In six weeks the number was a million. Their principal duty would be to fight the enemy's airborne troops as they landed.

On 4 June 1940, Mr Winston Churchill said: 'We shall defend our island, whatever the cost may be. We shall fight on the beaches, we shall fight on the landing grounds, we shall fight in the fields, and in the streets, we shall fight on the hills. We shall never surrender.'

The day after Mr Anthony Eden broadcast for volunteers for the defence of the country in the event of invasion, the Checkendon Local Defence Volunteers (LDV), (later given the title of Home Guard) was formed and, combined with Stoke Row, became the Checkendon Platoon under the title No. 3 Pln, 'B' Coy, 5th Bn, Oxfordshire Home Guard.

The Platoon soon reached a total of 100 men. This total fluctuated from time to time as men were conscripted to the regular Forces and others volunteered to join the Home Guard.

Shortly after its formation, duties began. At first they comprised Patrols every night in the week for the purpose of spotting enemy aircraft, or noting anything that was likely to be of use to the enemy. Then, at weekends, there was the strenuous task of digging trenches and erecting fortifications at vulnerable points and later there were inter-Platoon, Company and Battalion exercises. In the early stages Patrols had to carry sticks, as there were no arms, but in a short time a few rifles, with bayonets, were issued – these were then used by the Patrols.

In time, the Platoon was given a plentiful supply of weapons which included: Rifles and bayonets, Automatic rifles, Machine guns, Tommy guns, Sten guns and Northover Projectors. Small arms ammunition, Grenades and Bombs were also issued for use with the above. Rifles (.22s) were allocated for short-range shooting.

When exercises were commenced, a few of them were run in conjunction with the NFS (National Fire Service), the ARP (Air Raid Precautions) and First Aid units, in which women casualties were made up and taken away by ARP personnel to First Aid points, where imaginary wounds were tended. These wounds were identified by tabs tied to the casualty.

Later a Mobile Battle Platoon was formed, consisting of solo motorcycles and side-cars and motor-cars. This Mobile Team carried out a number of hard and realistic exercises with other Platoons and Home Guard units."

The Platoon also had a Wireless Unit, which did good work during the exercises. Many day and night exercises were carried out with the regular Army and Royal Air Force. They were performed in all weathers until the 'stand-down' of the Home Guard in 1944. The Final Parade took place at Henley on 3 December 1944, when there was a march-past of the whole Battalion. The Checkendon Platoon of the Home Guard included quite a number of men from Stoke Row.

Fred Powell recalled that, in the early days of the war, the LDVs had no rifles, so a retired Major in the village lent a Lee Enfield rifle and ammunition to his father, Albert Powell, who was also a Special Constable. (See photo on page 275). Mr Powell was later made responsible for guarding the wreckage of a plane that came down in a nearby field when he recruited eight or ten men to help him guard it.

The Checkendon Platoon of the Home Guard, which included men from Stoke Row. By kind permission of Checkendon Women's Institute.

The Women's Land Army

Not all the women who joined up for the Land Army worked locally – no doubt they were employed as near to home as possible, but Mrs Mavis Stevens (nee Armstrong), who was born in Consett, Co Durham and married George Stevens of Highmoor, worked on many farms in the South Oxfordshire area, as and when hands were needed. There is more about these splendid girls and the work they did throughout and after the Second World War in the chapter on the Farms.

Mavis Armstrong in the Women's Land Army, 1944. This portrait was taken on her 21st birthday. Kindly lent by Mrs Mavis Stevens (nee Armstrong).

Land Army girls in front of Henley Town Hall, June 1943. By kind permission of Mrs Mavis Stevens (nee Armstrong).

The Villages in Wartime

In one of the series 'Old Timer's Tales', Mr W French wrote in the *Stoke Row News* of February 1967 about his wartime memories:

"There must be quite a number of people resident in Stoke Row and its immediate vicinity who can well remember a few of the incidents that occurred during the period of the last war.

I was stationed in Nettlebed as a Police Constable from 1933-1938, when I was transferred to Stoke Row. War was declared on Germany on 3 September 1939 and for over a year it did not appear there was a war on. However, Hitler had other ideas and began sending over bomber aircraft. Many an evening I was on duty in the main street and could see the flares being dropped from German bombers over London and could hear the anti-aircraft fire and explosions as the bombs fell.

We were very often disturbed at night by German bombers which seemed to fly around Stoke Row and district, their crews looking for a suitable spot on which to drop their bombs. Many of these fell in the open countryside and little or no damage was caused. The first bombs dropped near Stoke Row fell in the grounds of Wyfold Court and only slight damage was done.

Much later during the war, a 'doodlebug' (V1 Flying bomb) flew over Stoke Row, its engine suddenly stopped and it fell in the woods just outside an American military hospital base on Ipsden Heath. About seven o'clock one morning several 'timed' (or unexploded) bombs fell at Timbers Farm, Nuffield, but all of them were dealt with and, apart from the deep holes they made in the ground, no damage was caused. Another 'doodlebug' fell in a field opposite Nuffield Church.

Many social evenings were held in Stoke Row Village Hall with a view to raising money for the war effort. They were well patronised by local residents, many of them generously bringing various items as gifts which were eventually auctioned, the highest bidder investing in War Savings Certificates. An occasional bottle of whisky, in short supply at the time, would raise as much as £90. (Over £1000 at today's rates).

Contests were also held to find the most talented local singer. I personally competed and on the first occasion was judged the winner; on the second occasion I was judged second best. The prizes were, of course, Savings Stamps.

Rationing was enforced and food, clothing and sweets were in short supply. Mothers and children found out which day the delivery sweets to the local retailers were expected and very often they could be found waiting for the arrival of the van. It did not take the shopkeeper long to sell all his supply of sweets. In spite of food rationing, several good tea-parties for children were held in the Village Hall. The American forces based on Kingwood Common often came to the rescue in providing extra butter and sugar and huge cakes for these children's parties.

In November 1946 I was transferred to Banbury on being promoted to Police Sergeant, in which capacity I carried on until retirement and pension in 1968, after completing 35 years of service. I still regard Stoke Row as one of my old homes."

Local War Effort

As part of the drive to raise War Savings Bonds, the people of Stoke Row ran a series of Fancy Dress Competitions in Stoke Row.

Alf Turner, senior, recalled "This was part of a Social Evening, which included a Mock Auction.

At these events someone would bring a prize, probably something hard to come by, such as a chicken or half a dozen eggs or perhaps even a bottle of Scotch and these would be auctioned.

Whoever won it had to buy Savings Certificates to the value of what they had bid and in this way the War Savings were raised a bit more, you see."

Colin Collis of 'Dogmore Cottage' as the groom and Colin Turner of 'Millstone Cottage' as the bride in a Fancy Dress Competition, 1941. Kindly lent by Alf Turner.

The Secret Factories

Reg Seymour of Sonning Common remembered that during the Second World War there were a number of mobile transport repair units (MTRU) hidden in the woods around Stoke Row. These were used for the repair of army vehicles.

There were also at least two 'secret factories' in Stoke Row during the Second World War. The largest one was on what today is known as the Vanalloys Business Park in Busgrove Lane and which had been the site of the old brick kilns.

Alf Turner, senior, told me "there was a firm of engineers in Reading called Hawkins and they did sheet metal work. At the start of the War they became very busy doing work for the Air Ministry and they needed to expand quickly into a place that was safer than Reading. When Mr Hawkins learned about the old brick-built warehouse on the former brick kiln site, he rushed up here to see it. At the time it was being used as a storage place for a Reading firm of car dealers who had many cars stored there, presumably waiting for the war to end! They had to clear them out quickly when Mr Hawkins commandeered it with the backing of the Air Ministry, as firms could then, since it was for urgent war work.

The Air Ministry sent down staff to start it up and they employed local women – some from Stoke Row and Highmoor but most of them came by bus from Reading.

In this factory they made fuel tanks for aeroplanes, mostly Miles Magisters which were being manufactured at Woodley. Later, when planes began to return from sorties full of holes, the workers had to repair these and test the tanks to make sure they were leakproof."

Mrs Louie Stevens (nee Wells) remembers mending and patching fuselages with aluminium after they had been through the panel beaters' workshop. She also remembers that her sister, Mrs Annie Britnell (nee Wells), had extremely small fine hands and could put them up an oil lamp glass, which is only about 2.1/2" in diameter. It therefore became her job to clean out the petrol tanks through two rows of about 100 holes which were only 3" in diameter. The girls called these 'pigeon holes'.

The Forewoman and Inspector was a Mrs Kettlewhite. "She had high standards and sometimes sent the work back if it was not up to scratch". Four of the local girls were two sets of Highmoor sisters, Louie and Annie Wells, Beryl and Joyce Stone.

The Crest Works at Stoke Row, 1941. Left to right: Robin Goodfellow, who was a butler at 'Bushwood', Stoke Row, Mrs Ivy Church (nee Norris), Bea Johnson. Middle row: Mrs Sadie Green, Mrs Flo Tucker, Mrs Florence Turner (wife of Alf), Miss Violet Pusey, Roland Page, Mrs Ethel Riley, Mrs Louisa Stevens (nee Wells), Ivy Butler, Rose Stallwood, Alf Turner, Flossie Brown. Seated: Mrs Sheila Miles, William Greener (the proprietor), Mrs Gracie Reske (nee Page), Joy Morris (evacuee) and a dog called Inge. By kind permission of Mrs Rose Textor (nee Stallwood).

They cycled up and down to Stoke Row to be at the factory sharp at 8.00 am. "If you were only a few minutes late, you lost 1/4 hour's money", Louie recalled. They usually had a cooked lunch at mid-day – the cook was a Mrs Welsford.

Meantime Mr Greener, with Roland Page, who owned the Stoke Row Garage, had a small workshop on the Crest Estate in a large shed which belonged to Tommy Cox and which had formerly been used for raising chickens. Greener and Page had been machining spindles for pulsometers, but they dropped this work in favour of subcontracting to Hawkins – drilling, tapping and turning cast parts to go on the fuel tanks being made in the Busgrove Lane factory. Very soon after the outbreak of war they asked Alf Turner to join them – he did so and stayed until 1948. The firm became known as The Crest Works and the people who came to work there were mostly local housewives and a couple of evacuee women. Mrs Gracie Reske (nee Page) remembers that she had just left school at 14 and was "glad to help the war effort". She stayed there for four years, nearly always on the same work.

Gracie also remembers that some of the women "embroidered the initials C W on their overalls." Mrs Louie Stevens (nee Wells) recalls "countersinking rivets, so the bolts could go on." Rev Isherwood's maiden sister, who was always known as 'Miss Kitty', had to do this vital war work too because she had no other job and no children.

Evacuees in Stoke Row

In 1992, Mrs Mary Foreman returned to Stoke Row School, where she had been Headmistress fifty years previously. As she walked through the rooms she kept uttering delighted cries. "How pretty and attractive this is, with these yellow walls and friezes – it was all cream paint when I was here and that was always dirty because the stove kept smoking all the time, because of the poor quality of the coal we had to have in the wartime."

She also recalled how, at one time during the war, perhaps because the Maharajah's Well was unusable by then, villagers came for their water to the school well, but when the numbers became too great, Mrs Foreman had to stop her maid, Connie, from drawing it and insist that people drew it for themselves.

Mrs Foreman said several times "I was very happy here", despite the fact that when she and her husband and only child, a daughter called Valerie, arrived on Saturday, 2 September 1939 from Marlow, it was only 24 hours before the Second World War was declared and there were no curtains, not even blackout blinds.

"On the Monday I was suddenly confronted with 60 children and their teachers – evacuees from London. Most of these children were Jewish and came from Battersea. They had had a very long journey by train from London to Reading and thence by coach to Stoke Row. They were tired, dirty and most of them had lice and fleas – it was a terrible time for all the women of Stoke Row – no-one knew what to do with them. Gradually the evacuees returned home, though some of them stayed on until the war ended."

Mrs Foreman's daughter, Valerie, was playing with Pauline Ruddle when a 'doodlebug' went over the school, just missing the chimney. This 'flying bomb' went on to land in the front garden of a house on Berin's Hill, Ipsden, the very one in which a teacher from London had been billeted. She later exclaimed "I came down from London to be safe and look what has happened!"

Rev Isherwood and his sister, Kitty, also had two evacuee children billeted on them in 1941. As neither of them were married and had no children of their own, they found it very difficult. Later on, one of Rev Isherwood's other sisters came with her grandchild and so the Isherwoods were relieved of the burden of caring for evacuees.

Mrs Foreman's husband was a professional electrical engineer, engaged on secret war work at Burghfield, near Reading and helped to set up the Admiralty headquarters at Bath. He was also a very practical electrician who provided lighting for the Village Hall socials and all the plays that Mrs Foreman produced with the schoolchildren. One of his great friends was Mr Boyd Neill, who lived in Stoke Row and had his own String Quartet which was often heard on the radio.

In December 1944 Mr Foreman was on his way home late at night, as he had been on shift work, and collided with a vehicle in an American Army convoy which was coming to one of their camps near Rotherfield Peppard. Mrs Foreman told us how she was informed: "I heard a great banging at the front door in the early hours of the morning and when I opened it there stood a policeman who had come to tell me the bad news. My husband was immediately taken to the Royal Berkshire Hospital, but he died a week later."

Her husband's death was a terrible shock and all the more so as Valerie was ill with whooping cough and pneumonia at the time. As she had no car or means of getting in or out of Stoke Row, Mrs Foreman decided to leave in 1945 and teach at St Paul's School, Wokingham.

Mrs Foreman had brought to show the children of Stoke Row Primary School a fully hand-written letter which she had received from Mrs Clementine Churchill, wife of the then Prime Minister, Mr Winston Churchill. In this she thanked the Headmistress and children of the School for the money they had raised for the 'Aid to Russia Fund', organised by Mrs Churchill and the Red Cross to help the starving people of Russia, especially those who had gone through the siege of Leningrad. A copy of it appears on the next page.

Mrs Eva Holloway (nee Clark) of Stoke Row remembered that her mother took in two evacuees, who arrived sometime in 1940. They were sisters, Joan and Margaret ('Peggy') Gosling. Joan did not stay long, but Peggy who was 11 years old when she came, stayed on until almost the end of the war. She attended Stoke Row School and when she left at the age of 14 she went to work at a private school at Homer, Stoke Row. She was probably born in 1928 and lived "in London". She left Stoke Row "with an English soldier" and was never heard of again.

December 1941   *10 Downing Street*
                                                              Whitehall
                                                                London

Dear Mrs Foreman

   *I write to thank you very much for the most generous contribution which
you have sent me from your School for my Red Cross 'Aid to Russia Fund'.
   The wonderful response I have had from all over the country is a great
encouragement, and I am most grateful to you all.*

Yours sincerely

                                        Clementine S Churchill

*Albert Powell, who lived at
2 Wellside Villas, Stoke Row and
was in the 'Special Police' during
the Second World War. When this
photograph was taken, he had just
been promoted to Sergeant.
By kind permission of his son,
Fred Powell.*

Evacuees in Highmoor

Don Shelswell and Ron Taylor, were aged seven and already close friends when they came down from Ealing to Highmoor on 1 September 1939. Having been assembled in the morning with their classmates at Northfield School, Ealing, they were parted from their weeping parents and brought by coach to Henley. Ron Taylor remembered that day very well: "Everyone was crying and I was covered in labels, with my satchel and gas-mask in its cardboard box, across my shoulders. The WVS and other volunteers met the coaches in Henley at about 11 o'clock in the morning and allocated us children to families around the area.

As in all these cases, some children were well received and made happy, some were resented and their surrogate parents found them difficult to deal with, which is not surprising as many of them were homesick and afraid of the countryside. It was so different from the town they had left. Once we were settled in though, we regarded the whole thing as a great adventure!"

Left: George Clements, his wife and evacuee Don Shelswell, with his dog, outside their home, 'Rose Cottage', at the foot of Witheridge Hill, in about 1940. With them are the sister and parents of the younger girl, Evelyn, who was staying with the Earle family at 'Bushwood', next door to 'Rose Cottage'. By kind permission of Don Shelswell.

Don Shelswell was sent to Mr and Mrs Clements at 'Rose Cottage', at the foot of Stoke Row Hill. The Clements were very kind to the London boy and he also became great friends with their nephew, Eric Edwards, for they were about the same age.

Don recalled that the 'privy' was at the north end of the garden. "It was built on a small mound. The slop bucket would sometimes overflow in the winter and then it froze so that you could not possibly get up even the small slope. Consequently I often went off into the nearby woods instead!"

Ron Taylor, who bore the nickname 'Golly' because of his hairstyle, was exceptionally fortunate as he was allocated to Fred and Edie Stallwood at The Woodman at Highmoor. They took to this little boy at once, especially as Edie had recently come home from hospital having lost her only baby in childbirth and was not likely to have another. Suddenly Ron was her little boy and she cared for him as she would have her own son. He recalled his arrival:

"In the beginning I was taken into the Tap Room of The Woodman and thought it was the lounge of the house, having never been into a pub before. I thought how strange it was at first, but Mrs Stallwood was very kind and took me up to my own bedroom. The Stallwoods were very good to me and I remember so clearly how we used to sit by the fire in the lounge and make marks with sticks in the soot and see whose sparks would go out the last. It was such a lovely pastime and typical of those simple games that people played before the advent of television."

During one of the visits from his parents, his father said, just as they were going, "I dropped a half-crown in the wood store, lad, can you find it for me?" Ron went into the store and found there a beautiful bicycle, all black and chrome, a wonderful gift. "They didn't see much of me after that," he laughed, "I was off on that bike!"

His mother wrote to him regularly, of course, as did his sister and he treasures these letters still. His mother also wrote lovely letters to Mrs Stallwood including one written on 23 June 1940, which said, in a depressed, downward-sloping handwriting:

. *"...I do hope he is a good boy and not getting too rude, especially as there are some terrible children down there (meaning the other evacuees). Will you please give him a big hug from me as we are always thinking of him and hope he will keep safe.*

Don't things look black for us, I wonder sometimes if we will be invaded, I hope not...

Yours sincerely,
Mrs Taylor"

It is hard for us today to imagine how far Highmoor seemed from Ealing, London. Although it meant only a journey by train to Reading and a bus to Highmoor, most people in London never went out into the country and looked upon Oxfordshire as we might look upon Scotland – rather remote and a bit 'different'. These two boys, however, soon felt very much at home. Although some of the children only stayed for a few months and others for a year or two, both Don and Ron remained in Highmoor until after the war had ended and became life-long friends.

More than fifty years later they came back to Highmoor and relived old memories.

277

Local boy, Eric Edwards, and London evacuee, Don Shelswell, at 'Rose Cottage', Highmoor, in the summer of 1942. Eric Edwards was the nephew of Mrs Clements, with whom Don was staying. By kind permission of Don Shelswell.

Master Michael Emblem, in his mini soldier's uniform, outside Rose Cottage, c 1942. His mother made the outfit for him whilst they were staying with her sister in one half of the cottage on Witheridge Hill which is today known as 'Half-Acre'. By kind permission of Don Shelswell.

The Americans

In the early part of 1944, American soldiers and airmen arrived in Britain to help us defeat the enemy. Camps were built for them all over the country and quite a number were constructed under cover of the woods in Stoke Row and Highmoor, as well as nearby Nettlebed, Checkendon and Peppard. Some traces of these camps can still be found today. One such outfit based here was Unit 4, Battery B of the 794 AAA (Anti-Aircraft Artillery) – a 40 mm gun Battalion. One of its members was Sergeant John Miller of Boston.

John Miller later wrote a small book, *My Life in the Army, 25 May 1943 to 9 December 1945.* I was 'introduced by post' through David Howells to John Miller in 1993, when he sent me a copy of his memoirs and a selection of photographs.

John was befriended by David Howells' relatives. "The nearest village was Stoke Row. I wasted no time in checking it out and met a very nice couple by the name of Roland and Edna Page. It turned out that Roland had a small four piece group that played in the local hall on Saturday nights for dancing. He asked me to join the group when he heard that I was a musician. I did, playing the trumpet while he played his saxophone. We really got the joint jumping with a swinging version of the *Hokey-Cokey*!

Mr Page had three bicycles and told me to use them when I wished. So, with a friend or two, I could pedal into Reading in the evenings, to attend concerts, dances or whatever...

One night, on returning from Reading, I had pushed on ahead of the other two fellows who were with me. I went to Roland's house to replace my bike, but the other two did not show up. I backtracked and found them in the hands of two local constables. 'What happened?' I asked. 'Riding a bike without lights' was the reply. It seems that the little gadget that took power from the front wheel did not work. They were let go with a warning and we returned to Camp. But the next day we were called out, lined up and marched in front of our officers and several policemen. We were given a talk by our officers on obeying local laws and honoring their rules.

We were only about 45 minutes from London and were given many passes, even 'overnights' to go there. I took advantage of this and spent many weekends 'in town', staying at the Red Cross lodgings for 25 cents a night. I got to know my way around the city in no time at all. I often visited the English NAAFIs, having tea and biscuits. I loved the 'tubes' and the double-decker buses and rode them every chance I got.

Another plus was the trips offered to various towns and places to have 'Tea with an English family'. I really enjoyed those Teas and attended quite a few with a buddy who was born in England but raised in the States. Nowheres in the world is there a more beautiful place to see than the English Chilterns. The countryside is so green, the quaint old villages, the stores, the people. And to think what they went through before we got there! Unbelievable. They had courage unparalleled."

John went on to fight through France and other parts of Europe and tells many stories of his experiences in his memoirs.

This photograph of Sgt John Miller was taken in a Reading street by one of the local newspapers. The caption read: "Got any gum chum?" By kind permission of John Miller.

One of the Nissen huts, still standing in Checkendon woods. This was used as a Polish Catholic Chapel and has religious transfers on the windows. Photo by the author.

John Miller returned to England several times after the war, with his wife. One occasion was in 1964, when the Duke of Edinburgh came to Stoke Row for the Maharajah's Well centenary celebrations. While he was here John bought a commemorative mug. During our correspondence he sent it to me with his best wishes. I care for it proudly.

Several of the Nissen huts and other buildings still stand in Checkendon woods. Erected by the American Army and later used to house German and Italian prisoners-of-war, they were used by the Polish Army after the war, to provide temporary homes for its soldiers and their families.

Tony Hall recalled seeing women dressed in black, wearing dark head scarves, European style, gleaning the fields near Ipsden at harvest-time, as they probably had done in their own country before the war.

Prisoners of War

Prisoners were taken by both sides during the Second World War. Although many of them found themselves in unpleasant camps, a few were more fortunate.

George Stevens of Highmoor volunteered for the Territorial Army in 1937. When the war broke out he was drafted into the Oxon and Bucks Regiment and, not far from Dunkirk, was wounded before being captured.

After many months of hardship, George finished up in German occupied Poland and was put to work on a farm. "This one was in the Danzig and was part of a very large farm, employing up to a hundred prisoners at the height of the season. These were Russian, English and Polish. All of them learned a smattering of German. They conferred in sign language and 'pidgin English' and got along together very well."

George related how they managed the food situation. "In time, the English group rose to being in charge of all the key jobs. One was the chief pigman, another the head shepherd, whilst yet another took charge of the dairy, so between us all we did pretty well for food.

For example, on one occasion, when a flock of geese was being driven to the local railway station, one of the prisoners saw to it that one 'went missing'. In order to conceal it from the guards, he sliced horizontally across a pile of frozen manure and made a hole for it in the middle!"

On another occasion "the prisoners were sent out on a hare hunt and killed over a hundred. These were then hung in an outhouse, but one of the British PoWs had become blacksmith for the farm and managed to make a spare key. When the guard lifted his nose later that day, saying 'Ich schniffen harzen!' they let him have a meal of the jugged hare, so he told no tales!"

Finally, working with about 500 other prisoners, they were clearing the local railway lines of bomb damage when they were released by the Americans and a joyful George was able to go home. He later married a Land Girl from Consett, called Mavis Armstrong, whose pictures appear earlier in this chapter.

George Stevens, Joseph Kashuba, a Polish cavalry officer, and Vic Darnell a fellow British prisoner of war, standing beside a ploughing engine on a farm in German occupied Poland during the Second World War.   By kind permission of George Stevens.

George Stevens (standing second from the right at the back) with colleagues in the Oxfordshire and Buckinghamshire Regiment in a German PoW camp in 1943. Photograph by kind permission of George Stevens.

When the war was over, a new use was found for the woodland camps - as temporary homes for Lithuanian soldiers. These photographs show a group of them standing behind national emblems which they had made from coloured stones, picked up locally. By kind permission of Tony Grismanauskas.

One last story needs to be told, and that is of a Fleet Air Arm pilot who lost his life saving the village of Highmoor, some time after the war was over. He was not on active service, but his story is one of heroism, nonetheless. In April 1950, a 'Seafire' (the naval version of the 'Spitfire') crashed in an orchard belonging to 'Upway'. The whole site was excavated in about 1990 by the RAF Association and nothing at all remains there now.

It was on a Sunday morning and it was thought that the pilot deliberately crashed the aircraft in this orchard to save killing people in the church and houses of Highmoor. The plane was totally burned out and left a huge crater in the ground.

A full report appeared in the *Henley Standard* the following week, but the story was summed up in a letter to me from Ron Pankhurst of Exeter, an historian with special interest in the Fleet Air Arm. I am grateful for details from his files:

"Seafire F15, SR611, 1832 Squadron, *HMS Hornbill*, (this was the then RAF Station at Culham, nr Abingdon, Oxon) crashed on Sunday 23 April 1950. The pilot, who was killed, was Lieutenant (A) Robert Caldwell MacLaren, RNVR. Date of birth 10 March 1920.

Lt MacLaren crashed in an orchard at Highmoor Cross, nr Nettlebed, Henley-on-Thames, Oxfordshire at 1054 Z (ie 10.54 am). He had lost control after a collision in formation on a training flight from RNAS Culham. The aircraft burst into flames on impact.

Husband of Moira Agnes MacLaren of West Croydon. His name is in the Fleet Air Arm Book of Remembrance in the Chapel, Fleet Air Arm Museum, Yeovilton."

1832 Squadron, HMS Hornbill, Culham, Oxon, 1950. Lt MacLaren is 5th from left.
By kind permission of Ron Pankhurst of Exeter.

15. The Manor Houses

Basset Manor, Dogmore End, Stoke Row

This is the house at the far western end of Stoke Row, in which Charles Reade is reputed to have written *The Cloister and the Hearth*. He was the brother of Edward Anderdon Reade of Ipsden, who arranged for the Maharajah's Well to be sunk. Charles was a scholar and a barrister, with an advanced sense of social justice, as is evidenced by another of his many books, *A Woman-Hater*. In this book there are several references to Ipsden (called Islip) and Stoke Row (Hillstoke) and of the awful living conditions of the poor in these villages. Mrs Topley, a former owner, was told that Charles Reade did his writing in the summer house at the far end of the garden.

Basset Manor is a Listed Building, Grade II. According to the Sites and Monuments Record (SMR PRN 2029), the house was probably built in the 16th century and rebuilt in 1695, allegedly on the site of a Norman hunting lodge. It is believed to have been known as Basset Farm in 1650 but it was called Basset Manor House in 1695. The timbers on the ground floor indicate the rebuilding of a 16th century farmhouse.

Harry Higgs, proprietor of Higgs Brewery in Reading, owned Basset Manor in the latter part of the 19th century. S H Higgs had bought the Lion Brewery from George Moore in 1877. Mrs Eliza Higgs ran the business from 1887 and Harry Higgs took it over in 1892. Samuel Higgs ran the brewery from 1906, but the company ceased to brew after Strong and Co of Romsey acquired it and eight licensed houses in 1953.

Mr and Mrs Hopkinson, Col Guest and Mr and Mrs Bell (1944 - 1955) are known to have been among the owners in the first part of the 20th century.

Mrs Topley told me that she and her husband came to Basset Manor in 1955 and left in 1980. During this time a number of alterations were carried out – the study, which had been built out in a block shape, was made into a gabled wing. Mr and Mrs Topley also chipped off all the rendering with which the bricks had been covered for many years. Most of the work was done by Paddicks of Kidmore End.

Danny Greenaway, who lived at Berncote, Dogmore End, told me that the walls of Basset Manor, especially the herringbone brickwork, were only built 4.1/2" thick, which may account for why the house was rendered at one time, to reduce draughts. He also told me that in about 1920, rubble from a pair of demolished cottages at Dogmore End was used to fill in the pond at the front of the house. This area is now laid to lawn.

Mr and Mrs Asquith came from Shropshire with the Topleys in 1955 and acted as Gardener and Housekeeper and lived in the cottage at the side of the road. According to a letter written by Mr B Topley, who by then moved to Blewbury, to Col Wright of Stoke Row in January 1982, the cottage of Basset Manor had been a small private school. (See the chapter on Stoke Row School).

Basset Manor, Stoke Row, 1913. This shows the house as it was when the exterior walls were rendered. Photograph kindly lent by Mrs Topley.

Basset Manor, Stoke Row. Photograph taken for the Historic Buildings Record in 1987. By kind permission of Oxfordshire County Council, Department of Museum Services.

In the Stoke Row School Log Book, the Schools Inspector noted, in July 1886: "...There has recently been an influx of newcomers, owing to the closing of a private school." There is little doubt this referred to the boarding school that had been run at 'Dogmore End House', as it was then called, by a Mr Morris. He appears in the doorway of the Village School, in the photograph of the 1882 tea-party, in the chapter on the Wells.

Nevertheless, Mr and Mrs Morris must have remained at Basset Manor, for on 25 December 1896, the *Henley Standard* reported: "On Monday week a concert was given by Mr and Mrs Morris and the Misses Morris in the large diningroom of Basset Manor School, on behalf of the aged people in the district. The audience was large and fashionable, and the programme was exceedingly well carried out. The banjo trios of Mr and Mrs Collins and Mrs Galloway provided a rare musical treat."

Uxmore House

Both Uxmore House and the Barn are Grade II Listed Buildings. There has been a farm on this site since before the Dissolution of the Monasteries in 1529; the barn was a Tithe Barn. The fireplace in the house is almost certainly that of the original farmhouse, which has been extended and added to over many years.

Uxmore Farm originally belonged to the Prioress of Goring. At the time of the Dissolution it was taken from her and rented to John Lydall who was eventually given the property. There were many acres with the farm and there is thought to have been a large manor house which was allowed to fall into disrepair and was later demolished. It stood where the tennis court is now.

Aerial photo of Uxmore House, barns, outbuildings and cottages, taken in 1958. Traces of the original farm, house and driveway can be seen at the bottom and left of the photograph. By kind permission of Lady Hayman.

In *The Lydalls of Uxmore*, published in 1980, a copy of which was kindly given to me by Philip Kingsbury, whose mother is a Lydall descendant, Edward Lydall tells of his family's connections with the house and farm:

"Andrew Ledall is found established as the sitting tenant of the estate of Uxmore, having held it from the Priory of Goring until the Priory was dissolved by Henry VIII. This had been a small priory of Augustine nuns dedicated to the Virgin. It is said to have been given Uxmore (then called Ulkesmer, meaning the pool of the ox) as early as 1070. It subsequently acquired large possessions in the valley of the Thames and much influence in the remote uplands of Ipsden parish. In a return of the property of the dissolved Priory about 1538, the Prioress, Dame Margaret Woodall, showed the rent of Uxmore as being £4.10s. The property was sold on 24 February 1540 to John Rydley and then again in May of that year to Andrew Ledall. It was at this time that Andrew changed the spelling of his name to Lydall.

As a yeoman family it was not inappropriate to have as one's name the appellation of the hamlet where it originated. After the purchase of Uxmore, however, when the family was set to enter the ranks of the landed gentry, some rather grander origin seemed to be called for.

By changing one letter of the surname it was possible to forget the humble hamlet of Ledall (Ledhale) and, both evidence and spelling being treated in those days in an altogether more easy-going fashion, to claim descent from the Norman barony of Lyddal or Lydall. One could then assert, and soon come to believe, that one's ancestor came over with the Conqueror!"

The name of John (then written Jno) Lydall, 1762, engraved in the brickwork at the rear of Red Cow House, Stoke Row. By kind permission of Lady Hayman.

Later in this fascinating book, Edward Lydall reiterates details about John Lydall, as written by Edward Reade in 1881:

"He became notable by his having been appointed by Queen Elizabeth, in 1585, as Curator of a considerable estate attached by the Queen, from its owner having become a pervert (sic) to the Romish faith, which gave him sufficient influence to create Stoke Row a Liberty. He is also stated to have been recognized by Queen Elizabeth as 'Lord of the Manor'.

At first he described himself as 'Lord of the Manor of Uxmore and Stoke Basset, alias Stoke Mules' but this eventually became 'Lord of the Manor of Stoke Row'."

Mr Lydall continues to trace his family's history through the ownership of its many properties, including Uxmore. He tells how "the Lydall family fortunes had shown a steady rise, thanks presumably to efficient management as well as to advantageous marriages." He also mentions that the name of John Lydall 1762 is engraved in the brickwork of a cottage in Stoke Row. Unfortunately, "his elder son also, as usual, called John, is described as being a ne'er-do-well who married, not a wealthy heiress, but an illiterate village girl, who signed her name with a cross in the marriage register. The squire was outraged to such an extent that he disinherited his son." When John Lydall, senior, died, he left nothing to his ne'er-do-well's son, John, but his youngest grandson, Robert, was left £400 'for his education'. He later went off to the Isle of Wight to seek his fortune. The greater part of the estate was bequeathed to John's daughter Frances, who married Thomas Reade.

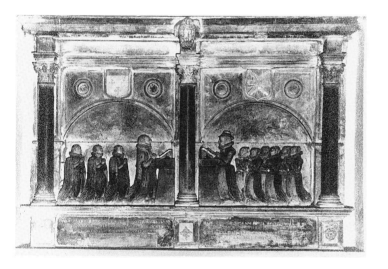

Memorial to Thomas Lydall of Uxmore (died 1606), his wife, their three sons and six daughters, in St Lawrence's Church, Reading. By kind permission of Lady Hayman

Frances and Thomas Reade had been appointed as guardians of the two grandsons. John married Mary Dodd from Mongewell when he was 21 and about that time "Uxmore was transferred to him... through the interposition of the Bishop of Durham... though there is no explanation as to how and why a prelate from the other end of England became involved in this matter." Edward Lydall continues: "John died in 1808 at the age of 36. In his will, when referring to 'the capital Messuage called Uxmore', he noted that it had been 'since taken down', that is to say, since his marriage. Presumably it had grown too big to keep up and had become derelict... Aerial photographs of Uxmore today show the foundations of a large rectangular building below the surface in a corner of what is now the paddock. It was obviously about four times the size of the still existing Queen Anne house which was Uxmore Farm and which has behind it, along with other buildings, a large tithe barn, now a scheduled monument."

In the original Norman part of Ipsden church, there is a tablet set into the floor which reads:

Here lyeth ye Body of
JOHN LYDALL
Gent. of Uxmore in this
Parish who departed
this Life
10 October 1728
aged 65

and beside it, another, which reads:

In the Memory of John Lydall
of Uxmore who departed this life
20 October 1808 aged 36 years

In Ipsden churchyard there is a gravestone to his widow:

In Memory of
MARY relict of
JOHN LYDALL
Esquire of Uxmore
in this Parish
who died
30 Dec 1848
aged 77 years

The Lydall family continued to own Uxmore Farm until John Lydall sold the house and land to a Mr Ramsbottom in 1841, when the family fell on hard times. The last of the Lydalls was a banker in Henley. Mr Ramsbottom sold the property to Robert Fleming of Joyce Grove, Nettlebed in about 1903.

From then on it was let to a Mr Cousins, then to a Mr Hewitt and finally to Robert Hayward, who lived in the house and farmed the land, first as tenant and subsequently as a purchaser (in 1917) of the freehold, from 1889 until he died in 1925. He had nine children, seven of whom were born at Uxmore. He became greatly attached to the property and while he lived and worked there he obtained a considerable amount of information about it from old villagers and title deeds.

On Robert Hayward's death, the property was sold to one of his sons, George, the purchase price remaining on mortgage. He became financially involved, the Trustees foreclosed, and the property was sold.

The house, cottages, farm buildings and land were acquired first by Ledley Brown, then by Mrs Walmsley, from whom Major F P Landon bought them in 1929. He sold the cottages and all except six acres of land in 1944. Inside Ipsden church there is a wooden wall plaque:

In memory of Nancy Landon, wife of
Major Francis Palmer Landon of Uxmore
and younger daughter of
Sir Thomas Wilmot Peregrine Blomefield, Bart, CB
born 16 May 1883, died 30 July 1953
R I P

In the June 1966 edition of the *Stoke Row News* there was an interesting snippet, under the heading of 'Plane down at Uxmore':

"In 1913, pilot Robert Slack, flying a French 'Morane-Saulnier' aircraft, came down with a broken petrol pipe in the field which is now opposite the Star Brush factory. It was before the August Bank Holiday weekend, and he became a guest for a few days at Uxmore House and telephoned from Woodcote for spares.

A 'Model T' Ford truck from Hendon arrived with these about two days later. The pilot and his aircraft caused a great sensation locally, people were out over the holiday weekend to catch a glimpse of them and Uxmore fences suffered considerably. Mr Slack was killed in a motor accident not long after leaving this district."

On the death of Major Landon in 1963, the house and 5.73 acres were bought by Mr (later Sir) Peter Hayman whose wife is a niece of the late Mrs Landon.

Mrs Landon's daughter, Miss L N Landon, retained about 1/2 an acre of the orchard, where she built a bungalow; she died in 1996.

Sir Peter and Lady Hayman lived at Uxmore House until Sir Peter died in 1992, and Lady Hayman moved to a smaller house in Stoke Row.

In 1992, Michael and Judy McFadyen bought Uxmore House from Lady Hayman. They have since made several alterations and small extensions to the house and improvements to the garden.

In 1997 they engaged Butlers of Peppard to virtually rebuild the old Tithe Barn, which was in danger of imminent collapse. The result is a beautiful building which will last for a few hundred more years.

Uxmore Farmhouse, c 1935, when Major and Mrs Landon were entertaining Stoke Row schoolchildren to a tea-party.   Photograph kindly lent by Mrs Rose Textor (nee Stallwood).

The ivy clad west side of Uxmore Farmhouse in 1943. Kindly lent by Lady Hayman.

The rural nature of Uxmore Farmhouse in 1900 can be detected by the presence of pigs in the paddock. Photograph by kind permission of Mr Brian Bastin.

Uxmore House, which today stands in 2.1/2 acres of beautiful gardens, with swimming pool, tennis court, workshop and studio. Photograph by kind permission of Lady Hayman.

The fireplace at Uxmore House – thought to be the original one.
Photograph by the author with the permission of Lady Hayman.

The Tithe Barn at Uxmore, June 1997, after it was completely rebuilt, using 17,000 clay tiles and old timbers from elsewhere. Photograph by the author, with permission of the owners.

Highmoor Hall

The first mention of the manor house at Highmoor is in an Indenture of 28 March 1661 between John Harbert, alias Bowyer, Yeoman, of Reading and John Pearce of Hymer, Sieve Maker, for the price of £6.13.8d, for 999 years and at a Peppercorn rent to be paid at the Feast of St Michael the Archangel.

At this time it was referred to as Hymer House. By 1855 the name had been changed to Hymor Hall, but ten years later the spelling had been changed to Highmore Hall. In documents of 1912 it was called Highmoor Hall, even though the parish records continued to spell the name of the village as Highmore.

In the 18th century, the property was owned by Thomas Stonor, Lord Camoys, who leased it, by an indenture of 22 November 1756, to Rev David Phillips (Rector of Nettlebed from 1748 to 1762). Eight years later, on 19 February 1764, Lord Camoys leased land close to the house to one John Perkins.

Robert Brakspear, the Henley brewer, became an agent for various insurance companies between 1782 and 1801. His ledger is kept in the Oxfordshire Archives and among other entries relating to Highmoor is this one: "1789: William Sarney of Hymer Hall, house insured for £300, contents for £400 = £700 at an annual premium of 15/6d." (Stonor House was only insured for £500 at this time!)

Two years later the property had been devalued to a considerable extent: "1791: William Sarney, gentleman, of Hymer Hall, house insured for £250, at an annual premium of 5/6d." Only two years after that it was valued at even less: "1793: William Sarney, gentleman, of Hymer Hall, granary and stock insured for £150, at an annual premium of 4/6d."

The following year, Robert Brakspear arranged insurance for William Sarney of Hymer Hall, with William Toovey, for machinery, running tackle and fixed implements in a mill, called New Mill, timber built and tiled, in the parish of Rotherfield Greys for £300, at an annual premium of 15/-. This was referred to in another place as being a water mill, presumably it was by the river at Henley.

It would seem that no Vicarage was available to the Vicars of Nettlebed at that time, for again, on 29 May 1818, Lord Camoys leased The Hall to Rev Thomas Leigh Bennett, Vicar of Nettlebed (1814 - 1843) to whom there is a memorial tablet in Nettlebed Church. He was still the tenant in 1842.

In a Lease dated 25 August 1855, Rt Hon Thomas, Lord Camoys and Hon Thomas Edward Stonor leased land adjacent to The Hall to Alexander McDonald for 99 years, including farmland which had been recently occupied by William Coles or his under-tenant, John Frewen. Alexander McDonald died 1859.

The Misses Elwes came to Highmoor Hall on 8 December of that year, when William F Schneider (Executor of Alexander McDonald's will) leased the property to Miss Frances Justina Elwes – she stayed at the Hall for 23 years. In the beginning her sister stayed with her but later appears to have left Highmoor.

Miss Frances Elwes seems to have taken a great interest in local affairs, because she "paid for Deskbooks at St James' Church, Rotherfield Greys" soon after she arrived. In 1865, when Rev G H Munro of Rotherfield Peppard paid for the sinking of a well at Highmoor, 284 ft in depth, just by the Church, she paid for the erection of the pretty little Well House, more about which is written in the chapter on the Wells. Frances Justina Elwes died on 12 July 1882, leaving the Hall to her sister, Margaret Augusta Pipon, but by this time her sister had predeceased her on 11 March 1877, so the property went to their nephew, John Henry Elwes of Colesbourne.

John Elwes leased The Hall in 1883 to George Talfourd Inman of 2 Drapers Gardens, London EC, to whom there is a memorial window in Highmoor Church. In November of that year the deeds were changed from Leasehold to Freehold.

Mr George Inman bought the Hall and its gardens for £1400 and other adjoining lands for £300. In September 1887, he enclosed a piece of the Highmoor Common, on which he built a Lodge House and constructed lawns and gardens, with the permission of Lord Camoys, to whom he paid £5.00. Gradually, over the coming years, George Inman acquired quite a number of parcels of land in the village and thus considerably enlarged his estate. From this time on the Inmans played an active part in the life of Highmoor. References to their visits to the Village School are contained in the chapter on this subject.

Highmoor Hall today. The grounds are beautifully upkept and the whole place is suitably peaceful as a family home, a base for Christian conferences and Retreats. By kind permission of Paul and Anne Persson.

George Inman sold Highmoor Hall on 7 October 1912 for £15,500 to Mr Hugh MacIntyre of Buenos Aires, who was temporarily residing in Surrey. By then the estate comprised 153 acres.

Mrs Ada Britnell (nee Wells), whose husband worked there for many years, recalled that "there were quite a few people on the staff of Highmoor Hall. There was a butler and a cook, named Mr and Mrs Cheshire, who had a son called Tom. Phyllis Earle was the housemaid and my husband, Arthur ('Art') Britnell was one of the under-gardeners. The Head Gardener lived in the Lodge House. There was also a chauffeur. The MacIntyres had four daughters: Nancy, Minona, Margaret Mercedes, Philippa and lastly a son called Alistair. One of the daughters married an Irishman called Owen, but she died of 'milk fever' in 1935. Her husband took the baby back to Ireland."

During the First World War, the wife and daughter of Admiral Jellicoe, Commander of the Grand Fleet, stayed at Highmoor Hall. Noel Baker recalled seeing them in church in about 1916.

Hugh MacIntyre died on 8 June 1918, but his wife continued to live at the Hall, with her children. In 1920 she had the telephone installed – the number was Nettlebed 13. She also sold the Manorial Rights to Mr Arthur C Denham of 'The Little Manor House', Witheridge Hill for £106, probably in the early 1920s. The MacIntyre family owned Highmoor Hall until 1930.

Alistair MacIntyre, who grew up there during this period, told me: "There was not only a 'ha-ha' (deep ditch to keep out animals) at the rear of Highmoor Hall, there was also one at the front, so the family had a view right out to the road and the commons." They had two gardeners, a Mr Wise and a Mr Steele. As a boy, Alistair was rather frightened of Mr Steele, who was "a very severe man". He remembered, too, that what is now 'The Cottage', for staff at Highmoor Hall, was, in his time, just a woodshed. He also told me that Mrs Cheshire, wife of the butler, was an excellent cook.

On 12 November 1931 Highmoor Hall was put up for Sale by Public Auction. A copy of the Sale Particulars and Map (lent to me by Mrs Ada Britnell) detail the Hall to be of 17th Century origin, with 12 bedrooms, 3 bathrooms, 4 Reception Rooms and Ample Offices, Central Heating, Electric Light and Mains Water. The Estate at that time included "10 Picturesque Cottages, Building Sites, Beechwoods and Pasture Land." In fact, it was not sold until 1934.

Ada Britnell recalled the Christmas of 1932: "That year we went up to Highmoor Hall and watched, along with the family and staff, lantern slides of life at the Hall, taken and shown by Frank Baldwin. I think they must have been taken some years previously as they showed Mrs MacIntyre in a long gown."

The small brick-built building with arched sides at the rear of the house was, at the time of the MacIntyres, a Fernery. At the end of this building there had been a greenhouse in which peaches, grapes and nectarines were grown.

The rear of Highmoor Hall, in the spring of 1913. The buildings on the right, which were the kitchen quarters and the oldest part, ie the original farmhouse, dated back to the time of Charles I. From a coloured plate, this photograph was kindly lent by Alistair MacIntyre.

The same view today. The lantern has been removed from the one-time Fernery, at the end of which had been a greenhouse where peaches, grapes and nectarines were grown. This building is now a beautiful and tranquil little Chapel. Photograph by the author.

Mary Isabel MacIntyre, who had by then returned to Argentina, sold Highmoor Hall to Richard Henry Comyns, Silversmith, of 41-47 Beak Street, London EC on 14 September 1934 for £5,500. By this time the estate had been increased from 153 to 264 acres. Alistair MacIntyre believes that Mr Comyns had been living at 'Shepherds', Shepherds Green when he came to Highmoor Hall.

Very soon after he bought the house, he demolished the original farmhouse which had become the kitchen and scullery on the ground floor and the cook/butler's flat on the top floor. Just before the Second World War, on 30 June 1938, Mr Comyns sold Highmoor Hall to Herbert Cecil Cain of Warrington House, Hertford Street, London. The Cains were great friends of Sir William Fraser (later Lord Strathalmond) and his wife, who lived at 'Bucks Barn' on Witheridge Hill. It is possible that this is how the Cains were introduced to Highmoor.   Ada Britnell remembered that Mrs Cain had been "born in Yorkshire". The Cains stayed until 11 November 1951, when they sold Highmoor Hall to Stanley William Bailey Hailwood for £20,000. The telephone number by then was Nettlebed 268.

Ada Britnell remembered Mr Hailwood as "an industrialist with motor vehicle connections, who had lived at 'Ferry House', Goring-on-Thames. His son, Mike Hailwood, was a very well known racing driver. When he was only seven years old, little Mike was given a child-sized motorbike by his parents, and rode it around the grounds of Highmoor Hall. He became a champion motor cyclist and then went on to motor racing, becoming the World Champion, but was tragically killed in an accident on the road at the Hogs Back, Surrey, when out buying fish and chips."

Tony Hall, the local pig farmer, told me "Mr Hailwood, senior, had quite a number of pigs at Highmoor Farm. At one time there was a serious fire at the farm, but Mr Hailwood rescued all the pigs, notwithstanding the fact that the asbestos roofs of the pigsties were exploding and slithers of this material were flying around like shrapnel in a battlefield. Many people at the time considered Mr Hailwood to have been something of a hero in his efforts to save his animals. Later on he kept turkeys." (See also the chapter on Farms).

Mr Hailwood disposed of quite a lot of the land so, when he sold Highmoor Hall in October 1960 to Mr Michael Lewis, Company Director of London, it was for the same price as he had paid for it, £20,000.   Mrs Diana Earle and her husband, Wyndham Earle, bought the house in 1962 and she told me "Mr Lewis (who was Jewish) bought it as a gift for his wife, but she, preferring the social life of Mayfair, never entered the house and wouldn't live there. They were later divorced."

Mrs Earle also told me that the small sitting-room was always known as 'The Justice Room' and it may be that poachers and other petty thieves were tried here by George Talfourd Inman, when he was a Justice of the Peace. The Charles II motto over the fireplace was probably put there by Mr Inman as a part of the extension work when the room was panelled in the latter part of the 19th century, and is not an original.   It was Mr MacIntyre's belief that the very fine plaster ceiling in the Drawing Room was carved on the premises by itinerant Italian workmen.

The dining-room of Highmoor Hall, during the ownership of Mr and Mrs MacIntyre.
By kind permission of Alistair MacIntyre.

The drawing-room of Highmoor Hall, during the ownership of Mr and Mrs Wyndham Earle.
By kind permission of Mrs Diana Earle.

Part of the Grims Ditch (or Dyke) runs through the grounds of Highmoor Hall, but it was levelled in the 19th century to make lawns. The Hall itself lies in the Parish of Highmoor, but, since the Grims Ditch forms the boundary, the top lawn and entrance road lie in the Parish of Nettlebed.

Mrs Earle sold the Hall to another Jewish gentleman, Mr Benjamin Zeev Immanuel of London, for £50,000, but he also sold it very quickly, in June 1968 to Mrs Alice Louisa Bates, of Maidenhead, for £5000 less than he had paid for it!

Mrs Bates stayed for eight years, but finally she decided to move to a smaller house at Peppard. Highmoor Hall was then sold to Paul and Ann Persson as a family home and for "Christian purposes".

Paul and Ann have brought up their family at Highmoor Hall and provided part of their home for Christian conferences and Retreats.

The garden is very beautiful, with huge herbaceous borders of plants in matching colours and several water features. The whole place has an air of serenity – a tranquil haven for tired minds.

The west part of the beautiful gardens at Highmoor Hall, 1990.
By kind permission of Paul and Ann Persson.

301

In 1993, Paul and Ann Persson decided to build an Arts Resource Centre in the grounds of Highmoor Hall, known as 'The Spring'. Operating as a charity, occasional concerts are held, as well as regular workshops and exhibitions on such subjects as wood carving, stained glass, quilting, watercolour painting, calligraphy; many, but not all, have a Christian theme.

The exterior of 'The Spring' Arts Resource Centre at Highmoor Hall.
By kind permission of Paul and Ann Persson.

The interior of 'The Spring' Arts Resource Centre at Highmoor Hall. By kind permission of Paul and Ann Persson.

16. The Farms – Animal and Arable

Stoke Row Farms

It has been very difficult for me to find out a great deal about farming as such in Stoke Row and Highmoor, since the old way of life has long since gone and most of the farms which are still going, possibly with the exception of English and Stoke Row Farms, are only a ghost of their former selves. Generally, I have only the Directories to give me the names of owners in times past, so the following is somewhat fragmentary.

Certainly by national standards, most of the farms in this area were small ones, not much over 100 acres and usually much less. Reg Greenaway told me that you could not farm 40 or 50 acres today as arable, because the area is too small to take the large machines that are currently economical for 200 acres upwards. Also the ground is very flinty and this damages the machine blades. The steep banks of this hilly area add to the problems of cultivation. Years ago a farmer would farm 50 – 150 acres, some as arable, some with beef or dairy cattle, maybe half a dozen sows and a few chickens, but that type of farm has completely gone from this part of the world now. As farms are sold, the farmhouses become private residences with a few acres for horse paddocks, the barns and farm buildings are pulled down or converted into residences and the land is sold and attached to another farm, sometimes a distance away.

Church Farm, Cox's Lane

The farmhouse, now a private dwelling, is a Listed Building, Grade II: "Probably late C17 with C20 alterations." Its name denotes that it probably belonged to the ecclesiastical authorities at one time. Bill George told me: "One time I saw a plaque on the wall of one of the rooms to the effect that Church of England services used to be held there – it probably saved people having to go to Ipsden Church." The suggestion that it is so called because it is near to St John's does not necessarily ring true, since the farm is a lot older than the village church. However, Geoff Boyson noted in one edition of the *Stoke Row News*: "Arthur Smallbones thinks that John Simmons probably occupied Church Farm, which was earlier known as Atkins Farm."

At a Meeting of the Vestry of Ipsden Church on Easter Monday, 10 April 1871, the Upland Pound (where animals were kept when they had been found straying) and a 'public pond' were stated to be opposite to the farm "now occupied by John Simmons", ie in Cox's Lane. Notwithstanding the presence of the pond, a serious fire at the farm did a great deal of damage in June 1874, by which time it appears to have been owned (or rented?) by a Mr Richard Parsons. In the *Berks and Oxon Advertiser* of 5 June 1874, we find this report:

"On Saturday morning last, about one o'clock, a fire broke out on the farm premises of Mr Richard Parsons, near the Church and before assistance was at hand a horse, three pigs, twenty-one head of poultry, three turkeys and a quantity of implements were destroyed. The buildings being of wood, and thatched, were also quickly consumed. The damage done, without estimating the buildings, was upwards of £150. Mr Parson's loss is covered by insurance."

The Farmhouse of Church Farm, Cox's Lane, Stoke Row.
By kind permission of the OCC Department of Museum Services.

In 1891, *Kelly's Directory* lists Thomas Greaves as "Farmer, Church Farm." However, by 1895 the name had been changed to William Ash.

In the early part of the 20th century, the farm was thought to have been tenanted by Owen Walters, but certainly before the Second World War, it was owned by Captain Oliver. Reg Greenaway recalled: "He had about fourteen acres and a small herd of dairy shorthorns, the milk from which he used to sell around Peppard. He also had about half a dozen sows." The farm would not have been all that profitable, but Capt Oliver was thought to have had an Army pension and some private means.

English Farm, near Nuffield

The Farmhouse here is Listed as Grade II: "Probably late C17, refronted late C18." The Stables, Cattle Shed and Shelter Shed are also Listed as being "probably early C18.", whereas the Barn and Shelter Shed are classified as "late C17", as are two other barns, one of which has a date-stone 1806. This is traceably the oldest of the farms in the two villages. It dates back to the 12th century and is said to have belonged to the Englysche family, who owned this farm as well as other land around in Nuffield and the English Lane part of Stoke Row.

The leaflet about Holy Trinity Church, Nuffield states: "Benet English of English farm, in the east of the parish, was a prominent local figure, first mentioned in contemporary documents in 1310 and known to be still alive in 1351. There is a 14th century monumental brass in this Church in memory of Benet English. ...This is let into the floor of the nave, just below the chancel steps. The brass is of a demi-man in civilian dress of the reign of Edward III. He wears a close fitting 'cote-hardie', with long sleeves and over it is a 'chaperon' – a kind of short shoulder cape, with the hood thrown back behind. It is believed that the brass was laid down in 1360. The inscription is in Norman French and reads:

Benet Englise gist ici. Dieu de salme eit mercy.
Benet English lies here. God have mercy on his soul."

The 1360 brass memorial to Benet Englysche in Nuffield Church. By kind permission of the Vicar of Nuffield.

There is also a small brass in Ipsden Church, dated 1525, to the memory of Master Thomas Englysche and his wife. The small plaque is in medieval English and is hard to read.

The hand-held guide comments on the 16th century brass memorial to Master Thomas Englysche and his wife: "The present chancel is said by Pevsner to be late 12th century and memorial brasses dedicated to Sir Thomas Englysche and his wife are dated 1525. The Englysche family were land owners in the 15th and 16th centuries and there is still an English Farm near Ipsden Heath."

In *Crowmarsh* by Berenice and David Pedgeley, they state: "When Ralph Warcopp of English Farm (then in the parish of Newnham Murren), died in 1605, he left 20 nobles (one noble equals one third of £1)) towards setting the poor of Newnham Murren parish at work on 'hempen wool' – hemp fibres to make a coarse yarn."

Robert Brakspear, brewer, of Henley became an Insurance Agent for various insurance companies, between 1782 and 1801. His ledger is kept in the Oxfordshire Archives and among other entries relating mostly to the public houses owned by him and his family, there is one for Stoke Row. "1793: Thomas Deane, late Joshua Rutland, of English (farm) in the county of Oxon, gentleman, insured: House, wearing apparel, plate, printed books, outbuildings, stock, etc. for £1300, annual premium: £1. 16. 6d."

Relating to the occupation of English Farm by Thomas Deane, in 1799, "Joseph Groate of Badgemore, esquire," obtained a "Certificate of qualification for Deputy Lieutenant." This was on the grounds that he had: "Estates at Henley, Rotherfield Greys, Newnham Murren, Stoke Row and Mongewell, (the manor of English being in his own occupation) and farms occupied by Wells, Deane, Robert Appleton, William Dodd and John Cooper with a Rental of over £200."

So it seems unsure as to whether Mr Deane was the owner or tenant of English Farm, but in 1804 Robert Brakspear again insured: "Thomas Deane, of English, gentleman. English and Cox's farms: £1450 for house and contents", and once more in 1806: "Thomas Deane, of English, gentleman, insured: Brick built dwelling House, wearing apparel, plate, printed books, etc. for £1750, annual premium: £2. 2. 6d, duty: £2. 3. 9d = £4. 6. 3d."

In 1815, the Conveyance document relating to the Chapel at Stoke Row, was signed by, among others, "Thomas Dodd of English Farm, Newnham, Oxon. gentleman" and "Thomas Dean of Newbury, Berks, shopkeeper". This may have been a misspelling, or it may not have been the same man, but a memorial tablet on the interior wall of the Chapel reads:

> *Sacred to the Memory of Harriet, wife of Thomas Deane who departed this life in peace. January 25, 1819.*
> *"The memory of the just is blessed."*

An enclosure map, dated 1861 notes George Dean as farmer of English Farm. Little else is known about the farm or its owners, except that the land was thought to have been farmed by a Mr Horseford between about 1914 to 1920 and a Mr Pither from then until Robert Purdie came here in 1924.

English Farm House, showing the elegant Georgian facade.
By kind permission of David Purdie.

Before the Purdie family came to English Farm, the two lower front windows, which were bowed, were replaced by flat ones. These bow windows would have been a part of the refronting done in Georgian times. They may have been replaced by Mr Robert Fleming of Joyce Grove, in about 1900 because they were rotting.

The late Dave Purdie of English Farm told me about himself in 1992: "My parents, Mr and Mrs Robert Purdie, came to English Farm in 1924 from Scotland. The farm was then 418 acres. I am their son and a bachelor. I live here with my sister, Mrs Ruby Munday, widow, together with Mrs Munday's son, Robin, and we farm the property now." Mr Munday was a butcher, but lived at the farm with his wife before he died.

Mr Purdie, Mrs Munday and Robin Munday were all tenant farmers of Nettlebed Estates. Dave Purdie died in 1998, but at the time I interviewed him the farm consisted of about 400 acres, mainly given over to grassland for beef cattle and 60 acres of arable. The Purdies had about 300 cattle, which included 100 cows kept for breeding and not for milk, about 100 one year-old calves and about 100-200 cattle which were 2-3 years old, depending on the time of year." Mr Purdie preferred to fatten his cattle slowly, as "this gives far more flavour to the meat than modern methods of high pressure fattening." The Purdies sold their cattle at the markets at Banbury, Reading or Thame, to be bought by butchers and dealers who took the cattle to the abattoir.

At one time it was said that English Farm contained parts of the boundaries of four parishes: Stoke Row, Mongewell, Newnham Murren and Nuffield. Mr Purdie was told that oak (originally ships' timbers) from Stoke Row Church were used to make one of the barns at English Farm. It is possible they were either left over at the time of the building of the Church in 1845 or they may have come from the barn in which the Dissenters met, at the top of Stoke Row Hill, when it was pulled down prior to the building of the Chapel in 1815.

A bank, part of the Grim's Ditch, runs along a section of the northwest perimeter of the farm and it has been said locally that an earlier house stood on a site further to the north of the present house. Certainly the Sites and Monuments Record notes: "Earthworks, platforms and rectangular enclosures at English Farm, Stoke Row; probably part of a mediaeval section of English Farm, to the east of the present building." Sites and Monuments Record PRN 474 records: "Mediaeval Fish Pond at English Farm, Stoke Row."

There is a pair of cottages nearby, marked on old maps as 'Conduit Cottages' – just by these were a number of ponds and it is thought that these were used to supply water to the farmhouse and its buildings, by means of a conduit. Hence the name of the cottages, now privately owned and known as 'Barley Hill House'.

'The Barn', Heath End, English Lane is now a private house but it was originally part of English Farm. It too is a Listed Building, Grade II. "Datestone in south wall '1659 RW', probably reset from gable during reroofing in early C19. ...Included as a rare survival in this area of C17 brickwork, used for an agricultural building."

Ipsden Heath Farm

Although Victorian, this is not a Listed Building but it had been in the Hayward family for over 100 years until it was sold in late 1992. The last of this family, Percival John James Hayward, moved into the bungalow next door which he had built for his father some 30 years before.

Ipsden Heath Farmhouse is thought to have been built in 1889. John Hayward was in partnership with his father, John Cottrill Hayward, for most of his life and took the farm over completely in 1971 when his father died. In his turn his father had inherited the farm from his uncle, William Hayward who had owned it for 21 years. The farm consisted more than seventy-three acres, including Morgans Wood, though four acres had been previously sold off.

Before 1977 and certainly before the Second World War, the produce of the farm was mixed, ie cattle and arable, pigs, etc but in 1977 new regulations would have made it too expensive to continue with the dairy side, so the farm has since been given over to the raising of beef cattle.

The new owners are Richard and Maggie Stow. Mr Stow is a bricklaying contractor and, when I visited him in March 1993, had already made a considerable inroad into tidying up the land immediately surrounding the house and modernising and improving the house itself. Today it is a fine building and a comfortable home.

Ipsden Heath Farm House, c 1990 – John Hayward is standing by the gate.
By kind permission of John Hayward.

Newnham Hill Farm

In 1680 Matthias Chessall built a smallish house on top of Newnham Hill – this is actually called 'The Manor House' but most people think of it as the Newnham Hill Farmhouse as it goes with the farm and is owned at present by Bernard and Jane Brazil. It is a Grade II Listed Building: "Probably late C17."

Later, Mr Chessall built another, grander house about 100 metres to the north and now called 'Newnham Hill Farmhouse'. It too, is a Listed Building, Grade II: "Probably late C17 to rear, probably mid C18 to front." The Barn, at the side is similarly Listed as "Probably late C17."

In the early 1700s Mr Chessall appeared to get into financial difficulties, so he sold the larger house (to John Wells?) and built an extension on to the front of Newnham Hill Farmhouse.

Bernard Brazil, the present owner of Newnham Hill Farm, showed me an Indenture, dated 17 October 1867, between John Brazil of 36 Parkers Row, Bermondsey, Surrey, Porkman and Thomas Brazil of Newnham Hill, Newnham Murren, Oxfordshire. This Indenture related to a previous one, dated 5 October 1860, between Edward Wells, gentleman and John Brazil and John Ordell, gentleman (the latter was a Solicitor at Lincolns Inn). From this it appears that Matthias Chessall sold the property to John Wells.

In the 1867 Indenture, which bears John Brazil's seal, it seems that lands and property (formerly known as 'the Easts'), were sold by Mr John Brazil to Mr Thomas Brazil for £570.

Between 1860 and 1921, Thomas Brazil and his family lived at The Manor House, which was divided because it was possible to make each half of the house almost self-contained with a back and a front door. The Brazils farmed dairy cows, sheep and some arable. They were also very staunch supporters of the Chapel. William Brazil, senior, who later moved to Kidmore End, made his money from pheasant farming and shooting parties. He supplied pheasants to many hotels and restaurants in London and when he died, aged 97, in July 1955, he left a substantial bequest to the Chapel.

The Brazil family at Newnham Hill in 1871. The four gentlemen at the back were Thomas Brazil, William Gunston, William Brazil, senior and William Brazil, junior. The lady and boy on the left are unknown, but in front of her husband was Mrs Phillis Brazil and Mrs Phillis Francis (nee Brazil). Many ladies spelled the name Phyllis thus. The children were Ada and Henry Brazil. By kind permission of Bernard Brazil.

'The Manor House' on Newnham Hill, c 1890. The man by the wall is Thomas Brazil. By kind permission of Bernard Brazil.

One branch of the Brazil family was in the butchery business at Lewisham and was thought to have been linked to the one-time famous pie and sausage makers, Brazils of Amersham. This is Brazil and Hester's butchery at 47 Loampit Vale, Lewisham, London. Kindly lent by Sibel Betts (nee Delafield).

The Brazil family valued their employees and one very highly thought of was Bob Horwood. Here he is seen with his wife, Emma, and their baby daughter, c 1874. Kindly lent by Sibel Betts (nee Delafield).

William Brazil, Junior, with his father and Bob Horwood in about 1925. By kind permission of Bernard Brazil.

This delightful portrait of Bob Horwood was published in Country Life in about 1925. He was born in a cottage which today is known as 'Little Orchard' on Newnham Hill in 1848 and died there on 2 February 1929. He and his wife, Emma, are buried at Stoke Row Chapel; their grave is cared for by the Brazil Trustees. By kind permission of Bernard Brazil.

Bernard Brazil also told me: "There was a pond between the two houses, from which the inhabitants got their water – it was sieved to take out tadpoles, weeds, etc. In 1898, when Ada Cox lived at 'The Manor House', Newnham Hill, she caught typhoid at the age of 18 and nearly died of it. There was also another pond at the rear of the house, with steep sides, known as the 'Tea Pond', from which the local cottagers came to collect their water."

Between 1921 and 1950 Miss Caroline Chillingworth and her retired father lived at 'The Manor House'. In the 1970's the Fleming family took back the Farmhouse and rented it to the Brazil family. Today Bernard and Jane Brazil own 'The Manor House' and 10 acres around it.

In 1995 they returned most of the farmland to the Flemings of Nettlebed, who own it all as well as 'Newnham Hill Farmhouse' and 'Lilac Cottage' lower down the hill. As at English Farm, many fossilised shells have been found in the grounds of Newnham Hill Farm, which shows this high land once lay at the bottom of the sea!"

Stag Farm, Newlands Lane

As with most of the other farmhouses, this is one of the oldest buildings in the village and it is also a Listed Building, Grade II "Probably late C17 with C19 alterations." During the reroofing of this house a large quantity of straw was found by the tiler to be attached to the beams – he thought it possible that the building might originally have been thatched.

On 27 October 1877, Moses Lewis and others sold Stag Farm to Solomon Saunders and also in this year it is mentioned in the Stoke Row Inclosure Award. From this date it seems to have been sold quite frequently. On 18 September 1880, James Saunders and James Little sold the farm to Stephen Smith and three years later, on 28 April 1883, he sold it to Silas Saunders. I am not sure when Ebenezer West came by it, but on 26 November 1887 he sold it to William Crutchfield.

Mr Crutchfield may have needed money to improve the farm, to keep it going, or for some other reason because, on 10 November 1894, he mortgaged the property to Jessie Maria Anne Bulley. The mortgage was evidently repaid because the farm was reconveyed in 1898. We can presume that William Crutchfield continued to work for Stag Farm until he sold it on 12 November 1910 to Silas Saunders who, in turn, leased it to Joseph Biggs on 24 January 1916. Finally, on 26 June 1925 Albert ('Bert') Biggs bought the farm from his brother Joseph who had a son, Walter.

Joyce Cordery, the daughter of 'Wally' Biggs, told me that Stag Farm had been in her family for about a hundred years and she was very sorry indeed when she had to move from it.

Walter ('Wally') Biggs worked for his father, Joseph Biggs and his uncle, Albert Biggs, at Stag Farm and this photograph shows him milking a cow, about 1905. Kindly lent by Brian Bastin.

314

Stag Farm in about 1890. 'The more you look, the more you see'. In fact the whole Biggs family, their staff and some of their animals lined up for this photograph. Between the bicycle on the left hand side and the dog posing on top of his kennel on the right there are, in fact, thirteen adults, two children, a horse and a number of cows. It must all have taken some time to set up this photograph! Kindly lent by Joyce Cordery (nee Biggs).

Joyce was actually born at Newnham Hill Farmhouse. At that time her parents, Walter John Biggs and his wife Ada (nee Hayward of Uxmore Farm) lived there.

Ada Biggs was a schoolteacher and often helped Miss Varley of Highmoor School when there was no other staff.

Daisy ('D') Newman (nee Wells) was born in one of a row of three cottages at the top of The Rise, Nottwood Lane. These were condemned and pulled down in 1922. In fact, these cottages had formerly been connected and it is possible that the row may have been a farmhouse until they were made into farm workers' cottages in the 17th century, when the new house was built for Stag Farm. Mrs Newman recalled: "there was a door between the bedroom of our house and the one next to it, but it had been nailed up."

The farmhouse at Stag Farm originally consisted of two front rooms, which opened off a small hall as one came inside. A staircase, facing the front door, led up to two bedrooms, one each side of a small landing.

During the childhood of Wally Biggs, ie circa 1895, an extra staircase was built at the back to allow access to an extra two bedrooms which were built on at that time.

At the rear of the farmhouse was a large baker's oven, which had been built in long before Mr Lambourne erected his on the corner of the Common. At the rear, one used to go down a few steps from the kitchen into the Dairy, where Mrs Ada Biggs made butter and cream. Building dairies partially into the ground was common as it kept the room cooler. In the living room was a large inglenook fireplace, in which people could sit either side of the fire.

'Wally' Biggs, standing at the gate of his house, c 1960. Kindly lent by Mrs Joyce Cordery (nee Biggs).

The type of farming carried on at Stag Farm was mostly animals, eg cows, pigs, hens, ducks etc. There was no arable. The Biggs family rented fields in the neighbourhood, as well as their own. Mary Wilder of Henley (nee Goodwin of Witheridge Hill) recalled: "Wally Biggs used to bring the milk around to the villagers in buckets, suspended from a yoke on his shoulders."

The farm today is quite small, about 10 acres, which with the farmhouse are owned by Robin and Vivienne Jenkins.

Stoke Row Farm, Cox's Lane

Stoke Row Farmhouse, Barn and attached Shelter Sheds are all Listed, Grade II: "Probably early C18 with C20 alterations." 'The Old Farmhouse' in Cox's Lane was a large property. The farm originally belonged to the Stonor estate. When it was owned by Richard Blackhall, in the late 17th century, Congregational Protestant Dissenters met there (see the chapter on the Chapel). This building is now a private house.

Sidney and Ada Delafield (nee Biggs) moved here in about 1905, but in 1935 they sold the old farmhouse and moved down into the cottages in the farm itself.

Fred Powell told me: "opposite the Church were fields, which were a part of Delafields (ie Stoke Row Farm) and on them there was a wooden barn and a low outhouse, but even in the mid-1930s these were semi-derelict. There was clay pigeon shooting there in the 1930s with 100 or so participants and the local boys used to collect up the cartridges."

During the Second World War the farm employed several German prisoners of war, many of whom had been agricultural workers in their own country.

The Old Farmhouse, c 1920. It now belongs to Philip and Huberta Kingsbury, who have modernised it, but kept its charm. Kindly lent by Sibel Betts (nee Delafield).

Arthur Goodenough, who lived at Scots End as a child, told me: "I worked for Mr Delafield from the time I left school in 1934 until he went into the Army in 1941. Among other jobs I delivered milk in chrome-plated churns with a horse and cart all round Checkendon and Stoke Row down to the houses at the foot of Witheridge Hill.

At the end of the war I came back to work at Church Farm and again I delivered milk, but by this time it was bottled.

Very sadly, one day I found Mr Delafield shot, in one of the fields. It is thought his death was accidental and the verdict was an open one." Soon afterwards, Mr Delafield's brother-in-law, Mr Colias, took over the farm and Arthur Goodenough went elsewhere.

Wolfgang ('Fritz') Walitzek from Wiesbaden, working at Stoke Row Farm in about 1944. By kind permission of Sibel betts (nee Delafield).

Mrs Sibel Betts (nee Delafield), with her dog, at Stoke Row Farm during the Second World War.

In 1993 I paid a visit to the present owner, Mr Henry Camp, who had bought the farm in about 1960. He has improved the buildings and built a road into the farmyard. I noted that there was an old pump in the middle of the garden, about fifty feet from the back door of the original house. Mr Camp showed me the interior of the old sitting room, which was heavily beamed and beautifully kept.

Uxmore Farm

Kelly's Directory, 1883, named George Hope as Land Steward to Mrs Ramsbotham of Uxmore Farm. This was probably the gentleman who built The Hope public house at Stoke Row. In 1887 Charles Hewitt was listed as Farmer of Uxmore Farm.

George Hayward owned this farm in the early part of the 20th century and let it, for nearly twenty years, to Harry Wells.

George Hayward, the owner of Uxmore Farm, in about 1900. By kind permission of Brian Bastin.

Mrs Alice Moore (nee Wells) remembered much of her childhood in the cottages at Uxmore Farm. She was born in 1904 and as she grew up, she, her sister and brother all played with the three sons and five daughters of the owner, George Hayward. "Together we played rounders, tennis, croquet – even football in winter. We also trolled our hoops and skipped with ropes. Most of these games took place on the front lawn of the house."

She remembered, too, life in the farm dairy: "It was fascinating to watch the milk being put into the cooler. It went round and round all the glass pipes, finishing up in the churns ready for selling. The transport people picked up the churns and delivered them to the station and cheese factories. A certain amount of milk had the cream taken off; this was made into butter and curds and whey. We had lots of skimmed milk for making lovely rice puddings and porridge and there was always plenty to drink. We also had cocoa every night before we went to sleep."

The Haywards had their own threshing machine. Alice said: "It went from one farm to another – with a father and two sons having three farms between them, they would help each other at all times, which is the best thing to do. When it was thrashing time we used to find some lovely large swedes and potatoes and put them in the furnace of the thrasher and bake them all hot to eat. They made a lovely supper with pepper and salt and bread and butter – nothing could be nicer and very filling. The other people working with us loved them too and Dad would pop some into the furnace later in the afternoon to take home for our tea. In the oven at home there was a nice large pie dish of rice pudding, with butter and grated nutmeg all over the top. It did not just smell beautiful, it tasted good, too!

We always went to bed early, for my Dad had to be up at 5.00 am again next morning. At this time of the day he had to fetch all the rest of the horses and cows in their stalls ready for washing down, get the milking gear ready, give the horses their hay and fill their nose-bags with chaff, oats, barley and corn, ready for the work."

The farmworkers' cottages at Uxmore Farm where Mrs Alice Moore (nee Hayward) grew up. By kind permission of Peter and Jennifer Fletcher.

Alice Moore continued: "When we had a long hot, dry summer we had to suffer for it because there was no water in the underground tank (caught off the roof) so we had to fetch water from Stoke Row Well with yokes on our shoulders and two large buckets. Dad had to go with a large horse-drawn water cart, carrying 50 gallons of water to put in the cattle troughs for the horses, cows and pigs, large and small. Of course the hens, ducks, swans, turkeys and Gleaneys (the Oxfordshire name for guinea-fowl) also had to have water.

It was a very bad time for washing clothes, and impossible to rinse them thoroughly. We had prayers in the Schools, Churches and Chapels, all to no avail. The corn was all stunted, the growth was very short and resulted in a quarter of the quantity of grain, making it very hard for the farmers and people alike. There was very little bread about and you couldn't make bread without flour and you couldn't buy any, whatsoever. We used to have a lot of potato scones every day to keep us all going. Lots of cattle died from thirst besides the insects and fowls of the air. It was not an easy time anywhere, you even saw frogs and tadpoles lying everywhere, all dried up.

Mrs Elizabeth Wells, daughter of Dennis Higgs. She was married to Harry Wells, they had two daughters (see below) and a son who was always known as 'Neddy'. This family lived in one of the cottages beside Uxmore Farm.

Mrs Wells with her two daughters, Ada and Alice. Alice lived until she was well over ninety and her memoirs are quoted in this chapter. Both photgraphs by kind permission of her grandson, Patrick Walsh.

Sometimes my brother would go with Dad and help to wash the cows' udders with a cloth and hot water before the hand milking started at 6.00 am by the light of hanging lanterns. They cast eerie shadows as they walked backwards and forwards past our bedroom window. It took an hour and a half to milk the cows and put the milk into the coolers. Then the cows had to be turned straight out from the milking sheds into the grass fields."

Harry Wells, feeding pigs at Uxmore Farm, in about 1920. Kindly lent by Patrick Walsh.

Alice continued: "Then the sheds had to be washed down with hose pipes and Jeyes fluid, all the utensils and churns had to be taken to the Buttery to be thoroughly cleaned, rinsed and dried and everything put away until 4.00 pm. Every cow was milked twice daily and everything had to be cleaned twice daily too.

Farming is a ritual which must be properly carried out. It makes a lot of difference to the milk yield if the milking is early or late. Cows can be very stubborn, especially if a different pair of hands milks them, sometimes they hold back and refuse to yield – they have their likes and dislikes, the same as we do."

In the first decade of the 20th century, the wages of Oxfordshire agricultural labourers were some of the lowest in the country. In the *Stoke Row News*, March 1966, George Gibbins stated: "I started work at the age of 13 as 'horse boy' at Uxmore Farm. My wages were 3/- a week and I had to start at 5 o'clock and work on Sundays. Many a morning I've pulled a turnip for my breakfast. Cruel times they was!"

Across the country, life on a farm was very hard at this time and continued to be so right up until the Second World War, when successful agriculture became essential for the country's survival and wages improved.

Harry Wells at Uxmore Farm, in about 1919. The thinness of both the horse and his owner gives an dea of the harsh conditions of the time, as a result of water shortages and poor harvests. By kind permission of Patrick Walsh.

Harry Wells and his family, haymaking c 1919. Mr Wells is holding aloft a stook of corn. Once the corn had been stooked and had dried, it was then piled into ricks. By kind permission of Patrick Walsh.

Dennis Higgs, with beard and stick, hauling timber near Uxmore Farm, c 1920. Unfortunately, the names of the other men are not known. By kind permission of Patrick Walsh.

In 1946, Dennis Clark came out of the Army. He then "went to work for Mr George of Uxmore Farm who had been allocated one of the Council houses in Church View, which was just being built, the first house being nominated as a home for a farm employee. I was happy there and although I hadn't planned to stay, Mr George paid me at the factory rate of 5/- an hour. When bricklayers were earning 2/11 and carpenters 1/-, this was good money!"

In the end Dennis stayed at Uxmore Farm for ten years, during which period it was sold three times. Mr Winward, a multi-millionaire, bought it from Mr George for about £7500. Mr David Arundel from Castleford near Leeds in Yorkshire was the next owner, and finally local farmer Bernard Brazil bought the farm and owned it for about fifteen years.

In aerial photographs a large 'white lump' appears in the farm area – this was a 'round house' in which a horse was used to cut the chaff. It was originally tiled but Bernard Brazil told me that it had been roofed with corrugated iron. It was later pulled down, sometime before he bought it.

Peter and Jennifer Fletcher bought Uxmore Farmhouse from Bernard Brazil in 1968. Colonel Landon kept back 150 acres at the time and later sold these to Stewart Baylis, with Roger Chapman as Manager. The land and the old farm buildings were later sold to Bob Beacroft, Mapledurham.

Woodside Farm

This farm lies at the end of School Lane. It incorporates Woodside Cottages and once comprised 85 acres which Reg Greenaway rented from Harold Owen (brother of the First World War poet Wilfred Owen) of Rodgarden Shaw, Kit Lane, Stoke Row in about 1950. When Mr Owen died in about 1971, Mr Reg Greenaway gradually bought the fields from his widow.

On the bigger fields in Kit Lane, about 50 acres, Mr Greenaway grew corn (wheat, barley and oats). This he mostly harvested by hand, using a binding machine. The sheaves of corn were put into stooks and then stored in ricks until they were threshed in the winter, with a machine which Mr Greenaway usually hired. The grain was then stored in the buildings at the end of School Lane and used to feed the chickens and pigs through the winter. Reg Greenaway sold chickens, eggs and piglets.

He also ran a herd of about 50 beef cattle, about which he told me: "The benefit of raising beef cattle as opposed to dairy is that you do not have the problems associated with milking, like getting up very early and running a milking shed, especially today with all the hygiene requirements of the EEC. On the other hand the income is less regular and predictable."

Although this photograph is entitled South View, Stoke Row, it is neither the name of the road, nor of the pair of houses. It is, in fact, the end of School Lane and was taken before 1910, long before the Council houses were built in 1920. The building is Woodside Cottages, a pair of Victorian houses built by William Greenaway on the woodland he owned and farmed at the rear of the property and which became known as Woodside Farm.
By kind permission of Reg Townsend.

Originally the land at the end of School Lane was mostly wooded, but much of the wood was felled and the land given over to the raising of animals, such as pigs and chickens. Reg Greenaway employed just a couple of men, though sometimes he had helpers in the form of lads from Turners Court, which was a reform school at Nuffield. In 1995, Mr Greenway sold most of his land and now just keeps a few animals at the end of School Lane.

Highmoor Farms: Conway's Farm, Satwell

This farm has been created in recent years, and as such is supposed not to have had a name, but to have been made up of the buildings, barn, loose boxes, etc once connected to what used to be called 'The Old Kennels' and is now known as 'The White House'. It was home at one time to the Woodland Hunt foxhounds, with which the owner, Gerald de Pass, had strong connections.

During the Second World War, there were six camps next to Padnell's Wood, beside the farm. Italian, and later German, prisoners of war, as well as Land Army girls based at Cowley, worked on this farm. Mr Conway told me that the contents of a huge cess pit in Overland's Wood, which served the camps, was spread on the fields by the prisoners as manure during the war.

By 1996 the Conway family owned over 200 acres in this area – principally worked by Steven Conway. It includes Padnell's Wood, Overland's Wood, the Rocky Lane Farm orchards, and quite a number of fields.

There are two Nissen huts and a large old barn, used for storing hay etc, at the rear of 'The White House'. Mr Conway has some beef cattle but chiefly grows corn and hay.

Josefi Arditto Cadell, who was always known as 'Ginger' was an Italian prisoner of war who worked as a tractor mechanic at what is now Conway's Farm. Kindly lent by Mavis Stevens.

Gerald de Pass, helping with the haymaking, probably on one of the fields belonging to Satwells Barton, during the Second World War. On the trailer are Michael (son of Siegfried), Eddie Brown, Sam Gardiner and Siegfried Kamlot (a Lithuanian Jewish refugee, who later went to Israel and then to America). By kind permission of Mavis Stevens.

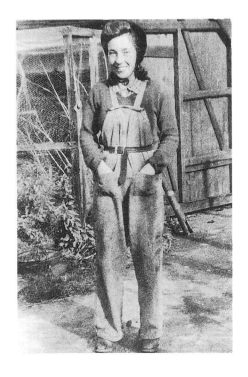

Jean Oxborough, in 'dungarees', a member of the Women's Land Army, she drove tractors in this area during the Second World War. Kindly lent by Mavis Stevens.

Mavis Stevens, a Land Army girl, who worked under the supervision of the Oxfordshire War Agricultural Executive Committee, (popularly known as 'The War Ag') driving a tractor and corn drill on Russells Water Common in about 1944. Mavis later married Highmoor-born PoW George Stevens when he came home from the war. By kind permission of Mavis Stevens.

A group of Land Army girls, some of whom worked at Highmoor from time to time, photographed at Colemore House, Peppard, during the Second World War.
By kind permission of Mavis Stevens, who is on the extreme left.

Highmoor Farm

Highmoor Farmhouse is a Grade II listed building: "Early C18, with late C18 main front." There is a date mark in one of the barns: 1740, so it is possible that the farm house was built around 1725. The oldest part is at the front and it is fairly obvious that it has been extended to the rear, first of all perhaps in about 1830 to 1840 and further back in more recent years, connecting the house with the barn at the rear of the property. In the cellar are notched beams, which may have been ships' timbers, with marks II matching II on a beam at right-angles to it and a III and III similarly.

In the cellar there is a recess which probably contained a boiler and some interesting alcoves with keystone bricks above them. In what was almost certainly the pantry at the rear, on the right, there are still game hooks in the beams and an alarm bell box which brought the attention of the maid to requests from the living-rooms and four upstairs bedrooms.

Highmoor Farm House – a beautiful example of a tastefully restored Georgian Farmhouse. By kind permission of James and Annabel Holder.

Also listed are: "Barns (approx 50 metres north: Grade II listed building: 2 linked barns. Probably early C18." And "Granary: Grade II listed building, approx 1 metre to north: C18. Staddle stones; timber-framing, weather boarding; plain old tile hipped roof. Central plank door. Malthouse Cottage and attached barn: Grade II: Maltings, now house and barn. Probably early C18 with C19 alterations."

Mrs Ruth Gibson of the Henley Archaeological and Historical Association, Vernacular Buildings Section, conducted a survey of Highmoor Farm in February 1984.

Her report noted that the farm had originally belonged to the Stonor Estate, as far back as 1775, when it was called 'Hatton's Farm'. "The 1844 Tithe Map shows the farm still in the possession of Lord Camoys of Stonor, with William Reeves as his tenant."

Kelly's Directory of 1848 lists Thomas William Reeves as Farmer, Highmoor Farm. According to the Gothick lettered gravestones in Highmoor Churchyard: Sally, wife of William Reeves of Highmoor Farm, died 6 February 1862 and William Reeves, died 17 July 1865 (aged 60?)

The census of 1881 gives only a couple more clues about life at Highmoor Farm and records John Janes as the farmer. However, it does also tell us that the farm comprised "230 acres, run by 8 men and 2 boys."

William Reeves, son of the above, died 5 February 1895, aged 70 and Sarafann Tubb, daughter of the above, died 2 December 1897, aged 68. Ruth Gibson thinks "it is possible that he had bought the farm at the 1894 Stonor Estate sale." By 1899 and again in 1903, Thomas Bryant was shown as farm Bailiff to Mr George Talfourd Inman of Highmoor Hall and later editions of *Kelly's Directory*, 1906 and 1911, also state Mr Inman as the owner of the farm.

Information about the farm itself after this time is rather sparse, but Ada Britnell told me about a barn fire at Highmoor Farm on 21 October 1910. She remembered the date well, since her mother had told her that she had gone out to witness the fire the night before Ada was born the following day!

In 1925 Dolly Franklin "left off gardening at Satwell House and worked at Highmoor Farm for Mr Edward Page." Unfortunately, she did not recall much about her employer or her time there, except that she had to work "jolly hard!"

Ruth Gibson met Sam Gardiner when she was investigating Highmoor Farm. This gentleman kindly lent me several photographs. He stated: "I first came to Highmoor in about 1930, with my father, Jesse Gardiner, when Mr Davies was the Manager and the farm belonged to Mr A C Denham, who lived on Witheridge Hill. The farm then had a milking herd of about 30 Shorthorns and Guernseys and there were two horses for ploughing. Barley, oats, kale and swedes were grown and there was plenty of hay.

In 1936 a modern milking parlour replaced the old one, which has now disappeared under the sunken lawn. Hand milking started at 5.00 am, and the van collecting the milk churns arrived at 7.30 am. Later, a milking machine and small bottling plant were installed in the milking parlour. The milk went to Cliffords Dairy."

"Threshing took place in the area behind the barns, when the steam engine from Wilders of Crowmarsh arrived. The ricks were stacked in the area known as the `modern farmyard'. Corn, for consumption on the farm, was first stacked in hired sacks in the barns, then carried through to the granary where they were emptied out into three large corn bins."

A delightful picture that shows a Harvest Home Supper at Highmoor Farm in about 1935. Arthur Denham and his wife hosted this happy gathering. Both these photographs were kindly lent by Mrs Mary Ramsay (nee Clements).

This photograph shows the number of men who worked at Highmoor Farm for Mr Denham in the 1930s.

Mr Robin Denham confirmed Sam Gardiner's version, when he told me about the time that his father owned the farm: "In 1935, my father, Arthur Denham, who was then living at the'The Little Manor House' on Witheridge Hill, bought Highmoor Farm. Within a few months he realised that the ploughman was using a single furrow plough and, in rainy weather, walked up and down the fields with a sack over his head. Very soon father bought a tractor for his farm."

Mr Denham also developed a herd of shorthorn cows, but lost a good deal of money on the project. He went into milk production and was one of the first farmers to have a T T (Tuberculosis Tested) Certified herd.

A man of vision, Arthur Denham was one of the first people in the country to breed 'large white' pigs in a Danish type piggery, an early form of what has become known as 'factory' pig farming, where the pigs were housed in a row of connected pens and cleaned each day. He had a Farm Bailiff and several farm workers and at one time it was managed by a Mr Lucas who had two sons. One was named Michael and the other went into the Fleet Air Arm during WW2 and was killed.

For a short time during the Second World War the farm belonged to Mr Brunner, whose family lived at Greys Court. Mr Cogbill was cowman here during the Second World War, he had a son called Ronnie who used to play with the evacuees.

In 1945 it was sold to Commander Colin Buist (RN) and his wife, who was always known as 'Gladdie'. Cdr Buist was Equerry to King George VI and also Chairman of the Coalite Company. In her biography of Celia Johnson, Kate Fleming mentions that the Duke and Duchess of Windsor, who were friends of the Buists, used to come and stay here. Mr Gardiner, who had left in 1937, returned as Manager. He said: "Commander Buist always took a keen interest in the farm."

After Cdr Buist retired from farming, "the fields were let to the Fleming Estate and most of the buildings no longer used. In 1981 the farm was sold."

Ruth Gibson continues: "It is interesting that many field names had not changed between 1725 and 1844. Mr Gardiner, however, knew only some of the old names, such as *Home Field* and *Stubble Close*. *Witheridge* had been divided into three, ie *Reservoir Field*, *Village Hall* and *Raglands Pond*.

Red Hangings still existed, but *Steep Hangings* is called *Banks*. Nos. 42 and 43 on the Tithe Map – not part of Highmoor then – are called *Shopfield* and *Windmill Field*. *Highmoor Pightle*, *Hammond's Corner* and *Holly Grove Field* did not belong to the farm in Mr Gardiner's day, but Highmoor farm's fields extended westwards past 'Little Farm' to Newnham Hill and the total acreage at the 1981 sale was almost the same as in 1844." I found myself wondering whether *Windmill Field* related to one being able to see both Stoke Row and Nettlebed mills from there or whether, in fact, there had once been a windmill on that hill, too?

Ian Posgate bought Highmoor Farm in 1981. By this time it was just a set of fields with no buildings, all of them having been previously sold for development into dwellings. The house was bought by Ann McKenzie-Hill who, in turn, sold it to Christopher and Fiona Bell. It is now owned by James and Annabel Holder.

Jesse Gardiner, who worked at Highmoor Farm in the 1930s. Kindly lent by his son, Sam Gardiner.

Sam Gardiner and Arthur Webb on a McCormick tractor at Satwell Farm in 1959. Kindly lent by Sam Gardiner.

*Left to right: Sam Edwards, the butler, Commander Buist and Mr McLeod
at Highmoor Farm in about 1950. Kindly lent by Sam Gardiner.*

*The barn and other outbuildings were bought in 1990 by a South African, a Mr Lubner,
who developed them. In 1995 they were put up for sale at £1,000,000, though they
finally sold for less than this sum. The new owners have made extensive improvements
and what was once an old barn is now a luxurious home. Photograph by the author.*

Satwell Farm

John and Frances Hives have owned 'Satwell Old Farm' since 1970. They bought it from Geoffrey and Hilda Barraclough who used to own 'Satwell House' and had converted the old farmhouse and cottages into one house in about 1965.

They showed me deeds given to them by a relative of Harry Burr (1854-1938) who had previously lived at 'Satwell House'. The documents were found in the attic of his London home after his death.

They contained an Abstract of Title for Dr Henry Kendall, dated 11 August 1870, which refers to an original document of 14 March 1777, relating to Thomas Mower Keats. The property was then transferred/sold/bequeathed(?) to Thomas Ovey and from then on it appears to have been split into five parts. The history of the early ownership of this property is really quite complicated! By 9 July 1815, the farm was certainly in the hands of Thomas Ovey, a hatter of Reading and his wife Elizabeth. At this time the property was in seven parts.

The Particulars, Plan and Conditions of Sale, relating to Satwell Farm when it was auctioned on 1 June 1875. Kindly lent by Johnand Frances Hives.

In 1830 the owner was Thomas Tullett, who became bankrupt and sold the property to release money for his Assignees. The money thus released was given in 1831 to Edward Tullett. There then came a Recovery relating to Miller, Hyde and Tullett, dated 26 November 1833. This was Hyde's copy and is very handsome, with embellishments around the edge and a large seal. However, in the same year Edward Tullett leased the property to Charles Hyde and finally sold it to Miss Ann Hyde in August 1833.

In Highmoor Churchyard there is an elegant sarcophagus-type tombstone, dedicated to:

> *Sarah Ann*
> *beloved wife of William Bird*
> *8.7.1829 - 11.2.1885*
> *William Bird*
> *late of Satwell Farm*
> *23.10.1880 - 12.6.1914*

Curiously enough, despite the elaborate nature of the tomb, this couple are not mentioned in the deeds at all and yet they would have been quite prosperous.

By 1866 it would appear to have been owned by Henry Kendall who, for some reason not stated, gave Power of Attorney to George Singer. A Sale document for Satwell Farm dated 1875 is among the papers now owned by Mr and Mrs Hives and states that the timber on the land was valued at £603 in 1875. Thereafter there is very little clue as to the ownership until 1936, when *Kelly's Directory* lists Mrs Raikes as resident, at least until 1942.

A set of Particulars, Plans and Conditions of Sale of the Satwell House Estate dated 29 July 1948, is among the papers and states that the property comprised 102 acres, including "a Modern Georgian Style House, overlooking Beautiful Pleasure Grounds and Hanging Woods, with a Productive Home Farm, including an Old World Farmhouse, a Pair of Cottages, Pasture and Arable Land, Cherry Orchard and Woodland."

Geoffrey and Hilda Barraclough bought the whole lot, but sold Satwell House about 1980, having developed the cottages into a tasteful residence.

Bob Bryan worked for 30 years for the Barracloughs at Satwell Farm. He told me: "They had a pedigree dual purpose herd of about 50 - 60 Red Polls – they were beef and milk cattle. The Barracloughs won prizes at the Smithfield Show and the Royal Show with these animals." Fred and Nellie Wrigley also worked there for some years.

The drive to the farm used to come down to The Lamb and meet the old road, which ran through Shepherd's Green before the new road (B481) was developed.

Stonehouse Farm

Mr George Page originally owned Stonehouse Farm. Mabel Cox (nee Page) who will be 105 in June 1999, was brought up there by her grandparents, Mr and Mrs George Page. She had recollections of helping her grandmother to make butter in the dairy. Later on George Page built himself a large house, 'Stonehouse', on the main road. (See the chapter on Health).

Mrs Mercy Cook (nee Treadwell) remembered when the old farmhouse was pulled down. She lived in the original 'Stonehouse Cottages', the only remnants of which are now incorporated into the garages of 'Stonehouse'. *Kelly's Directory* of 1936 names John Phillips as farmer but other than that I could find out little more about this farm until the outbreak of the Second World War.

Brian Wells, who grew up at Highmoor, recalled Mr Mendel Jedlin, an East European refugee who kept pigs, cows and other animals at Stonehouse Farm from about 1942. "He also grew many vegetables including ridge cucumbers in greenhouses. All these vegetables he sent to Reading market, where they were highly valued during the wartime. In the last years of the war and for a short time afterwards, Mr Jedlin employed German prisoners of war on the farm."

Mr Jedlin sold this pig farm to Mr Dickinson soon after the war and in 1960 Mr Dickinson passed it to his daughter and son-in-law, Tony Hall, who carried on the business until he retired in 1994.

At the height of his business Tony employed four men and had some 1500 pigs, about 150 of which were sows. At one point the pigs contracted swine fever and all the herd had to be killed and destroyed. Tony told me: "It was a terrible job, but we did get some government compensation." He then gave me some interesting figures that compare the raising of pigs in 1960 with doing the same these days:

"In 1960 1 ton of barley cost £18 – a 'finished' pig made £22. In 1995 1 ton of barley cost £105 and a 'finished' pig made £70."

He pointed out that the land around here, being so full of flints, wears out the blades of the machinery very quickly. Also it is not suited to today's arable farming methods as it is so hilly and banked that the large machinery now used on most farms could not get around economically. Another factor is the proximity of the woods which means that rabbits and pigeons come out and feed on the corn.

When Tony Hall came here from Sussex, "there were nine or ten men working on the local farms then, today there is not one. In fact it would not be feasible to run a pig farm on so small an area, in a residential village like Highmoor which is now not so much an agricultural area as a rural suburb."

In 1997 Tony and Mary Hall had all traces of the old pig farm removed and converted a barn, in which they used to keep the straw, into a very tasteful little house which they aptly named 'The Straw Barn'.

Witheridge Hill Farm

This farm was originally part of Highmoor Farm and for some years it was probably run as a farm, alongside its neighbour at Highmoor. In more recent years however, the farmhouse has become a private residence and the fields are let out to neighbouring farmers. The earliest record I can find for it is 25 March 1890, when George Talfourd Inman of Highmoor Hall, bought for £1,000 "the farmhouse, together with farm buildings, five cottages and gardens, arable pasture and woodlands, known as Witheridge Hill Farm." At that time it was in the occupation of William Reeves. He bought it from Anne Champion (widow of William Samuel Champion of Henley-on-Thames) and others. These buildings and fields were later incorporated into Highmoor Farm.

Witheridge Hill Farmhouse, a pencil drawing made in 1927, when it was known as 'Hilltop' and owned by a Miss Gask, who was renowned locally as an expert plantswoman. This picture is reproduced by kind permission of Mrs Muriel Browning.

Highmoor Hall Farm

Some mention should be made about Highmoor Hall Farm, although it is no longer in existence as such.

This farm was attached to Highmoor Hall and although little or nothing is known about its previous history, Tony Hall informed me that, during the time Mr Hailwood owned Highmoor Hall, around 1950, a very large pig farm was established there. "In the mid-1950s a serious fire broke out and destroyed all the buildings. Sadly, many of the pigs were killed too." However, the buildings were rebuilt and a turkey farm set up. This was part owned by Bowdens. Later on, there was a chap making furniture there." (See also the chapter on Manor Houses). Today this is a private house.

17. Hilda Trevelyan and Sydney Blow

These two names may not be familiar to many people today, but in the earlier part of the 20th century they were household names to those interested in the theatre – especially Hilda Trevelyan, who became most famous for her role as the first 'Wendy' in *Peter Pan* – a part she played for almost twenty years.

Her husband, Sydney Blow was an impresario and wrote two books of personal memoirs: *The Ghost Walks on Fridays*, subtitled: *In and Out of the Stage Door* in 1935, and *Through Stage Doors, or Memories of Two in the Theatre* in 1958. Both were written at Witheridge Hill, where the Blows lived in several houses at different times.

Sydney's brother, Detmar Blow, was an architect of some renown and helped the Blows when they bought and refurbished a thatched cottage on Witheridge Hill which later became The 'Little Manor House', then another, known today as 'Witheridge Hill Cottage', between the School and the Rising Sun, and after that our own house, 'The Old Place'.

Finally they built themselves a bungalow on the Hill which they named 'Jane's' after their housekeeper and life-long friend, Jane Heath.

A portrait of Hilda Trevelyan, taken in about 1920. Kindly lent by Michael Reed.

The manner in which the Blows found Witheridge Hill is an extremely interesting one and is related in *The Ghost Walks on Fridays*. "We scoured the Home Counties with no result, until an advertisement came to our help." (This advertisement had been placed in *The Lady* in about 1912 by John H Baker, the Master of Highmoor School on Witheridge Hill, who referred to it in *The School on the Ground Floor*.) Sidney Blow continued: "Hilda was having her hair waved and reading *The Lady* at the same time, when she spotted an advertisement that read: 'A Thatched Cottage on the Chilterns facing miles of Beechwoods. Facing south and in a sheltered position, 400 feet up on Witheridge Hill. £10 per annum.'

We blew the expense and took the cottage. And here is a curious coincidence. Years afterwards, in turning out some old photographs and picture postcards, we came across a postcard of Witheridge Hill, with the same thatched cottage on it. On the back of the card had been written in my own hand: 'A delightful place, where we should like to live one day.' The date that followed was many years prior to our taking up our abode there.

It came about in this way. After the second year of *Peter Pan*, Hilda said she felt she wanted to have a holiday in some quiet country spot. But where should we go? She suggested all sorts of places, but I urged her to make no plans but to leave the holiday to fate. 'There is nothing like an unplanned holiday – not knowing where you are going to,' I said. Hilda did not agree; she is a deal more cautious than I am, but

eventually she gave in and I introduced her, not without many misgivings on her part, to the scheme which starts with your selecting some London terminus at random.

You then arrive at that terminus with luggage to last you a week. You next choose any letter of the alphabet and then find out from the platform indicator which is the next train out. You note the name of the last station on that route which begins with the letter you decided upon, and buy your tickets.

Sidney Blow in his retirement years. By kind permission of Michael Reed.

You take the train; you arrive at your random destination, you hire a conveyance and direct the driver to take you to the most charming inn in the most lovely surroundings in the neighbourhood. And you have a week's delight of unplanned happiness – that is, if you are the right couple to play the game.

In the case of Hilda and myself, we chose Paddington and H was to be the letter. The first train happened to be a Henley train At Henley my instructions to the driver of the conveyance led us to arriving at the Maltster's Arms, Rotherfield Greys, an inn not far from Witheridge Hill, where we spent a lovely week. During our walks there we came across the cottage that was destined to be our country home. It was then we bought the picture postcard. There is nothing like a country cottage to blow the theatre cobwebs away from one. There is always a new joy and a new joy and a new thrill each day in the garden you 'do' yourself. Of course the love of the garden must be yours, otherwise you will never make a success of it or enjoy it. A garden can get a big hold on one."

Hilda Trevelyan in the garden of the original Witheridge Hill Cottage – it was in this garden that she had a little thatched 'Wendy House' built – it still stands there today. By kind permission of Michael Reed.

Sydney Blow made many references in his books to their life at Witheridge Hill. Philip ('Pa') Braham, a musical director and composer of *Limehouse Blues* and other well-known songs, with his wife, Faith, bought a cottage nearby, which they named 'Fipps Cottage'.

Several of their 'show business' friends also bought cottages around Witheridge Hill, including the famous dancer and singer, Jack Buchanan, who was a frequent visitor at 'Fipps', was a very generous and kind man. Quoting again from Sydney Blow's book *The Ghost Walks on Fridays*: "Jack has a heart of gold. He will do anyone a good turn if he can. When my friend Philip Braham died, and his wife opened a delightful restaurant in Reading, Jack promptly rallied round and served behind the snack bar on the opening night. There was a long queue waiting outside 'Sallie's' that evening and it had to be controlled by the police. They were all marshalled in good order and patiently waited their turn to be served by Jack Buchanan with a hot-dog or cold-cat." ((See the chapter on the Gentrification of Cottages).

One of Haviland's 'Series of Theatrical Portraits', this painting of 'Wendy' in Peter Pan, was published in The Illustrated London News, on 1 January, 1910. By kind permission of Mrs Green.

Sydney Blow's books are delightful to read, he seems to have been such a pleasant person and recounts many amusing stories, but it is his accounts of Hilda Trevelyan's life which are the most interesting, for she was an actress of some note, chiefly in plays by J M Barrie, not only in *Peter Pan*, but also in *What Every Woman Knows*, in which she made a name for herself.

Her career started in *Little Mary* and it was at a performance of this play that J M Barrie first saw the girl that he turned into the immortal Wendy, said to have been Barrie's favourite in the part. From *The Ghost Walks on Fridays*: "When the rehearsal of *Peter Pan* started, you can well imagine the astonishment in the minds of the company. Was there ever such a household as that of the Darling family? No play so far had had a big dog for a children's nurse. No fairy so far had come flying through a casement window into a night nursery. Not on the stage, anyway. Fairies strode majestically on and were very often five foot ten inches high, with tiny wings and shimmering with diamonds and bejewelled wands. The first *Peter Pan* company was staggered when they learned that Peter, just an ordinary boy, made his first entrance flying with **no** wings, right through the window and landed on the nursery floor. Hilda used to meet me in the breaks of rehearsal and tell me scraps of the many odd things that happened on the Duke of York's stage. She was quite at a loss to know what the play was about. During a lunch together she announced that she was going to learn to fly. "What!" I said, "are you a fairy, too?"

342

'I don't know yet; we haven't got that far. It's all very strange and puzzling.' And yet, as we know, she did 'fly' and the whole thing was a wonder at the time, so long before 'special effects' gave us the terrifying thrills we see in modern entertainments."

In *Through Stage Doors*, Sydney Blow quoted from a well-known critic of the time, J T Grein:

"She is the most modest of artists. She is rarely lured into an interview and then scarcely speaks of herself. She expresses no opinions in – mainly futile – symposia when actors and actresses are supposed to have the last word in wisdom and omniscience. We don't know what she wears, nor where she walks, dines or maybe dances. Yet we all know and love her, this unobtrusive little 'country mouse', who has more heart and intelligence than a random dozen actresses. When she does not act, and wisely she selects only parts into which she can throw herself, she retires and is not heard of.

Yet she dwells in memory, a clear cut cameo to be treasured and cherished. From the day that she leapt into fame in Frederick Fenn and Richard Pryce's '*Op o' my Thumb* – a slip of a girl, so tiny that she was nothing to look at – but she looked at you with those big eyes of hers and made you laugh and cry at will – her portrayals stand out when so many others are forgotten. And when we talk of Barrie, our most poetic playwright, up looms the name of Hilda Trevelyan, with visions of *Peter Pan*, *A Kiss for Cinderella*, *What Every Woman Knows* and *The Twelve Pound Look*."

A photographic portrait of Hilda Trevelyan by Rita Martin, taken in about 1916. By kind permission of Michael Reed.

J T Grein continued: "...There are perhaps many ways to play *What Every Woman Knows* but there is the right one – the Barrie-Trevelyan way, the way of dominating the crowd without ever creating a soupcon of a mailed fist. ...thus Hilda Trevelyan, the artist, whose supremacy is not born from effort or effect, but from the exquisite gift of insinuation which conquers."

Not much is known of the Blows after about 1935, but there is a stone in Highmoor Churchyard extension, which commemorates their life at Witheridge Hill, stating simply:

Hilda Blow – 1877 - 1959
Sydney Blow – 1878 - 1961

It is actually the top of a stone seat on which they used to sit and look over the Chiltern beechwoods which they loved so much. Sitting there, Sydney Blow often said to his wife: "Drink it all in, Hilda, drink it all in."

A delightful photograph of Hilda Trevelyan and her husband, Sydney Blow, in the garden of their home on top of Witheridge Hill. Kindly lent by Michael Reed.

18. Ills and Pills

In small villages like Stoke Row and Highmoor, which were, in the terms of the 19th and early 20th centuries, far from the town, most illnesses and accidents were dealt with at home. The doctor was only called for when the patient seemed to be almost at death's door.

One accident which was felt to warrant a journey to the hospital, was in the 1890s, when 'Grandad Green', who was born in 1850, lost part of his right arm in an accident with a reaping machine at Newnham Hill Farm. The machine had taken off two parts of his forearm, first the hand to the wrist and then to the elbow, before he could be rescued. He was taken to Reading Hospital in a horse and trap, and survived the accident. On the way they stopped at the barn of the 'Old Red House' at Sonning Common and there cobwebs were applied to his wound. It is said that the effect of this was very beneficial.

'Grandad' Green, after his accident. He is holding his right sleeve with his left hand. By kind permission of Carol Evans.

Rev Cyril Isherwood, Vicar of Stoke Row Church, writing his memories in the *Stoke Row News*, 1979 - 80, remembered that "The Doctor, then, as now, came from Nettlebed, but for every call that he made, a bill was sent, as there was no free attendance, and bills could be a considerable item. The first motor-car we saw was a small two seater and was used by a Doctor from Nettlebed. I can only describe it, as I remember, as a glorified perambulator, with just room for two, sitting up high outside, with no cover to shelter from the rain (as was the case with our carriage) and it was started by turning a handle at the front, but as there were no gears, the car started to go at once so, unless there was somebody already there, you had to be quick to jump on and take control."

One of the people to whom the villagers turned when there was illness in the family in the 1920s and 1930s, was 'Granny' Stratford, who had been the nurse to the Fleming family at Joyce Grove. She saw her patients in the Well Cottage and she used to make a pure white ointment from rose-petals, which had a lovely smell. This she sold to the local mothers for skin diseases, like impetigo, which was quite prevalent then, probably due to poor food and unhealthy living conditions.

There were also a number of congenital deformities. Mrs Alice Moore told me that her sister, who was also born at Uxmore Farm, "had six toes", although it appears that one of her toes just had an extra stump growing out of it. As a small child, Mrs Ada Smith (nee Evans), used to go to Stag Farm to collect the milk in a big jug. "I was always fascinated by the fact that the farmer, Mr Wally Biggs, had an 'extra thumb' which appeared to be a fairly loose growth from the knuckle of his true thumb, about 1" - 1.1/2" long." Other villagers also remembered that "Mr Biggs had two thumbs". However, his daughter did not recall it and it may be that he had it removed when she was young.

Ted Evans of Sonning Common told me about a man who worked at the Star Brush factory. "He was born without most of his fingers, but he could lift a whole load of chains with just his little finger, he had developed such strength in it."

'Granny' Stratford, outside her home, No. 1 The Rise, Stoke Row, about 1920. By kind permission of Mrs Jenny Norris (nee Wixen).

In his wonderful little book *Stories and Pictures associated with Kidmore End & District*, which was published in 1982, Dr A J Reed told of life in this area before the Peppard and Nettlebed practices were established. I am grateful to his nephew, Mr A C Lovern, to quote from this booklet. In the first chapter Dr Reed talked about general practice in the area:

"The late Jim Knight told me that when his next door neighbour was taken ill in the night, he was called to give a helping hand and, seeing that a doctor was required, he had to walk to Henley, rouse the doctor and eventually he and the doctor drove back to Peppard in a pony and trap. This method of 'calling' the doctor at the beginning of this century has been confirmed to me by several old people in this area." Dr Reed continued: "The first doctor to start general practice in the Peppard District was Dr Esther Colebrook, born 1870. She qualified in 1896, which was, in itself, a great achievement.

Dr Colebrook started the Peppard Chest Hospital and she was followed into general practice by Dr Robinson. A lady remembered how she 'was given some leeches by the doctor and these she took back to her employer, who, because he was a sick man, had to have them applied to his forehead. After they had done their work, she returned them to Dr Robinson'."

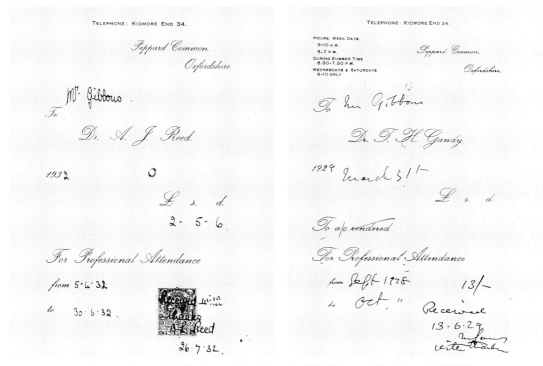

Examples of bills from Dr Gandy (1929) and Dr Reed (1932).
By kind permission of Isobel Bourne.

Dr Reed continued: "Following Dr Robinson, Dr Gandy became the General Practitioner in the area and as the years passed, so the practice grew. Dr Gandy worked in all the villages around the area, Checkendon, Stoke Row, Binfield Heath and so on. He was a hardworking, conscientious man. He was interested in the little known subject of psychotherapy. I remember Dr Gandy. He introduced me into what was then known as the Peppard practice.

He was generous and kind especially to those less able than himself and, soon, I learned that he was a specialist in helping lame dogs of the human variety over difficult stiles and those stiles could be difficult human problems as well as illnesses.

He was somewhat unorthodox in his approach to patients. It was not unusual for him to visit patients wearing 'plus-fours', with his hands grubby from meddling with his offending motorbike.

Wherever he went he was welcomed and his approach quickly signalled through to the kitchen department of the house where the kettle was soon made to boil and a pot of tea prepared. When I was being introduced, we had cups of tea in every house and I did admire Dr Gandy's ability to drink many cups of tea and to hold his fluid. He liked his pipe and so he smoked on his visiting rounds. Many people still remember Dr Gandy as a good and helpful doctor and the great interest he took in all local activities."

In 1931 Dr Reed purchased the Peppard practice and the house from Dr Gandy, as was done in those days. He worked for a time at the Royal Berkshire Hospital and also at the Peppard Chest Hospital and the Borocourt Hospital. His slim volume gives a fascinating insight into medical practice in the area during the days before the Second World War.

Dr Reed also explained how the Nettlebed and Peppard practices became linked: "For many years, when Dr Pooley of Nettlebed was away, I looked after the practice. In the early days of the war Dr Pooley was taken ill and, unfortunately, he died." When Joan Watkins (nee Powell) of Sunnyside was a very small child, in about 1920, she was bitten by the family dog on the cheek, leaving her face in a very nasty mess. The dog was shot and Joan was taken to Dr Pooley. He stitched up the wound and told her she would wear the scar for the rest of her life and, at 77, it was still visible.

Continuing Dr Reed's account: "I was asked to take over the practice and this I did. Dr Rostron, with her usual ready cooperation and enthusiasm, went to live in Nettlebed and did most of the work there. This is how the Nettlebed practice became united with the Peppard practice."

During the Second World War, Dr Reed worked very hard and very long hours. "We all did, and I am grateful that I was well enough to do so. Two afternoons each week I was operating at the Royal Berkshire Hospital. Two wards at Borocourt were set aside for war casualties from London and staffed by special nurses. Bishopswood Camp and Kennylands Camp were built and filled with children and staff. Italian prisoners of war were placed in a camp at Rotherfield Greys.

English, Polish and Americans troops were all over the place and all sorts of organisations arrived in the area, like the Women's Land Army and so on. When I look back on this period of time I do not know how I managed everything, but most people say that who survived that dreadful holocaust. I had around me a very faithful team of comrades, doctors, nurses and physiotherapists and my smallest wish was carried out as soon I had made the request."

Les Franklin had other memories of the local doctors, though. "Dr Gandy, who practised from the house on Gravel Hill, Sonning Common, pulled teeth as well. It was said of him that 'If you could stop crying he would get you laughing!' (This referred to 'laughing gas' anaesthetic). Dr Reed came after him. He charged 2/6d for a visit and he would always demand the 2/6d before he would see the patient!"

Fred Powell recalled: "In the 1930s there was a Doctor's surgery held in a room at the rear of the London House Stores. Dr Reed came up from Sonning Common, but both he and the patient could be seen through the lace curtain of the window. He had six different coloured medicines in bottles which he kept in a small cupboard. He would fill a small bottle and lick the label. You got the colour he thought appropriate or sometimes a cocktail of all six! He told us that the more bitter it tasted the more it did you good! Later on, the Doctor's Surgery was held in a small room at the side of No. 4 Ishree Terrace. This room had once been the Reading Room for the village and was later turned into a garage for the house.

In the 1950s a surgery was held in The Hope public house. You waited on benches in a verandah-type place behind. The Doctor held his surgery in the Lounge Bar, but you had to go to Nettlebed for the medicines."

From 1951 onwards the Doctor's Surgery was held in the Chapel Schoolroom, by Dr Robin Williamson and Dr Jack Foster of Nettlebed, before the Medical Centre was built at Nettlebed. After that patients went up there in a minibus."

In 1948, Dr Reed left the Nettlebed practice and it was taken over by Dr Hubert Pim and Dr Robin Williamson. Dr Hubert Pim was, in turn, succeeded by his son, Dr Joe Pim, and now Dr Jim McWhirter and a team of doctors run the practice at Nettlebed. Dr William Bird and his colleagues have an equally excellent medical centre at Sonning Common.

Not far from Stoke Row, along the Reading Road is a new housing development that was once the Peppard T B Sanatorium. Its history is a fascinating one and was related by Carol Evans in a long illustrated article in the *Henley Standard* in May 1998:

"The hospital was started in 1902 by Dr Esther Carling (formerly Colebrook) of Reading, who became world famous as one of the first doctors to pioneer the open air treatment of tuberculosis. Peppard, lying on the edge of the Chiltern Hills, proved to be a perfect location with plenty of good, fresh air, away from the pollution of towns.

Dr Colebrook (as she then was) bought the former Kingwood Farm for her new hospital with donations received after her successes in treating tuberculosis sufferers at 'Maitlands', a house in Wood Lane, that still bears a plaque attesting to her achievements. She and her engineer husband, Henry Carling, who she married in 1904, stayed at Peppard Sanatorium until 1938, as Superintendent and Medical Officer.

Dr Harley Stevens succeeded Dr Carling as Medical Superintendent and his name is preserved in the new road 'Stevens Lane'. But, after the war and the discovery of antibiotics, the number of TB cases fell dramatically. The hospital then began to specialise in other chest diseases, with modern equipment and operating theatres. By then it was known as the Peppard Chest Hospital."

The Maitland Sanatorium at Peppard in about 1910. Dr Esther Carling is reading a book. By kind permission of Ken Stevens.

The Peppard TB Sanatorium, or Peppard Chest Hospital, as it was later known, covered a large area.

A J Reed's book contains a chapter on the Peppard Chest Hospital, and in 1938 the Carlings themselves wrote a small book, covering the period 1897 to 1938. A brief summary of its life from 1938 to 1970 was later appended.

Some of the patients lived in this area, and also a number of Stoke Row and Highmoor residents worked there.

Mrs Eva Holloway (nee Clark) of Stoke Row, had a long and close association with the Peppard Chest Hospital, going back to when it was a Sanatorium. Some years before the Second World War, a party was given for the children of the staff at Christmas. As her mother, Mrs Queenie Clark, worked in the laundry, little Eva was invited and can still recall "the thrill of receiving a gift from Father Christmas – it was very rare for a child to see him in those days!"

After the war, she herself went to work there, although by then the TB side of the work was changing to that of general chest diseases. Eva started in the laundry in 1945, where her mother was, by then, Supervisor. However, when her son was born in 1949, Eva left the laundry and looked after her young family. Her mother retired in 1968, at the age of 60.

In 1958, when her children were older, Eva returned and stayed on until the hospital closed down in 1980. She remembered life at the hospital laundry as being a happy one. "Even though my mother was the Supervisor, I was granted no privileges and had to work just as hard as the other girls."

She also told me about the machinery used in the laundry: "There were two big washing machines. The ironing of the sheets was done on a huge 'Callendar' roller; it took four girls to work it. Then there was a press for all the nurses' uniforms, aprons and hats, which had to be starched after they were washed. A lady called Mrs Monger, who lived in Stoke Row, had sole responsibility for 'finishing off' these garments after the pressing. Everyone liked her, she was very popular."

In Eva's early days at the sanatorium, quite a number of the TB patients died. "The mortuary was just beyond the laundry and we sometimes saw 'the pram', as we termed it, go past the window. It was like a bier with a black cover." On a lighter note, she recalled that life in 'Kinderscot', the children's ward, was very happy and "everyone loved going in there."

While Eva worked at the hospital, Matron Elliot was in charge of the hospital and ran it very efficiently. "She was tall, slim, erect and always held her head high. The patients adored her, but the staff found her to be very strict – a traditional matron, in fact. One day Eva's Grandma fell down some steps at her home. When her mother phoned to the hospital to ask that Eva help her grandmother, the Matron refused to let her go. "I went all the same," Eva told me, "but I got carpeted the next day! Matron couldn't understand why I had to go, when my grandmother had daughters; she thought they should have gone!"

Ten years before the hospital closed, the Norman White Ward was opened, in 1970. This was used mainly as a cottage hospital and provided, among other services, convalescent care for local patients. It was much missed when it closed down.

In the laundry of the Peppard Chest Hospital in about 1942. The lady on the left is unknown, next to her is Mrs Queenie Clark, little Mrs Monger and, seated on the basket, is Jess Howell. The other ladies' names are unknown. By kind permission of Mrs Eva Holloway (nee Carter)

Borocourt Hospital

A little to the north of the Chest Hospital was 'Borocourt' which, in 1930, was developed as a community hospital for mentally handicapped patients. The name was comprised of the first letters of the authorities responsible for it, ie: Buckinghamshire, Oxfordshire, Reading and Oxford, plus the latter part of the original name of the mansion, Wyfold Court, which had lain empty since the death of Lady Wyfold in the mid-1920s.

According to Dr Reed: "Just before the Second World War various villas were built and about 1.1/2 million pounds spent on structural work, making this a very modern hospital where doctors and nurses could do good work and patients have comfortable quarters, with many amenities, like workshops, gymnasiums, modern kitchens and diningrooms. There was also an excellent Day Hospital Scheme where suitable patients could spend the day at the hospital and return home at night."

Dr Reed went on to speak of Dr Gerald O'Gorman who did much excellent work as Physician Superintendent. He died in 1998. Quoting from a booklet published when Borocourt closed: "At its height, in the 1960s, Borocourt was home to more than 600 people. In addition to the medical and nursing staff, there were Occupational Therapists, Physiotherapists, plumbers and gardeners, cooks and porters, secretaries and clerks, telephonists, electricians, social workers and more." In the early 1990s Borocourt was closed down under the new 'Care in the Community' scheme.

Today the house and grounds are being developed into a residential area. However, like the Peppard Chest Hospital, a number of local people worked at Borocourt. Maureen Green of Stoke Row was a patient there for 33 years, in the Remedial Section. As a young woman she found the sight of the enormous mansion to be breathtaking. "I'd never seen anything like it!" she said. Hers was one of the success stories of 'Care in the Community'; when Borocourt closed down she soon found work in the laundry at Huntercombe Hall. Maureen has inherited her mother's cheerful disposition and does the most beautiful embroidery; she has recently made very attractive tapestry kneelers for St John's Church.

Miss Maureen Green at Wyfold Court, which has now been
developed into apartments and large houses built in its grounds.

Mrs Gill Wood, now a retired carer, was an assistant at Borocourt. She kindly wrote to me, explaining her role there:

"I started work in the Occupational Therapy Department in 1979, having answered an advertisement in the local paper for an OT Helper with Playgroup experience! (At the time I jointly ran the Woodcote Playgroup).

Initially, I worked full-time with the less abled patients, doing art, craft, puzzles etc. We also had sessions in the Gym. Later I moved to Social Education, helping with reading, writing, basic arithmetic and money skills sessions. In the early days people came off the ward for the whole morning or afternoon, making rugs, baskets, trays, etc. At this time I had little contact with ward staff.

As the years went by, attitudes changed, uniforms disappeared and the whole atmosphere was more relaxed, with all levels of staff working together. Gradually, I reduced my hours until I worked three days a week in the Social Training Flat, preparing patients for Life in the Community. We did everything you would do in a normal home – washing, cooking, ironing, etc.

The Occupational Therapy Department was situated in a converted stable block with a cobbled courtyard. It consisted of a large craft room, art room, woodwork section, training kitchen, Social Training flat and several smaller rooms and offices.

Later on sessions became shorter, with patients moving between the factory, the OT Department and the wards. Their occupations became much more varied, they did light packing jobs sometimes. Looking back, I enjoyed my work at Borocourt, I remember we had some happy times, especially when we made trips to Caversham to do shopping and had coffee at the baker's shop."

Wyfold Court, Peppard. This stately Victorian house and 250 acres of land was converted in 1930 as a community hospital for mentally handicapped patients and was known as 'Borocourt'.

A direct outcome of the work at Borocourt, which continues today, is a group called 'Riding for the Disabled', based at Wyfold. In 1998, a group of the volunteer helpers went out to Mongolia on a sponsored trek and succeeded in raising over £4000 for this cause. Cynthia Davidson of Stoke Row later outlined its story:

"It was during the summer of 1971 that the long association between the former Borocourt Hospital and the 'Riding for the Disabled Association' began. Riding therapy was provided for residents of the hospital, with ponies hired from a local riding school.

354

The riding took place in the safe 180 acres of grounds and woods. By 1979 land was set aside to accommodate horses on site and in 1983 driving, with donkeys and carts, was added to the activities provided by the group.

The Wyfold RDA Group, run entirely by volunteer helpers, endeavours to enable disabled riders to benefit in their general health and wellbeing. Clients gain confidence in learning to ride a large animal, they improve physically by exercising and adjusting posture and balance and are able to gain certificates and badges in recognition of their progress.

Following the sale of the hospital, the new owners have generously allowed us to remain in the grounds. In order to secure its future, Wyfold RDA has raised funds for purpose built facilities which will enhance the service already being given."

Disabled people riding at Wyfold.
Photograph kindly lent by Cynthia Davidson.

Stonehouse Guest House

Perhaps we should not leave this subject without making mention of a convalescent home at Highmoor. In the 1930s, when tuberculosis was still rife, Mrs M H King ran a Guest House on the B481, and her card made it sound very attractive:

"The unrivalled Health Resort high in the bracing Chilterns, catering as it does for convalescents and the aged, stands in its own gardens and orchards, which provide the finest Fresh Fruit and Vegetables, Eggs and Poultry. Fully modernised, and with ideal Sunbathing and Open-air Sleeping facilities, Stonehouse nestles in quiet, restful Woodlands, though if desired, glorious Golfing, Riding and Water Sports are close at hand. Terms are from 3 guineas per week, with special arrangements for long residence, and enquiries are welcomed."

Whether such a claim would could be made today, as it borders the very busy B481 Nettlebed to Reading Road, is another matter! Commander and Mrs McDougall lived here for many years, but the house has recently been sold.

Stonehouse Guest House, Highmoor. In the 1930s this was advertised as 'A Health Resort on the Chiltern Hills'.

19.   Transporting People and Goods

In the *Stoke Row News*, June 1967, Geoff Boyson informed us that "the first stage coach service from Wallingford to Henley operated in 1773. The coach was the 'Wallingford Machine' and a pair of horses were always available at 'Well Place' to help haul it up Berins Hill. The word *Machine* had a very novel connotation at that time, the start of the Industrial Revolution. The coach probably followed the old Roman track from Wallingford to Henley, over Berins Hill."

However, only the landed gentry and the few wealthy people in the area would have used such a service; most folk would have used 'Shanks's Pony' (walked) or, perhaps once or twice a year, used a carrier.

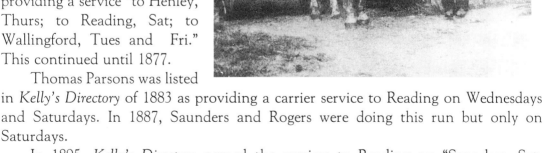

William Wixen, his carrier's cart and his horse, 'Robin', which was an old pit pony, bought at Henley March Fair, 1920. By kind permission of Mrs Jennie Norris (nee Wixen).

The first record of a carrier in Stoke Row was in the *Post Office Directory* for 1854, when Mary Ann Turner was listed as providing a service "to Henley, Thurs; to Reading, Sat; to Wallingford, Tues and Fri." This continued until 1877.

Thomas Parsons was listed in *Kelly's Directory* of 1883 as providing a carrier service to Reading on Wednesdays and Saturdays. In 1887, Saunders and Rogers were doing this run but only on Saturdays.

In 1895, *Kelly's Directory* named the carriers to Reading as: "Saunders, Sat, and Rogers, Sat; Jeffries, Mon, Wed and Sat; Peter Frewin, Tues, Thurs and Sat." By 1899, Brown & William Lester had taken over from Jeffries, but otherwise this set of carriers maintained the same trips until about 1911.

Saunders had dropped out by 1915 and by 1920 two operators were mentioned as going to Reading – William Lester and Albert Tucker. William Wixen went to Wallingford, calling at Nettlebed. Mr Lester and Mr Wixen carried Stoke Row and Highmoor people to the nearby towns for most of the 1920s and 1930s.

Highmoor had another carrier, too. Noel Baker told me about Mr Bailey, from Nettlebed, who came to Highmoor and went on Reading. "He performed a useful task in carrying out commissions in Reading, where some villagers would hardly ever visit."

Tom Wells of Highmoor is shown here with a horse named 'Blackbird', driving a cart through Nettlebed. High Street. By kind permission of Mrs Hilda Pitt (nee Shurey).

The following extract was taken from the wonderful Checkendon Women's Institute Scrapbook, compiled in 1955, describes a day out with a carrier and is reproduced with their kind permission:

"You left the village at 9.00 am in a van with a canvas cover for protection from the weather and drawn by a stout horse which jogged steadily along, stopping frequently to pick up a passenger, a parcel and often, an order for some shopping. A crate of chickens for market and baskets of fruit may have been tied on the tailboard.

Pleasant conversations with your fellow travellers and with the carrier, who was an authority on all local matters, made the time pass happily. By 11.00 am you were in town. The carrier 'putting up' his horse and van at his favourite hostelry, you could now leisurely do your shopping, while the poor carrier was meantime rushing around to fulfil all the shopping commissions he had received, for which, when delivered, he charged 2d or 3d.

3.00 pm saw you all back at the inn yard, laden with packed baskets. You all took your seats among the packages of meat and fish, groceries, repaired shoes and merchandise of every kind. Clip, clop, you came up the Caversham Road. Now, the return journey was uphill, so if the load was heavy or the horse ancient, you got out and walked up the hills, often giving a push behind to help along.

Halfway home brought you to the roadside inn, probably The Bird in Hand, where a stop was made. Here a welcome cup of tea, or something stronger, could be bought. The horse was given his nosebag and all settled down for a quiet five minutes and then on again, with all the stops to deliver the parcels.

In winter, the candles on the van would be lit. Through the winding lanes and over rough stony roads, you would arrive home again between 6.00 pm and 7.00 pm, not forgetting to pay the fare of one shilling. This carrier service was provided three times a week."

Wealthier families had conveyances. One of these was the Rev Herbert Harben Appleford, Vicar of Stoke Row, seen in this picture with his wife in about 1905. Kindly lent by Mrs Kay Browne, whose husband was related to theCox family of Stoke Row.

Another photograph kindly lent by Kay Browne shows her husband's grandparents, James and Emily Cox (nee Proctor) of 'The Rest' (later 'Bodgers' and now 'Virginia Cottage') of Stoke Row, out for a drive with their pony and trap. James Cox had a very prosperous building business and also acted as an undertaker when required.

John Whitehead very kindly wrote a most interesting article about the buses which operated to and from Stoke Row for the February 1997 edition of the Stoke Row News. I have summarised some of the information contained in it:

"In the early 1920s, the established horse-van carrier's service between Stoke Row and Reading was being operated by old Bill Smith, who worked to The Boar's Head, Reading. At this time a Mrs Ellen Shaw of Stoke Row operated a similar service, from No. 1 School Lane, Stoke Row. This also went also to Reading, but by a different route and to The Forbury.

Mrs Shaw, widowed in the early 1920s, had been married to a farm labourer and had at least one daughter and one son, George. William Richard Jackman, who at first worked for a relation, Bill Greenaway, ran a business in Stoke Row, hiring out horses and farm carts and, later, agricultural engines and threshing machines etc. He eventually married Mrs Shaw and then took a hand in running her family business. In about 1925 it changed from a horse-drawn conveyance to a motor van." Mrs June Cope (nee Shaw) read John's article and commented: "The carrier & bus business (The Triumphant Bus Company) was, I understood, started by Ellen Shaw to provide them with a living as, by 1922, Horace George Shaw had developed consumption, from which he eventually died."

This photograph was kindly supplied by Paul Lacey from his huge collection of pictures of Thames Valley buses and charabancs. He told me that this was a "Thames Valley car no. 197 (HE 2336), a Leyland 'Pup' Z7-type, with a 20-seater body by Ransome Sims and Jeffries of Ipswich. It was purchased by Thames Valley in May 1929. Only one of a batch of seven acquired was used at Stoke Row, but not this one, which worked for the Fingest shed on the Lane End service. Shedded buses rarely featured in photos!"

John continued: "Later they bought a new vehicle, also a new Chevrolet, powered by a 4-cylinder engine and fitted with a 14-seat 'country bus' body, painted dark blue and white. It is remembered as being rather square and unattractive. It had small windows, a passenger doorway at the front on the nearside and double van-type doors at the rear. The seating was inward facing, each side seating seven.

George Shaw had left school by now and gone to work at the 'Star Brush' at Stoke Row. He had an accident at the saw bench, losing the tops of two of his fingers and, with the compensation he received he was able to finance the purchase of a second bus. This was, perhaps, how he came into the business which became known as W R Jackman & Son. Again June Cope observed: "Alice Whittamore (nee Shaw) used to relate that she went to collect the new bus from Great Western Motors and paid for it with the money she took with her in the brown leather bag she had strapped round her waist (for collecting the fares) and she drove it back to Stoke Row. I believe the compensation George got was £15. I don't know if this would buy a bus – I think it was more likely bought on hire purchase."

John went on: "This second vehicle, believed to have been a Dodge, was much more like a bus than the first and was, by all accounts, an attractive little vehicle with a polished chrome radiator and finished in a livery of light blue lower panels, bonnet and wings, with cream window surrounds and roof. It is also thought to have been a 14-seater.

George Shaw took over the running of the Stoke Row to Reading service and Bill Jackman used the original vehicle on private hire duties, which mainly consisted of the transport of the inevitable cricket, football or darts teams. It was about this time that Mrs Jackman suffered a stroke.

From 1st April 1929, the Thames Valley Traction Co Ltd started running into the area, using a vehicle based at the Stoke Row 'dormy shed', erected in a field at the side of the church. Only the first bus in and the last one out ran through Stoke Row."

Another bus company was also operating in the area at this time, namely House's of Watlington. This photograph shows a Napier wagonette which Houses ran through the early part of the 1920s. Joe House, who ran the business with his brother, Dick, can be seen at the rear. This bus, technically a 'wagonette', built in 1919, was later fitted with Michelin pneumatic tyres, which were some of the first to be used in the south of England. The driver always took several spares with him as they often became punctured. An Oxford Bus Company manager jealously warned Dick House: "You won't run on those for long!" but eventually pneumatic tyres became standard. By kind permission of Arthur J House.

A Thames Valley bus, No 16, Thornycroft T-type 29 seater bus, built in 1919, stopped outside the Unicorn at Peppard on its way from Stoke Row to Reading, in the summer of 1925. The driver was Jack Lambden. By kind permission of the Paul Lacey Collection.

A Commer 'Avenger' that Houses ran from Watlington, through Highmoor to Henley in about 1948. Kindly lent by Arthur J House.

Continuing John Whitehead's account:

"However, George Shaw had already signed up with the Army as a reservist, so he was called up when the war broke out. Either the Woodcote to Henley service was curtailed forthwith, or at the end of September 1939, when a stringent petrol rationing scheme was brought into effect, or Bill Jackman carried on alone as best he could. The final departure of W R Jackman & Son from the scene is not yet clear, but it was probably in 1940, possibly due to the problems of wartime restrictions, in particular petrol allocation, tyres and spares. The service may have become hopelessly unremunerative, but it seems that both the bus service and the carrier's business ceased, never to return."

June Cope still has her father's badge, and sent me a drawing of it, done by her grand-daughter, along with a few more memories. "Before the Second World War my father, George Shaw, worked for the Thames Valley Traction Co. He was a driver, sometimes doing conductor duties, as Charlie Butler from Peppard was killed during the Second World War."

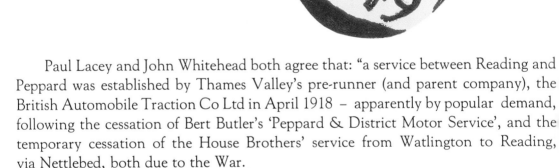

George Shaw's bus driver's badge.

Paul Lacey and John Whitehead both agree that: "a service between Reading and Peppard was established by Thames Valley's pre-runner (and parent company), the British Automobile Traction Co Ltd in April 1918 – apparently by popular demand, following the cessation of Bert Butler's 'Peppard & District Motor Service', and the temporary cessation of the House Brothers' service from Watlington to Reading, via Nettlebed, both due to the War.

However, B A T had to withdraw the facility the following month, due to severe fuel shortages. The service was duly reinstated after the war, but the most significant development, as far as this study is concerned, occurred on 22 May 1925, when the route was extended to Nettlebed, via Stoke Row and Highmoor. The service was covered by two single-decker Thornycroft buses, one provided by Reading garage, plus another which commenced its working day as the first journey (9.55 am) from Nettlebed Post Office.

The latter car was out-stationed at the Cherry Tree yard at Stoke Row. The names of the crew have not come to light; whether they were from Stoke Row or volunteers from Reading also remains unknown." I was told by Fred Powell that the crews often cycled back and forth to work, even from Reading.

Miss Minnie Heath recalled the years of the Second World War and how the villagers had to guard the 'dormy shed': "We had been given 'stirrup-pumps' for doing fire-watching service at this shed throughout the war. It remained on the Company's books until about May 1946 and is believed to have been used by the military for war work of some nature."

The 'Dormy Shed' at Stoke Row, which was sited on the land that lay between 'The Haven' and 'The Vicarage'. Two bungalows, 'Longways' and 'Bron Eirean' have since been built on this piece of land. This photograph was kindly supplied by Paul Lacey from his collection.

Returning to Paul's account: "Incidentally, the facilities at the 'dormy shed' were quite minimal. All refuelling and routine maintenance was handled during layovers at Reading (where the conductor paid in his takings daily), with the crew being responsible for maintaining a clean exterior and interior.

The driver also had responsibility for draining the radiator during winter months, a hay-box being provided, together with a lamp to keep the engine from freezing overnight. The roof was raised in 1935 to take a double-decker bus, then employed on the route. The 7 route remained a single-decker working, probably when the shed closed in 1940, thereafter warranting a double-decker, due to the influx of evacuees and the military. The 'dormy shed' was finally lost in a fire in 1947."

365

In about 1950, a single decker bus, belonging to Houses and going from Reading to Nettlebed via Highmoor, was turned over into a ditch. It was being driven by Wilf Dicks who, according to Sam Gardiner, "had had more than his fair amount of lotion!" The above double-decker also overturned on Witheridge Hill about that time. By kind permission of Freda Fairbairn.

Road Mending

Ted Evans, who grew up in Stoke Row, recalled: "Before the days when the roads were laid with tarmacadam, the potholes were filled with cart-loads of flint stones that had been picked off the fields by women and children. Then the whole lot was covered with chalk. Steam-rollers would come and flatten them out, but it was your own carriage wheels that had to do the rest – they had iron tyres then.

Sometimes we would see two old men sitting by the roadside by a pile of large flints, with hammers, breaking up the flints (a very slow business) and wearing horn glasses to protect their eyes. There was very little traffic, only occasional farm carts or a private carriage, or someone on horseback.

This surface got very dusty in the hot dry weather and so the men of the village would spray it from a water tank. The water was drawn from the pond opposite the Cherry Tree and sprayed out through a hose with a nozzle. To prevent the nozzle becoming clogged with dust it was tied to a shovel which glided along the road."

Benjamin Stevens, with the Oxfordshire Council's 'Invicta' steam roller, c 1935.
Shadrack Allum is second on the left. By kind permission of George Stevens.

Road mending near Highmoor, c 1935. The man with the horse is unknown,
but the one sitting on the vehicle bearing the tar barrel is Tom Wells.
Standing beside him is Moses Stevens. By kind permission of Mrs Louie Stevens.

Road mending was much improved by 1952. This shows men at work at Highmoor. By kind permission of Mrs Joy Green.

Not every one went by public transport. The next pictures show several modes of conveyance that were popular, especially among the less wealthy which, of course, meant most of the villagers.

Violet Pike and Joyce Pitt with the donkey and cart which was kept at 'Binksholme' (now 'Clayhill') at the top of Stoke Row Hill and was used for transporting chair parts made at The Cherry Tree. By kind permission of Mrs Joyce Martin (nee Pitt).

Many men, and a few ladies, too, had bicycles and this enabled them to get to more distant places of work with less effort than by 'Shanks's Pony'. Here one is seen leaned by the hedge outside 'Belmont', next to 'Well Cottage' at Highmoor. Kindly lent by Mr McLeod.

For most ambitious young men in the 1920s and '30s, the ideal in life was to own a motorbike, on which one could go so much further and faster than on an ordinary push-bike. This photograph depicts Susie Wixen and her sister Jenny with *Charlie Saunders, who had recently acquired one of these prized machines. By kind permission of Arthur Wixen. (*See also the chapter on Pubs).

Once you could afford a motor car though, you were really 'made'! Jack Day reckoned he had "the first car in Stoke Row" and labelled this photograph accordingly. Actually Rodney Page had owned a 1904 Argyll in 1920. (See chapter on Shops).

Tom Sarney, Mrs Margaret Day and Jack Day, proudly sitting on the running-board of his two-door Chevrolet Sedan, c 1928. By kind permission of John Day.

Later, Roland Page owned several sports cars and was especially proud of his MG M-type Midget, which was made at Abingdon between 1929 and 1932. By kind permission of David Howells.

The Stoke Row Garage

I could not conclude this chapter without mentioning the Stoke Row Garage, which has been filling up local cars with petrol and seeing to their many ailments since the 1930s. This was originally a wooden building, with one or two pumps and owned by Harry Munday. He sold it to Roland Page, who had started his career there as an apprentice mechanic and then began his business at Stoke Row, selling and servicing motorbikes. He was also an amateur radio enthusiast and a special constable.

The garage had underground tanks which had been used during the Second World War for the storage of paraffin for tractors and other agricultural use by the Agricultural Board. Alan Cox recalled an amusing story: "The Foden lorries that were bought by the Star Brush from the army after the Second World War were very 'soupy' and took 150 gallons of petrol. George Hearns not only sold petrol from what was just a tin shack then, but he also acted as the village barber. One Sunday morning in the late 1940s he was half-way through cutting my hair when one of these great long trailers came in for its weekly fill-up. In those days the petrol pumps were worked by hand and you had a lever which you had to move backwards and forwards. It took so long to fill this lorry up that I had to go home with one side of my hair cut, have my dinner and then go back in the afternoon to have it finished off!"

In 1948, William Townsend bought the garage and ran it with the aid of George Hearns. Eventually, about 1950, Mr Townsend sold it to Mr Hearns, who, sadly, was killed in a Go-Kart accident in 1970. Thereafter his wife, Lucy, ran it until 1981, when she sold it to Brian Husbands. He owned it for about eight years and then sold it to Chris Girdler in 1989. A new canopy was fitted in 1994. Now owned by Trevor Gibbins and Cliff Barrett, the garage still offers an excellent and personal service.

Author's photograph of Stoke Row Garage, taken in 1993, before the canopy was fitted.

20. The Gentrification of Cottages

One of the most significant changes in villages in this country during the past fifty years, apart from the advent of the ubiquitous motor-car and television, is what the Americans call 'the gentrification of houses'. Unlike France where there are far fewer people per square mile, and where the owners of dilapidated properties tend to let them go to ruin and just build new ones beside them; we in this country have so little land and are always short of houses such that any building, be it an attractive old house or cottage or just a pre-war cedar bungalow, an old barn or farm outhouse, is looked upon, usually by developers, as being 'ripe for conversion'. In addition to this, any orchard or piece of land not specifically designated as 'agricultural land', and sometimes even then, is also the subject of the envious eyes of anyone with money to invest. And so by looking at photographs past and present, we can see that, even since the end of the Second World War, these villages have altered considerably and if we return to the end of the First World War, almost beyond recognition.

Most old houses in Stoke Row and Highmoor were put up during the latter half of the nineteenth century following the sinking of the wells. Prior to that the lack of water discouraged all but the most hardy from settling here. Therefore most of our 'local cottages' were in fact pairs of semi-detached houses put up as quickly and cheaply as possible, in Victorian times, using local bricks and sometimes flints.

My dictionary defines a cottage as being 'a labourer's dwelling, built of local materials'. This certainly used to be the case. Most cottages in both Stoke Row and Highmoor were owned by just a few landlords who let them to tenants. Some were owned by farmers and were 'tied' to the job – hardly any labourers possessed their own dwellings. One of the Franklin boys, on returning from the First World War in 1918, had the chance to buy our house for £100 and was advised "'not to tie a millstone around his neck!"

One of the most obvious areas of change has been around Witheridge Hill, where there are about a score of houses which used to be owned mainly by George Page, of 'Stonehouse' at Highmoor, or by the owner of Highmoor Hall. Before the First World War they were let for about 2/6d to 3/- a week – today they have expensive cars outside; some have swimming pools and tennis courts as well.

John H Baker, Head Master of Highmoor School 1907-24, in his book *A School on the Ground Floor* related how the change began. "A year or two previous to the Great War of 1914, *the outlying property of a big estate was advertised for sale and included an old thatched cottage. It overlooked the hillside and beyond the valley road, with a view of a great beech wood rising to the village of Stoke Row. The beauty of the view can be imagined; in spring a vast expanse of greenery, in autumn a scene of brown and golden tints." (*This was probably the Highmoor Hall estate which was partly sold off by Mr George Talfourd Inman, prior to the purchase of the Hall by Mr Hugh MacIntyre in 1912).

Mr Baker continued: "I communicated with the agent and offered a hundred pounds for the cottage. Back came the reply that the owner thought it best to let the property be sold at the sale with other items.

Not to be outdone I increased my offer to a hundred and fifty pounds. Success was achieved, the offer was accepted and a tenth of the price, fifteen pounds, was forwarded as a preliminary payment. I resolved to raise the rest of the money by a mortgage. I got in touch with a scholastic insurance society and invited an inspection of the property with a view to obtaining an advance. One morning two gentlemen arrived at the scene by taxi and made a survey. They had come from the city and the rural charm of the locality greatly impressed them. One of them exclaimed enthusiastically, 'This is the most truly rural survey I've ever made!' They were duly entertained at the School House and intimated that they were favourably inclined to recommend the advance of a hundred pounds on the thatched cottage. The family financial barrel was well scraped and the balance of the required cash was secured, supplemented by a small loan by a relative."

The original of 'The Little Manor House' on Witheridge Hill.
Mrs Denham is in the garden. Kindly lent by Robin Denham.

Mr Baker continued to explain: "So the country schoolmaster had become a man of property, lightly burdened with a mortgage of a hundred pounds, to be repaid with moderate interest charges over a period of years. The cottage being untenanted was cleaned and distempered with the help of a neighbour and made ready for letting. No applicants came forward so the cottage was advertised in *The Lady*. Shortly after, one fine Sunday morning, a taxi drove up to the School House and a lady and gentleman alighted. *The visitors turned out to be well known theatrical persons. (*The purchasers' side of the story can be found in the chapter on Sydney Blow and Hilda Trevelyan). The lady was appearing in the leading part of a Barrie play then enjoying great popularity in London. She was entranced with the cottage especially with the view from the windows and the secluded position.

The visitors agreed to rent the cottage for the very modest sum of ten pounds a year. These were the days when country cottages, with only primitive sanitation and no bathroom, were let at very low rents. Four shillings a week or less was an average rent among village tenants at that time."

Arthur Denham and his wife bought the house in the early 1920s, and with the advice of the architects Collcutt and Hamp, enlarged and improved it considerably. They named it 'The Little Manor House', and it became the subject of a 'before and after' photographic article in the *Ideal Home* magazine October 1925.

'The Little Manor House', photograph taken in 1984 by the author.

'The Little Manor House', photograph taken in 1984 by the author.

This was the view from the top of Witheridge Hill as described by John H Baker in his book. "It overlooked the hillside and beyond the valley road, with a view of a great beech wood rising to the village of Stoke Row." By kind permission of George Stevens.

Few people today can believe that before the Second World War Witheridge Hill bore hardly any trees, most of it was covered in gorse, which was carefully burnt off each year - every cottager had an animal or even several grazing on this Common land. The 'new road' can be seen on the right. This picture is from a 1913 Sale catalogue.

'Fipps' in the 1930s, when the Brahams had built on a thatched porch, under which they could sit and gaze across the tree tops to Stoke Row. Photograph by kind permission of Mary Wilder.

Next door to 'The Little Manor House' is 'Fipps Cottage'. A photograph of the original cottage can be seen in the chapter on the shops. The unusual name was given to the house by Faith and Philip Braham who rented it from 1916 and bought it in 1920. It is derived from Faith, Ivan, Philip, Puddy, all of whom were a group of friends who worked in the theatre and often spent weekends there together.

Philip ('Pa') Braham, who was a musical director, wrote many famous songs and music, including *Limehouse Blues*. He also wrote much music for the famous entertainer, Jack Buchanan, said to be "England's answer to Fred Astaire", who often visited 'Fipps Cottage'. There were many parties at the house in those days and the couple were neighbours of Sydney Blow and his wife, Hilda Trevelyan.

George Stevens recalled, "Philip Braham worked in London and the couple had a flat in Charing Cross Road. Mr Braham would come down to 'Fipps' on a Saturday night after the show to be with his family. Many of their theatrical friends would come down to spend Sunday, especially in the summer and at Christmas, when they stayed for a couple of days but always had to get back to the London stage by Boxing Night."

George remembered too how the Stevens children and their friends "loved to stand on orange boxes and peep over the fence at the 'goings-on' of the grand folk from London!"

The same house, with its lovely garden in 1990.
Photo by the author with the kind permission of David and Fiona Barnes.

At Easter the Brahams used to hide hundreds of chocolate Easter eggs for the village children to find in the garden of 'Fipps Cottage'. This photograph shows the family's Nanny looking on as the children search for these treats. Kindly lent by Fiona Barnes.

Mary Wilder told me: "My uncle, Philip Braham was involved in a car accident near Remenham. His car somersaulted twice into the field below. He suffered severe bruising and cuts and didn't work again in the theatre for a year. He died of angina some few years later, aged 53, at his flat in Charing Cross Road, where he lived during the week." The ashes of all the Braham family were scattered in the garden of 'Fipps' or on Witheridge Hill, so much did they love this area.

Lady Westmacott lived at 'Fipps' throughout the Second World War. She was the daughter of Lady Maclean of Nuffield. Mrs Joan Earle told me: "three little girl evacuees came to stay at Fipps during the first year of the Second World War but when things quietened down, they went back to London."

'Fipps' was, for a long time, in the possession of Eric Hives, the architect, and his wife, but for the past almost twenty years Sir David and Lady Barnes have owned this property.

Two cottages next to 'Fipps' were gutted in 1938 by Jack Buchanan, who turned them into a modest but 'modern' house for Mrs Faith Braham, after her husband died, so she could derive an income from letting it. It was called 'Bucks Barn' after Jack Buchanan. Lord Strathalmond and his wife lived there for a while during the war and so did the industrialist Sir Harry Methven. Later it was owned by the Van de Berghs, Ross and Vanessa Andrews, and a Mr and Mrs Kelly who sold it to the present owners in 1989. Each owner in turn has enlarged and improved both the house and the garden.

A carrier's cart approaches the original pair of cottages that now form the basis of 'Bucks Barn' on Witheridge Hill. Photograph by kind permission of Ada Britnell.

The rear of 'Bucks Barn' in 1988. Photograph taken by the author.

This photograph of 'Garden Cottage', being explored by John and Mary Goodwin and Valerie Braham, was taken in 1928. Kindly lent by Mrs Mary Wilder (nee Goodwin).

*The same house in 1984. Photograph by the author,
with the kind permission of David and Judith Hubback.*

Mary Wilder (nee Goodwin), who grew up at Garden Cottage, told me: "My mother bought 'Garden Cottage' for £150 from her brother-in-law, Philip Braham, in 1927. Renovations were carried out by Mr Cox of Stoke Row at a total cost of £350. All the dormer windows were put in at the time of rebuilding and the rear of the cottage looked the same in 1928 as shown in the photograph overleaf. Mother let the cottage from 1934 until her death in 1949." During the Second World War, Nancy Price, the writer, lived in this house. It was sold in 1970 to David and Judith Hubback. Judith wrote a book about psychoanalysis whilst she was there.

As 'Garden Cottage' is adjacent to 'Fipps', David and Fiona Barnes bought and substantially improved the property in 1992, almost rebuilding it. Considering that this had originally been erected as a simple labourer's cottage, it is not surprising that, when it was completely stripped inside, the builders found 'floating joists', much faulty brickwork and many cracks as a result of bulging walls. The whole house needed a great deal of work done on it, from the foundations to the chimneys. The result is a charming cottage, with pretty dormers. Mary Wilder wrote: "...the work they had carried out to the cottage saved it, and in so doing David and Fiona Barnes were the saviours of our childhood and my brother and I will, for always, love them."

*The rear of 'Garden Cottage' in 1928. Photograph kindly lent by
Mrs Mary Wilder (nee Goodwin) niece of Mrs Braham.*

*The same view of 'Garden Cottage' today. Photograph by the author,
with the kind permission of David and Fiona Barnes.*

'Rose Cottage', at the entrance to Newnham Lane, comes just within the boundary of Highmoor parish. Mrs Mary Ramsay (nee Clements) lived with her parents in this house in the 1920s and '30s. "It was owned by Mr Denham then. He had it reroofed and redecorated in 1928. We had a 'privy' up the garden, but it was very modern, with a bucket and not just earth!"

Mick Ralphs owned Rose Cottage between about 1974 and 1976. He played in a pop group called 'Bad Company' and also with 'Mott the Hoople'.

Michael and Susan Snow bought the house from him in 1976 and stayed until 1988. It was for Susan's horses that the stables were built in the garden and she practised 'dressage' in the paddock at the southern end of the property, which she used as a 'menage'.

In more recent years Andrew Nolan and his Australian wife, Linda, owned the cottage but it was bought in 1997 by Gill Oxenburg who demolished the old conservatory and had this little cottage enlarged by the addition of an L-shaped wing to match. Matthew Young was the architect and Fred Pratt the builder – the result is quite charming.

Gill Oxenburg left in the spring of 1999 and the house has recently been purchased by Peter and Wendy Keal, who have recently added a three-bay garage, beautifully crafted in oak by Heart Of Oak at Nuffield.

This is the oldest existing photograph of 'Rose Cottage', probably taken by Collier, circa 1910. The 'privy' (or 'up the garden') is the tiny box with a pitched roof, adjacent to the house. Photograph by kind permission of Mrs Hilary Fisher.

*'Rose Cottage' in 1928, after it had been restored.
From a hand-tinted photograph given to the author by Mrs Mary Ramsay.*

'Rose Cottage' in 1930. Photograph kindly lent by Archie Earle.

'Rose Cottage' today. The new wing was designed by local architect, Matthew Young, in keeping with the half-timbered original cottage. Photograph taken by the author.

'Bushwood', at the foot of Stoke Row Hill, circa 1930. Kindly lent by Archie Earle.

'Bushwood', which also comes just within the Highmoor boundary, is often confused with another house with a similar name near to the Crooked Billet. This 'Bushwood' was built in 1816. When they were looking at the house, Archie Earle clearly told them that when he demolished the old kitchen at the back of the cottage in the 1970s, he found a coin with the date 1816 embedded in the lime mortar. This was a practice carried out by workmen in order to record the date of construction of even the most humble properties. It had been in the Stallwood and Earle families for about a hundred years when Archie Earle and his wife, Joan, sold it in 1994 to Terry and Dianne Duggan, who came from Australia.

The Duggans enlarged and modernised the house and rebuilt the old stables into garages. They also imported an old barn from Winnersh, Berkshire and had it built into the at side of the house where it has now not only been saved from demolition, but has become a delightful sittingroom.

This skilled work was carried out by F J Williams, the Henley builders. In her interior design work Dianne made use of a great number of artefacts which she found lying about the place, old tools, gates, wooden panelling, and an oven door, etc.

One of the items she found and mounted on the kitchen wall was a board which was inscribed: 'SNOW - 25 APRIL 1908'. Archie Earle told her that his grandfather had written this at a height of six feet, to mark the snowline that year.

'Bushwood' today. The main extension to the east of the house has been reconstructed from timbers of a barn which had been discarded. By kind permission of Dianne Duggan.

The old, once thatched, stables at the side of 'Bushwood', in about 1941.
The group includes 'Evelyn', a little girl evacuee, her father and James Stallwood.
By kind permission of Archie and Joan Earle.

'Bushwood' - the stables have been rebuilt as garages and a log store.
Photograph taken by Dianne Duggan and used with her permission.

Not all the 'gentrified' houses in the district are around Witheridge Hill. Most old houses in both Stoke Row and Highmoor have been altered and improved, but those dealt with in this chapter are the ones which their original owners would hardly recognise. One such is 'The Barn' at Highmoor.

Mrs Ada Britnell recalled that her grandfather, James Saunders, owned this barn, along with 'Woodland Cottage' next door. It had originally been owned by Mr MacIntyre of Highmoor Hall. However, in 1930, Lenna Archer's father bought the old barn, which has a date stone of 1567, and converted it into a lovely house.

Lenna recalled: "The work took nearly two years, including the layout of the garden. My family spent four very happy years there – in fact, I celebrated my 21st birthday there and put out a cartilage in my knee whilst playing tennis on the court."

Mr Michael Worster, a retired solicitor, told me that he and his mother bought 'The Barn' in 1939 for the sum of £1500. Between 1946 and 1948 the Worsters extended the house westward, creating a bedroom for Mrs Worster and a kitchen below it. "Mr Cromie, the famous cinema architect, who lived at Highmoor Park, next door, drew up the plans and the work was done by Paddicks, the builders of Kidmore End."

Building materials were still restricted for some years after the Second World War and so Mr Paddick bought a war damaged barn and used the timbers from that.

Mr Worster told me how it was done. "The roof timbers were laid out on the lawn and changed around until the correct layout was found. From the wood that was left over, they created a staircase. One of Paddick's men used a spoke shave to hand carve every one of the oak banisters. Because the craftsman started in the middle of the run of banisters the spacing was perfectly symmetrical."

In 1948 Mrs Worster and her son had the house raised to two storeys. "We also took down the original garage which, at that time, was at the end of the drive and faced the gates at the front – the builders turned it round 45 degrees to the position that it is in today. The front door was bought by Paddicks from a house in Sonning Common, which had been built by Lutyens.

Mrs Worster was sister to the film producer, David Lean, who bought many 'film world' guests to 'The Barn', including the famous actress Anna Neagle. Michael Worster also told me that, during the Second World War, a Mrs Rosemary Ducros (nee Reece) sometimes stayed with his mother. "This lady was one of the first women to fly aircraft from the manufacturers to RAF stations. When she went to bed she always wore her flying helmet and at least seven blankets!"

Subsequent owners have all enlarged and improved the house and the present ones, Dennis and Diana Allport, keep it in beautiful condition.

'The Barn' at Highmoor, during the course of reconstruction in 1930.
Photograph kindly lent by Mrs Lenna Green (nee Archer).

*'The Barn' when it was finished, in 1932. Photograph
by kind permission of Mrs Lenna Green (nee Archer).*

*'The Barn', 1948. Mrs Worster doing her tapestry in the sunshine while Paddicks'
men raised the roof to two storeys. By kind permission of Michael Worster.*

The 'man from Paddicks', who hand made the oak stairs and banister rail at 'The Barn', in 1948. By kind permission of Michael Worster.

'The Barn' today. Author's photograph, by kind permission of the owners.

'Giles Farm' at Stoke Row has been changed almost beyond recognition.
This picture, taken in about 1914, shows 'Mabel', Alice M D Cox and Eileen Cox.
Kindly lent by Mrs Kay Browne, whose husband, Beric, was the little boy.

'Giles Farm' in 1960, when it was left by Mrs Melville to her niece,
Mrs Nancy Cotterell, who kindly loaned this photograph.

Mrs Nancy Cotterell at 'Giles Farm', c 1960. Photograph kindly lent by Mrs Cotterell, who often opened her garden to the public in aid of charities.

'Giles Farm' in 1992. Author's photograph. The house and garden have since been extended and improved by the present owners.

Although more houses have been enlarged in Highmoor than in Stoke Row, there are a number in Stoke Row which have been converted from a pair of semi-detached cottages into a single dwelling. Many enlarged houses could have been included in this section but either no photographs of the originals have been found in good enough condition, or it is impossible to take the same view today, because of trees and/or more recent buildings.

However, the most altered house in Stoke Row must surely be 'Dogmore Cottage' at the top of Stoke Row Hill. This was originally a pair of Victorian semi-detached houses which belonged to the owner of the large neighbouring house, 'Dogmore'. In 1985, the tenants, Percy and Ivy Collis, moved to a Council bungalow at Sonning Common, although they died soon afterwards. The property was sold to Alwyn Dyer, who very sympathetically renovated and extended it. The present owners, Henry and Sheila Casley, have put on a conservatory and another garage in the form of a barn, as well as creating a delightful garden.

'Dogmore Cottages' in 1980. Mr and Mrs Collis are in their garden.
Mrs Collis's parents, Mr and Mrs Johnson, had lived in the right hand of the
pair, but by the time the author took this photograph that part was unoccupied.

Mrs Ivy Collis, by the fire at 'Dogmore Cottage', 1980. Photograph by the author.

The front of 'Dogmore Cottage' in 1986, soon after renovation work was completed.
Photograph by the author.

The rear of 'Dogmore Cottage' today. The roof of the original cottage can be seen at the back on the left hand side. Photograph by kind permission of the present owners.

Finally, we come to our own house, 'The Old Place'. It is believed that this house started out as a squatter's cottage, erected on the edge of common land on the Stonor estate. Although a dwelling appears to be marked on a map at Stonor dated 1630, the Stonor papers are not available to the public and so further research was not possible in this direction.

There are quite a number of references in the Oxfordshire Archives to the Blackall family, with a variety of spellings, and I think that one branch of them lived in this cottage. The problem of endeavouring to trace families through the Census returns is that the dwelling is usually just referred to as a 'cottage at Witheridge Hill' and this of course could be any one of several.

However, not long after we had moved here in 1979, I met Miss Dolly Franklin and brought her to our home, where she had lived from 1908 to 1930. I tape-recorded her story, which I found fascinating.

Dolly was born at Checkendon but her mother came to this cottage when their father left home. Her two elder sisters were in service and 'living in'. Her two older brothers were working on local farms but still lived at home. As Dolly was the eldest of the three younger children, she became responsible for them while her mother went out to work, even though she herself was only eight years old when they moved to this house.

"The Parish Guardians wanted my mother to put us three young 'uns into an orphanage, but she wouldn't. She managed to keep us all together on 3/- a week Parish Relief." Mrs Franklin had small contributions from the two older boys but supplemented her income by working as a laundress. To do this she left home each morning at 7.00 am and thought nothing of walking two miles to Uxmore House before she started work. After a day's labour, for which she received 1/-, she walked home and I'm sure she was glad to find that Dolly had prepared the evening meal.

Mrs Ellen Franklin. This is obviously not a happy photograph and may have been taken in connection with the Parish Relief. By kind permission of Peter Franklin.

Ellen Franklin was, by all accounts, a sweet and remarkable woman. Born in 1866, she recalled her father saying "Pennyfarthings are the Devil's work!" One of her favourite proverbs was: "A wash is as good as an hour's rest." Goodness knows she had little enough rest with two hungry farm lads and three young children to feed. The meat and vegetables were all cooked in separate string bags in a huge iron pot that hung over the open fire. That fire had to be maintained, even in the summer, if one was to make a cup of tea. Dolly said: "Water for tea and washing we heated in a tin drum, which we bought for 6d."

Collecting and storing firewood was one of the children's main tasks. They gleaned it from Bere Wood, opposite the house, because Witheridge Hill then was all grass and furze, as grazing cattle, goats and donkeys ate everything as soon as it grew.

"Every week I was sent to the butcher at Sonning Common to buy a few scrag ends for the pot. We had plenty of vegetables, which we grew in the garden, we never grew flowers. The boys had the meat and the little ones often just had the 'goodness' (ie the gravy)." If the family were lucky, they had a suet pudding, rolled in a cloth and hung in a net bag in the main pot.

Dolly remembered how the whole family bathed on a Saturday. "The water had to be drawn from the well. It was hard work to keep that well clean and in good order. Sometimes it ran dry, especially in the long hot summers, like 1921 and my sister and I had to go up to Highmoor or even Satwell House and bring water back in buckets."

There were two main rooms. The ground floor room was divided by a wattle and daub partition. The family lived in the half that had the fireplace and kept in the other half "our barrows, our boots, our vegetables and all that sort of thing." Access to the upper floor was by means of a simple stairway, no space was wasted. Again, upstairs the room was divided with a thin partition. Mrs Franklin slept in the first part, with the baby in a cot at the foot of her bed and the two little girls slept in another single bed beside her. The two older boys went through a space in the wall (as downstairs, there were no doors), where they slept together in a small double bed. They all conducted their ablutions in a lean-to 'wash house'.

Dolly Franklin, reminiscing by the fire at 'The Old Place', 1980. Photograph by the author.

Of course, the sanitary facilities were 'up the garden'. When the family came in 1908, the Vicar persuaded the landlord to build them a brick 'privy' in lieu of the 'guzzle hole', a large hole with a plank spanning it, which had existed beforehand. "Even so, we still had to dig our way up there when it snowed and that was very often then!"

For all this, Mrs Franklin paid 2/9d a week. "When she got behind with the rent one time, Mr Page made her pay 3/-, but he didn't change it back when the eleven weeks were up!" Dolly recalled with some bitterness.

When the two older boys went off to the First World War, Ellen Franklin was left to fend for herself, Dolly, Annie and Jack. Dolly always had bad eyesight and related how her whole life was affected by the fact that her mother could not afford spectacles for her. "When the Health Inspector came to Witheridge Hill School, he said I should have glasses, which would cost 5/-. Mother said it was a fortune and she couldn't possibly find that sort of money, so I was 25 years old before I could afford to buy myself a pair." (See the chapter on Highmoor School).

397

'Old Place' in 1938. By permission of the Oxfordshire Archives.

"I never learned to read and write properly and so when I left school, I was 14 then, I just minded cows for a year. After that the Vicar's wife took me on to scrub floors at the Stoke Row Vicarage. Another of my jobs was to keep the iron cooking pots clean with sand. It was very rough on your hands – they were often almost raw!"

Eventually Dolly got sick of this job and managed to get work as a gardener for Mr Burr at' Satwell House' – she stayed there for ten years. As her brothers were away in the Army she had to grow their own vegetables and clean out the 'privy'! Dolly earned £1 a week then, but she was warned: "Don't speak to your employers unless they speak to you first." The postman came past the cottage every morning, prompt at 7.00 am, sitting up high on his cart. The Franklins used him as an alarm clock as he went along the lane beside the cottage, and up to Kingwood Common. "I had to be at work at 8 o'clock and woe betide me if I was late!"

Her brothers came home from France several times during the War, usually arriving in the middle of the night, as they had to walk from Reading Station. "I remember at the of the war, George came home and our Jack saw him coming down the hill. He shouted to Mother, and ran to the gate, but George called out: "Tell Mother to bring a bowl of water and clean clothes for me by the hedge. I'll wash before I come in, I'm alive with lice!" This resulted from life in the trenches.

'The Old Place' in 1995, before the greenhouse was replaced by the conservatory.

The well head, now an ornamental garden feature, this used to be across the well, which, though now filled in, used to be under the present diningroom. Photograph taken by the author.

Two views of the sittingroom at 'The Old Place', taken in 1998. Author's photographs.

When she left 'Satwell House', Dolly worked for a while at Highmore Farm for Mr Edward Page and then, in 1925, she helped the Head Gardener to create a garden at the 'The Little Manor House' on Witheridge Hill for Mr Arthur Denham. In 1930, the Julius Blow and actress wife, Hilda Trevelyan, bought 'Old Place' (as it was then called) and so Dolly and her mother had to rent another cottage at the top of the hill.

After the Blows had modernised the house (to 1930 standards) and lived here a while, they built 'Janes' and sold this house to a Mrs Cecily Stewart-Anderson, who lived in London, and kept it as a second home, coming here for the summer and for a brief spell at Christmas. They stocked the garage with masses of tinned food during the Second World War, in case they should need to evacuate themselves here permanently, but they did not actually do so.

In June 1948, a new 'lean-to' kitchen was built and an Aga installed. However, the chimney was not properly flued and so one Sunday morning, while Mrs Anderson was out, the house caught fire. Of course, it was sometime before her neighbour, Mrs Freda Fairbairn, noticed the smoke and by the time the Fire Brigade arrived the house was almost totally destroyed. "Mrs Anderson was quite distraught by the fire." Mrs Fairbairn told me. "She sold the wreck to my husband. In 1951 he had it rebuilt by A E Nunn of Henley, to a design by Stephen Bertram, MBE, ARIBA."

Mr Fairbairn then sold the house to a Mr and Mrs Cox, who lived here for six years before they sold it back to Cecily Stewart-Anderson, and she lived on here until she died. Her daughter, Mrs Kelly, inherited the house and used it as a weekend retreat. Finally, Mrs Kelly sold it to Mr and Mrs Bateman in 1977. They put in central heating and other improvements before we bought it in 1979. We have tried to keep the cottage much as it was in the 1950s, with the exception of building a conservatory in dark wood on the side of the house.

The author in the garden of her home, 'The Old Place' in 1997. By kind permission of the Henley Standard.

21. Conclusion

And so dear reader, I do hope you have enjoyed this book. I have had a lot of fun writing it and apologise for any errors or omissions. I have tried to check all my facts but this is often difficult, especially when one is learning them from elderly people whose memories are often not as vivid as they themselves would like them to be. However, I am most grateful to all those kind people who, with first-hand knowledge, have proof read individual chapters. Unfortunately, it is not possible to rectify errors already printed but I would be glad to hear of any nonetheless.

It has not been my aim to write a long-term history. As Stoke Row and Highmoor were, in the late 18th century, "only a few poor houses", there is not a great deal to be discovered about these villages before then. Nor will the reader have found any references to suicides, illegitimacies, incest, etc, for although I have been told of them, I do not think it right to make such events public. People ask if I am against change, but this is not so, for one of the joys of doing this research has been the revelation of just how lucky I am to be living in this day and age of physical comforts. Perhaps one of the few benefits there were to living in past times was the companionship of a big family and the helpfulness of neighbours when there was trouble. Nevertheless, I do think it is necessary to record these changes before they are lost and to keep some note of life as it is today. An excellent example of this is the recent *Stoke Row Village Appraisal.* One of my favourite sayings is: "Today is the history of tomorrow!"

If I were asked: "What would you like to see passed as an Act through Parliament?" my answer would surely be: "All photographs should be provenanced." Many people have said to me that they think it unnecessary to put details on photos, because "*we* know who they are." And I have replied: "Yes indeed, but will your grandchildren know who, what, when, where and why?"

It is my hope that all my findings, including my collection of newspaper cuttings going back to 1930, will go into the Oxfordshire Archives. These records include video and audio tapes but of course they will only last as long as machines are still available to play them. Time has proven that only paper and photographs, if preserved in acid-proof boxes, will keep for centuries. I also hope that the Oxfordshire Museum Service will be willing to take the small collection of artefacts that I have acquired – not enough in themselves to create a museum, but they all have local interest.

I am always interested to hear of new contacts and of course new sources of photographs. One of the pleasures of this hobby has been to avail people living today of photographs of their families or houses that they had perhaps never seen. This especially applies to newcomers who love to have copies of pictures of their house as it was, in say 1910, or of the people who lived there in the 1920s and 1930s. All in all, this whole project has been a great joy!

Angela Spencer-Harper,
'The Old Place', 1999.

Notes

Notes